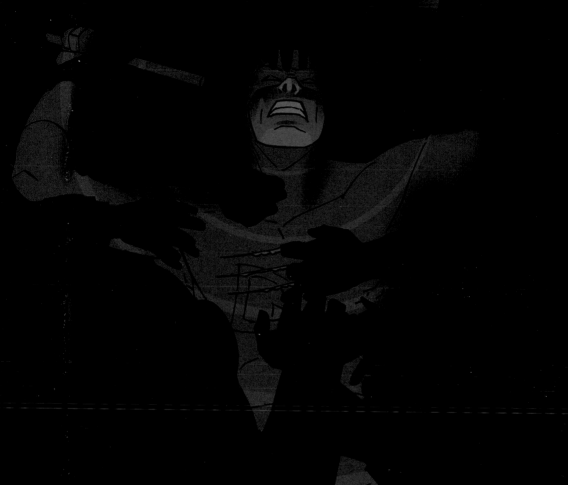

WHEN MATT MURDOCK WAS A KID, HE LOST HIS SIGHT IN AN ACCIDENT INVOLVING A TRUCK CARRYING RADIOACTIVE CHEMICALS. THOUGH HE COULD NO LONGER SEE, THE CHEMICALS HEIGHTENED MURDOCK'S OTHER SENSES AND IMBUED HIM WITH AN AMAZING 360-RADAR SENSE. NOW MATT USES HIS ABILITIES TO FIGHT FOR HIS CITY. HE IS THE *MAN WITHOUT FEAR.* HE IS... *DAREDEVIL*!

———————

DAREDEVIL'S PROTÉGÉ BLINDSPOT WENT UP AGAINST THE MASS-MURDERING INSTALLATION ARTIST KNOWN AS MUSE ALONE. DAREDEVIL SHOWED UP JUST IN TIME TO SEE MUSE GOUGE OUT BLINDSPOT'S EYES — AND WHILE MUSE ENDED UP IN THE HANDS OF THE AUTHORITIES, NOW MATT MUST LIVE WITH HIS GUILT...

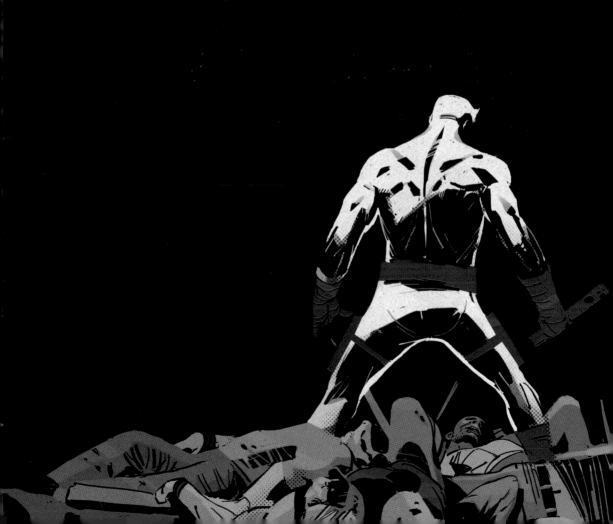

DAREDEVIL
IDENTITY

CHARLES SOULE
WRITER

GORAN SUDŽUKA (*Nos. 15-16*), **RON GARNEY** (*Nos. 17-18, 20*) & **MARC LAMING** (*No. 19*)
ARTISTS

MATT MILLA (*Nos. 15-20*) & **MIROSLAV MRVA** (*No. 19*)
COLOR ARTISTS

VC's CLAYTON COWLES
LETTERER

DAN PANOSIAN (*Nos. 15-16*), **RON GARNEY** & **MATT MILLA** (*Nos. 17-18*), **DAN PANOSIAN** (*No. 19*) AND **MIKE DEODATO JR.** & **FRANK MARTIN** (*No. 20*)
COVER ART

CHRIS ROBINSON
ASSISTANT EDITOR

MARK BASSO
ASSOCIATE EDITOR

MARK PANICCIA
EDITOR

COLLECTION EDITOR **JENNIFER GRÜNWALD**
ASSISTANT EDITOR **CAITLIN O'CONNELL**
ASSOCIATE MANAGING EDITOR **KATERI WOODY**
EDITOR, SPECIAL PROJECTS **MARK D. BEAZLEY**

VP PRODUCTION & SPECIAL PROJECTS **JEFF YOUNGQUIST**
SVP PRINT, SALES & MARKETING **DAVID GABRIEL**
BOOK DESIGNER **ADAM DEL RE**

EDITOR IN CHIEF **AXEL ALONSO**
CHIEF CREATIVE OFFICER **JOE QUESADA**
PRESIDENT **DAN BUCKLEY**
EXECUTIVE PRODUCER **ALAN FINE**

DAREDEVIL: BACK IN BLACK VOL. 4 — IDENTITY. Contains material originally published in magazine form as DAREDEVIL #15-20. First printing 2017. ISBN# 978-1-302-90562-0. Published by MARVEL WORLDWIDE, INC., a subsidiary of MARVEL ENTERTAINMENT, LLC. OFFICE OF PUBLICATION: 135 West 50th Street, New York, NY 10020.

Printed in Canada. DAN BUCKLEY, President, Marvel Entertainment; JOE QUESADA, Chief Creative Officer; TOM BREVOORT, SVP of Publishing; DAVID BOGART, SVP of Business Affairs & Operations, Publishing & Partnership; C.B. CEBULSKI, VP of Brand Management & Development, Asia; DAVID GABRIEL, SVP of Sales & Marketing, Publishing; JEFF YOUNGQUIST, VP of Production & Special Projects; DAN CARR, Executive Director of Publishing Technology; ALEX MORALES, Director of Publishing Operations; SUSAN CRESPI, Production Manager; STAN LEE, Chairman Emeritus. For information regarding advertising in Marvel Comics or on Marvel.com, please contact Vit DeBellis, Integrated Sales Manager, at vdebellis@marvel.com. For Marvel subscription inquiries, please call 888-511-5480. **Manufactured between 5/26/2017 and 6/27/2017 by SOLISCO PRINTERS, SCOTT, QC, CANADA.**

10 9 8 7 6 5 4 3 2 1

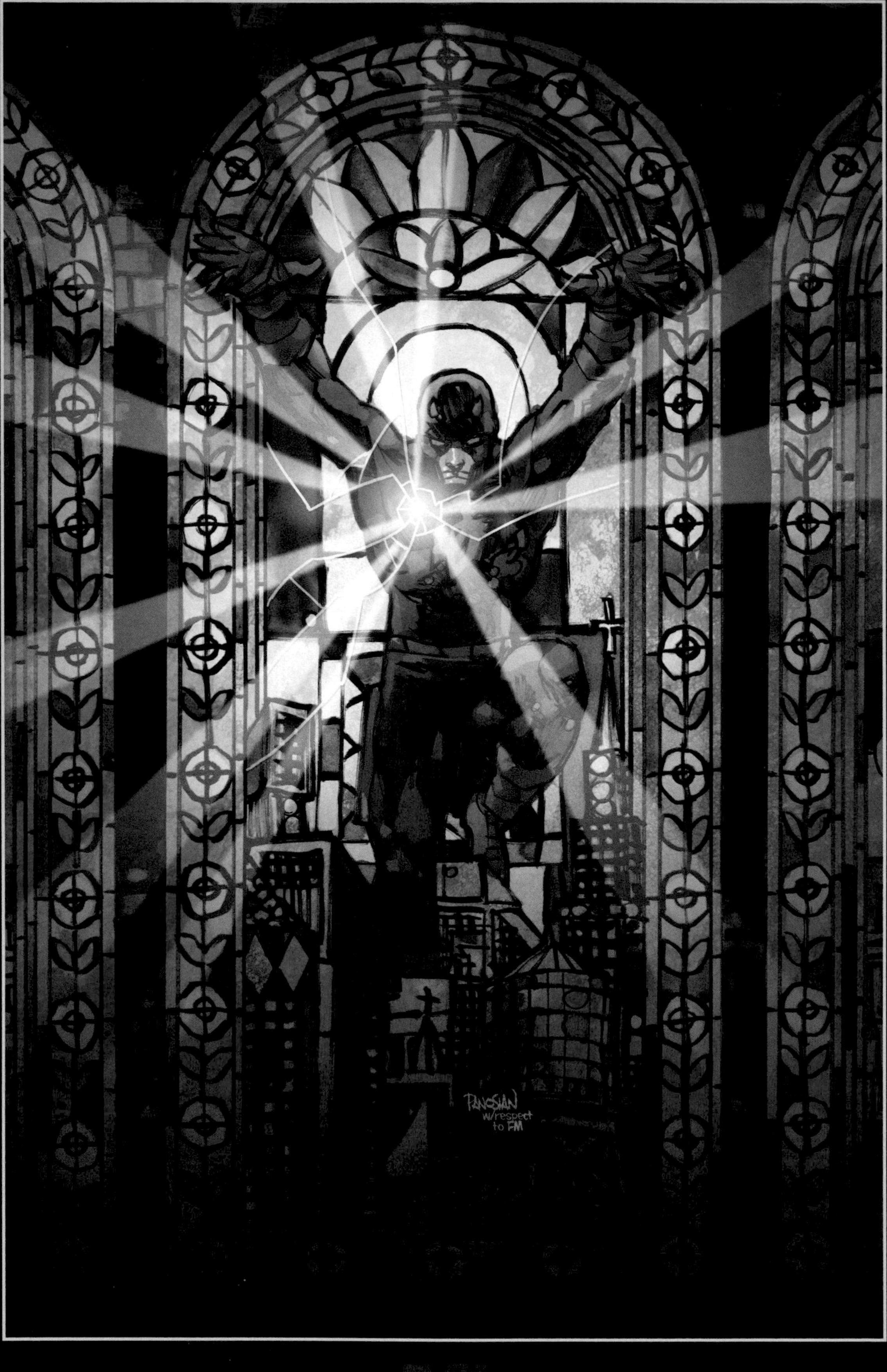
PANOSIAN
w/respect
to FM

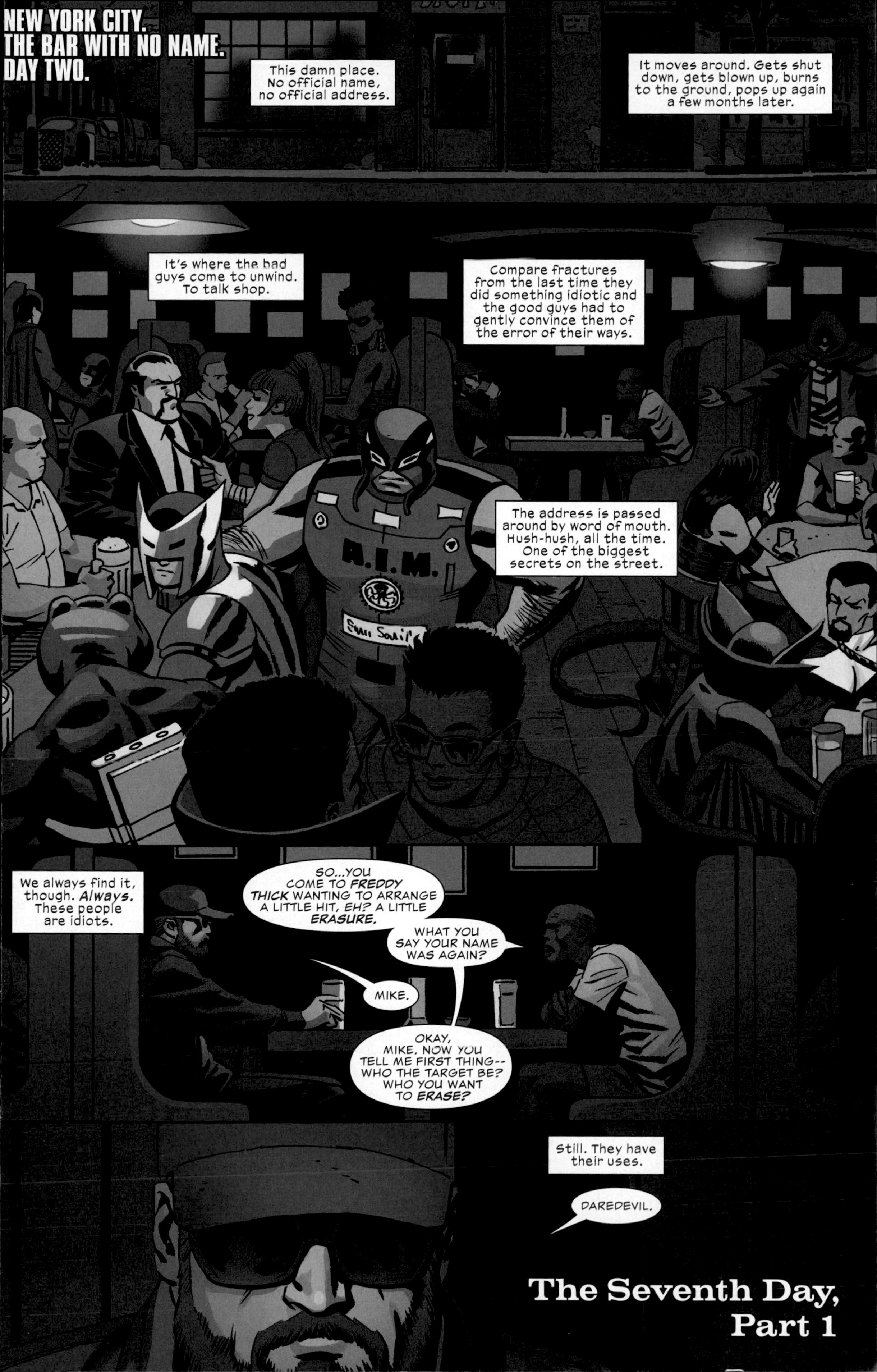
NEW YORK CITY. THE BAR WITH NO NAME. DAY TWO.
This damn place. No official name, no official address.
It moves around. Gets shut down, gets blown up, burns to the ground, pops up again a few months later.
It's where the bad guys come to unwind. To talk shop.
Compare fractures from the last time they did something idiotic and the good guys had to gently convince them of the error of their ways.
A.I.M.
The address is passed around by word of mouth. Hush-hush, all the time. One of the biggest secrets on the street.
We always find it, though. Always. These people are idiots.
SO...YOU COME TO FREDDY THICK WANTING TO ARRANGE A LITTLE HIT, EH? A LITTLE ERASURE.
WHAT YOU SAY YOUR NAME WAS AGAIN?
MIKE.
OKAY, MIKE. NOW YOU TELL ME FIRST THING-- WHO THE TARGET BE? WHO YOU WANT TO ERASE?
Still. They have their uses.
DAREDEVIL.
The Seventh Day, Part 1

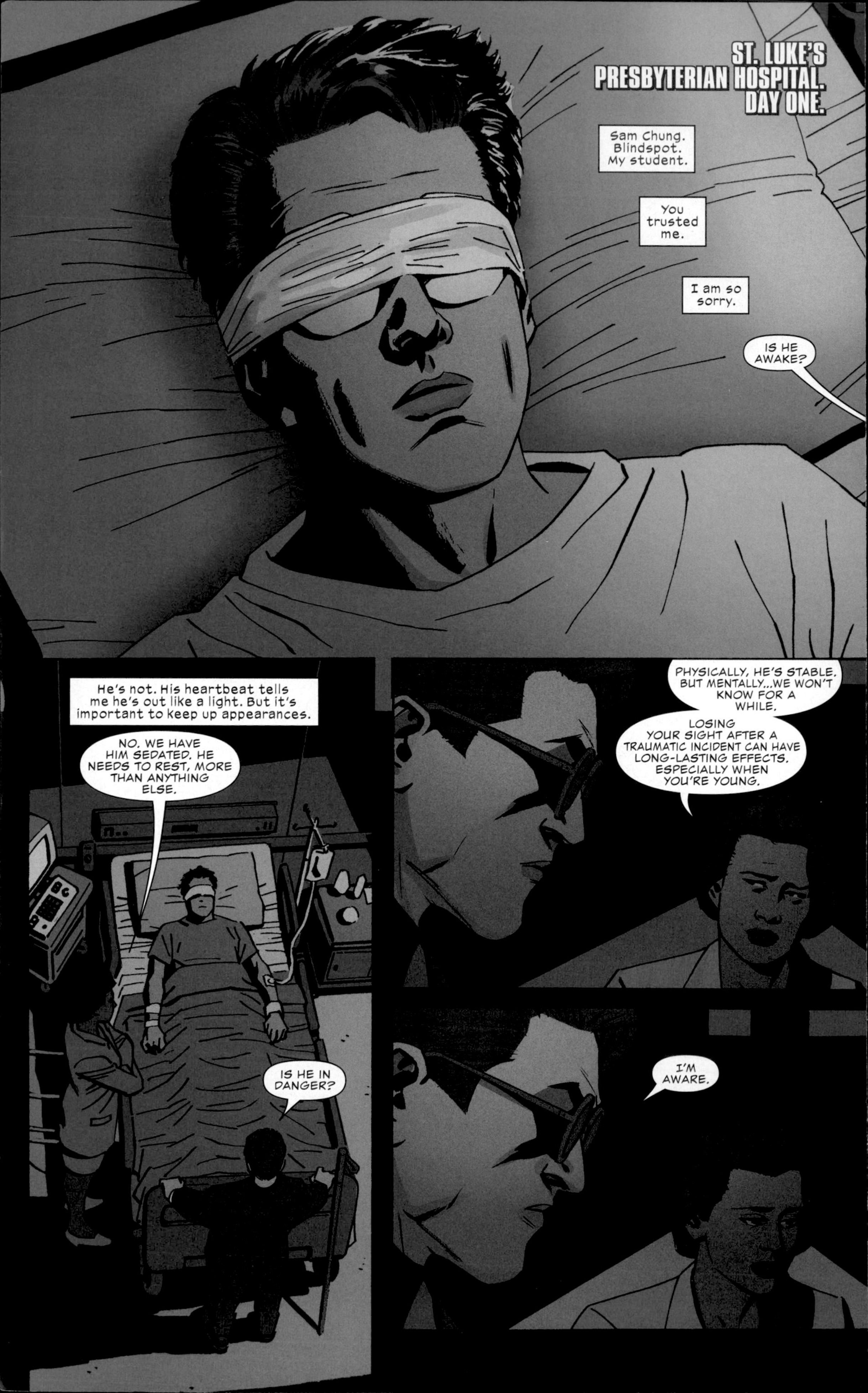
ST. LUKE'S PRESBYTERIAN HOSPITAL. DAY ONE.
Sam Chung. Blindspot. My student.
You trusted me.
I am so sorry.
IS HE AWAKE?
He's not. His heartbeat tells me he's out like a light. But it's important to keep up appearances.
NO. WE HAVE HIM SEDATED. HE NEEDS TO REST, MORE THAN ANYTHING ELSE.
IS HE IN DANGER?
PHYSICALLY, HE'S STABLE. BUT MENTALLY...WE WON'T KNOW FOR A WHILE.
LOSING YOUR SIGHT AFTER A TRAUMATIC INCIDENT CAN HAVE LONG-LASTING EFFECTS. ESPECIALLY WHEN YOU'RE YOUNG.
I'M AWARE.

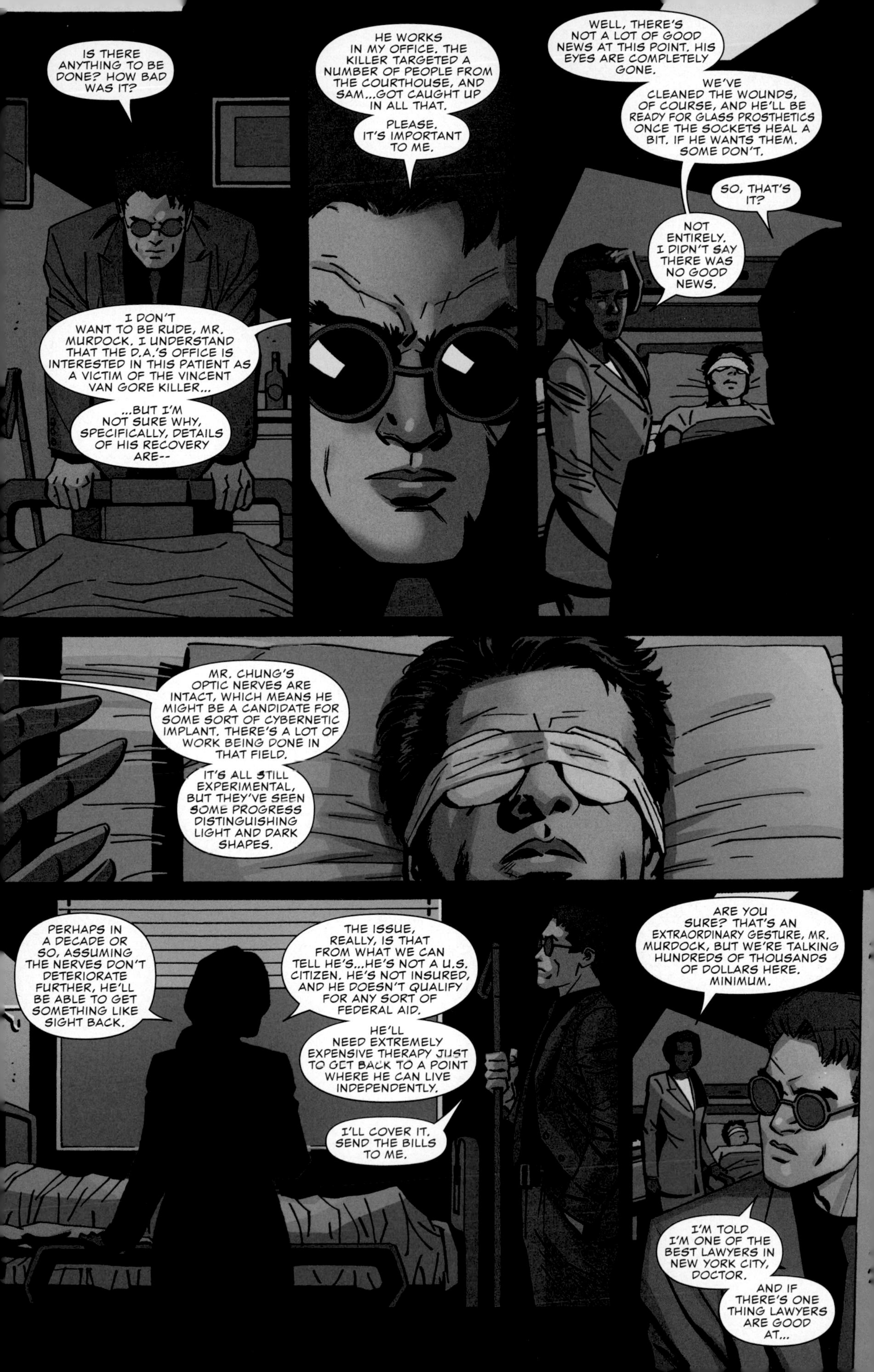
IS THERE ANYTHING TO BE DONE? HOW BAD WAS IT?
HE WORKS IN MY OFFICE. THE KILLER TARGETED A NUMBER OF PEOPLE FROM THE COURTHOUSE, AND SAM...GOT CAUGHT UP IN ALL THAT.
PLEASE. IT'S IMPORTANT TO ME.
WELL, THERE'S NOT A LOT OF GOOD NEWS AT THIS POINT. HIS EYES ARE COMPLETELY GONE.
WE'VE CLEANED THE WOUNDS, OF COURSE, AND HE'LL BE READY FOR GLASS PROSTHETICS ONCE THE SOCKETS HEAL A BIT. IF HE WANTS THEM. SOME DON'T.
SO, THAT'S IT?
NOT ENTIRELY. I DIDN'T SAY THERE WAS NO GOOD NEWS.
I DON'T WANT TO BE RUDE, MR. MURDOCK. I UNDERSTAND THAT THE D.A.'S OFFICE IS INTERESTED IN THIS PATIENT AS A VICTIM OF THE VINCENT VAN GORE KILLER...
...BUT I'M NOT SURE WHY, SPECIFICALLY, DETAILS OF HIS RECOVERY ARE--
MR. CHUNG'S OPTIC NERVES ARE INTACT, WHICH MEANS HE MIGHT BE A CANDIDATE FOR SOME SORT OF CYBERNETIC IMPLANT. THERE'S A LOT OF WORK BEING DONE IN THAT FIELD.
IT'S ALL STILL EXPERIMENTAL, BUT THEY'VE SEEN SOME PROGRESS DISTINGUISHING LIGHT AND DARK SHAPES.
PERHAPS IN A DECADE OR SO, ASSUMING THE NERVES DON'T DETERIORATE FURTHER, HE'LL BE ABLE TO GET SOMETHING LIKE SIGHT BACK.
THE ISSUE, REALLY, IS THAT FROM WHAT WE CAN TELL HE'S...HE'S NOT A U.S. CITIZEN. HE'S NOT INSURED, AND HE DOESN'T QUALIFY FOR ANY SORT OF FEDERAL AID.
HE'LL NEED EXTREMELY EXPENSIVE THERAPY JUST TO GET BACK TO A POINT WHERE HE CAN LIVE INDEPENDENTLY.
I'LL COVER IT. SEND THE BILLS TO ME.
ARE YOU SURE? THAT'S AN EXTRAORDINARY GESTURE, MR. MURDOCK, BUT WE'RE TALKING HUNDREDS OF THOUSANDS OF DOLLARS HERE. MINIMUM.
I'M TOLD I'M ONE OF THE BEST LAWYERS IN NEW YORK CITY, DOCTOR.
AND IF THERE'S ONE THING LAWYERS ARE GOOD AT...

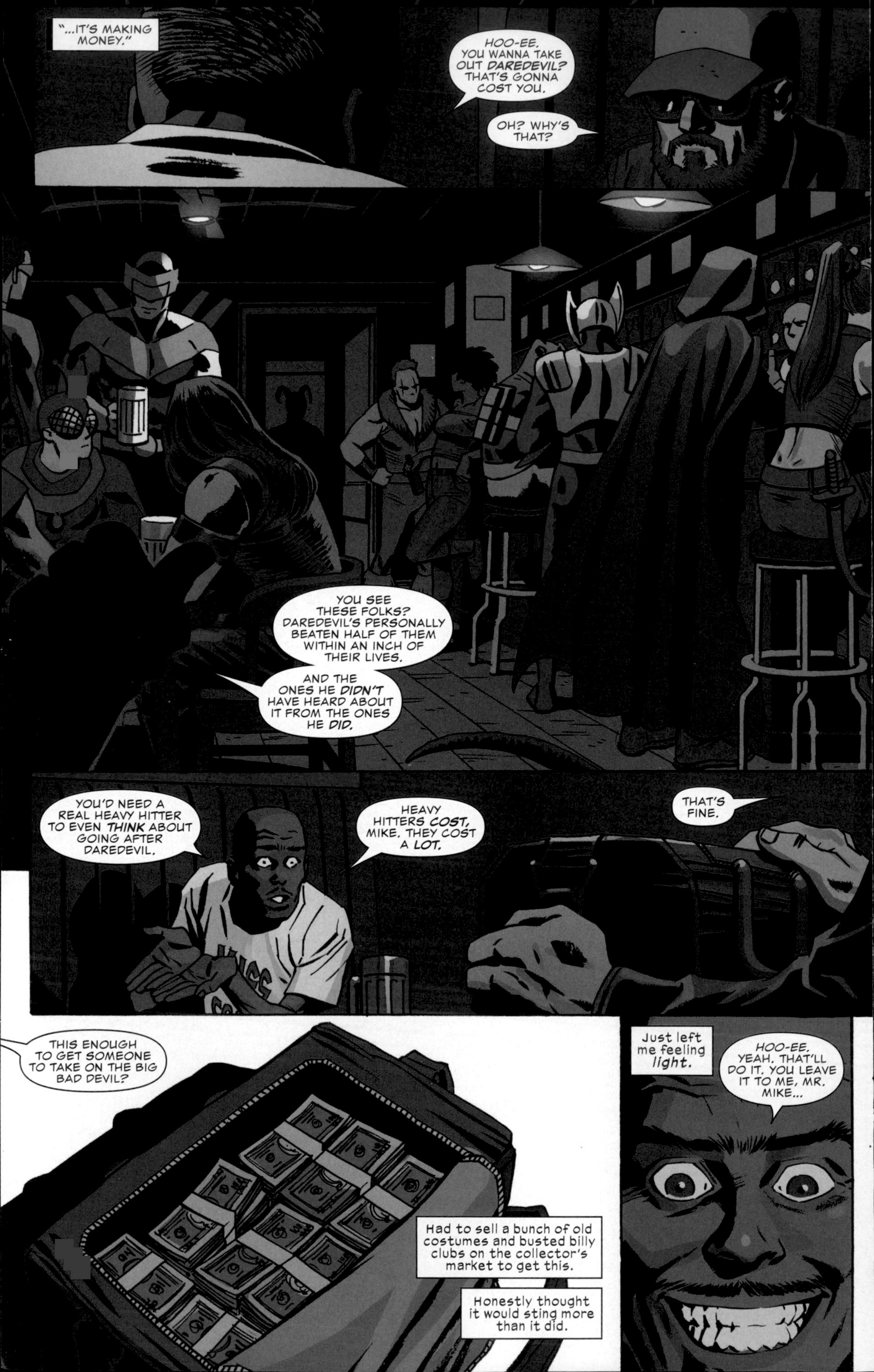
"...IT'S MAKING MONEY."
HOO-EE. YOU WANNA TAKE OUT DAREDEVIL? THAT'S GONNA COST YOU.
OH? WHY'S THAT?
YOU SEE THESE FOLKS? DAREDEVIL'S PERSONALLY BEATEN HALF OF THEM WITHIN AN INCH OF THEIR LIVES.
AND THE ONES HE DIDN'T HAVE HEARD ABOUT IT FROM THE ONES HE DID.
YOU'D NEED A REAL HEAVY HITTER TO EVEN THINK ABOUT GOING AFTER DAREDEVIL.
HEAVY HITTERS COST, MIKE. THEY COST A LOT.
THAT'S FINE.
THIS ENOUGH TO GET SOMEONE TO TAKE ON THE BIG BAD DEVIL?
Had to sell a bunch of old costumes and busted billy clubs on the collector's market to get this.
Honestly thought it would sting more than it did.
Just left me feeling light.
HOO-EE. YEAH. THAT'LL DO IT. YOU LEAVE IT TO ME, MR. MIKE...

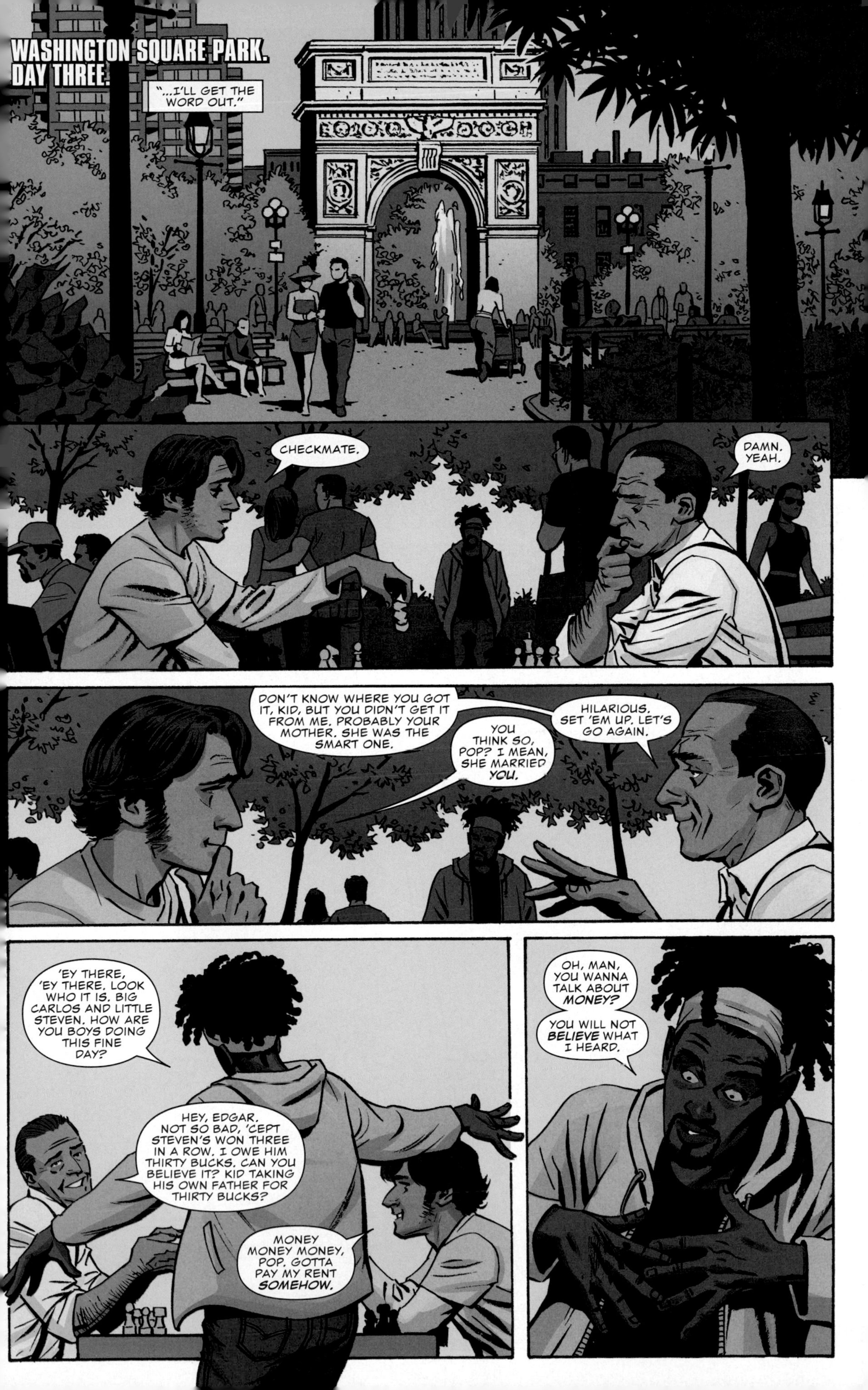
WASHINGTON SQUARE PARK. DAY THREE.
"...I'LL GET THE WORD OUT."
CHECKMATE.
DAMN. YEAH.
DON'T KNOW WHERE YOU GOT IT, KID, BUT YOU DIDN'T GET IT FROM ME. PROBABLY YOUR MOTHER. SHE WAS THE SMART ONE.
YOU THINK SO, POP? I MEAN, SHE MARRIED YOU.
HILARIOUS. SET 'EM UP. LET'S GO AGAIN.
'EY THERE, 'EY THERE. LOOK WHO IT IS. BIG CARLOS AND LITTLE STEVEN. HOW ARE YOU BOYS DOING THIS FINE DAY?
HEY, EDGAR. NOT SO BAD, 'CEPT STEVEN'S WON THREE IN A ROW. I OWE HIM THIRTY BUCKS. CAN YOU BELIEVE IT? KID TAKING HIS OWN FATHER FOR THIRTY BUCKS?
MONEY MONEY MONEY, POP. GOTTA PAY MY RENT SOMEHOW.
OH, MAN, YOU WANNA TALK ABOUT MONEY?
YOU WILL NOT BELIEVE WHAT I HEARD.

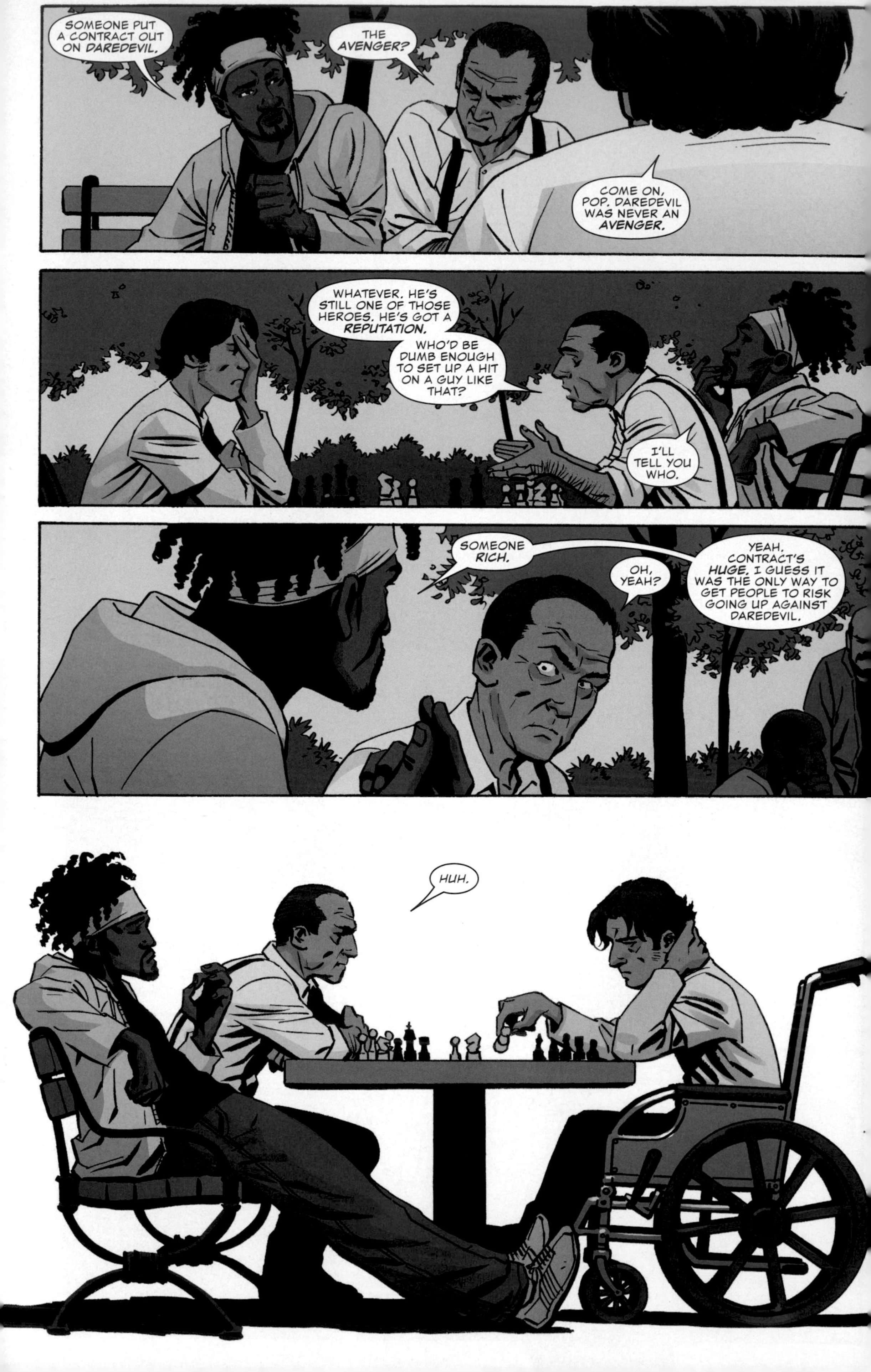
SOMEONE PUT A CONTRACT OUT ON DAREDEVIL.
THE AVENGER?
COME ON, POP. DAREDEVIL WAS NEVER AN AVENGER.
WHATEVER. HE'S STILL ONE OF THOSE HEROES. HE'S GOT A REPUTATION.
WHO'D BE DUMB ENOUGH TO SET UP A HIT ON A GUY LIKE THAT?
I'LL TELL YOU WHO.
SOMEONE RICH.
OH, YEAH?
YEAH. CONTRACT'S HUGE. I GUESS IT WAS THE ONLY WAY TO GET PEOPLE TO RISK GOING UP AGAINST DAREDEVIL.
HUH.

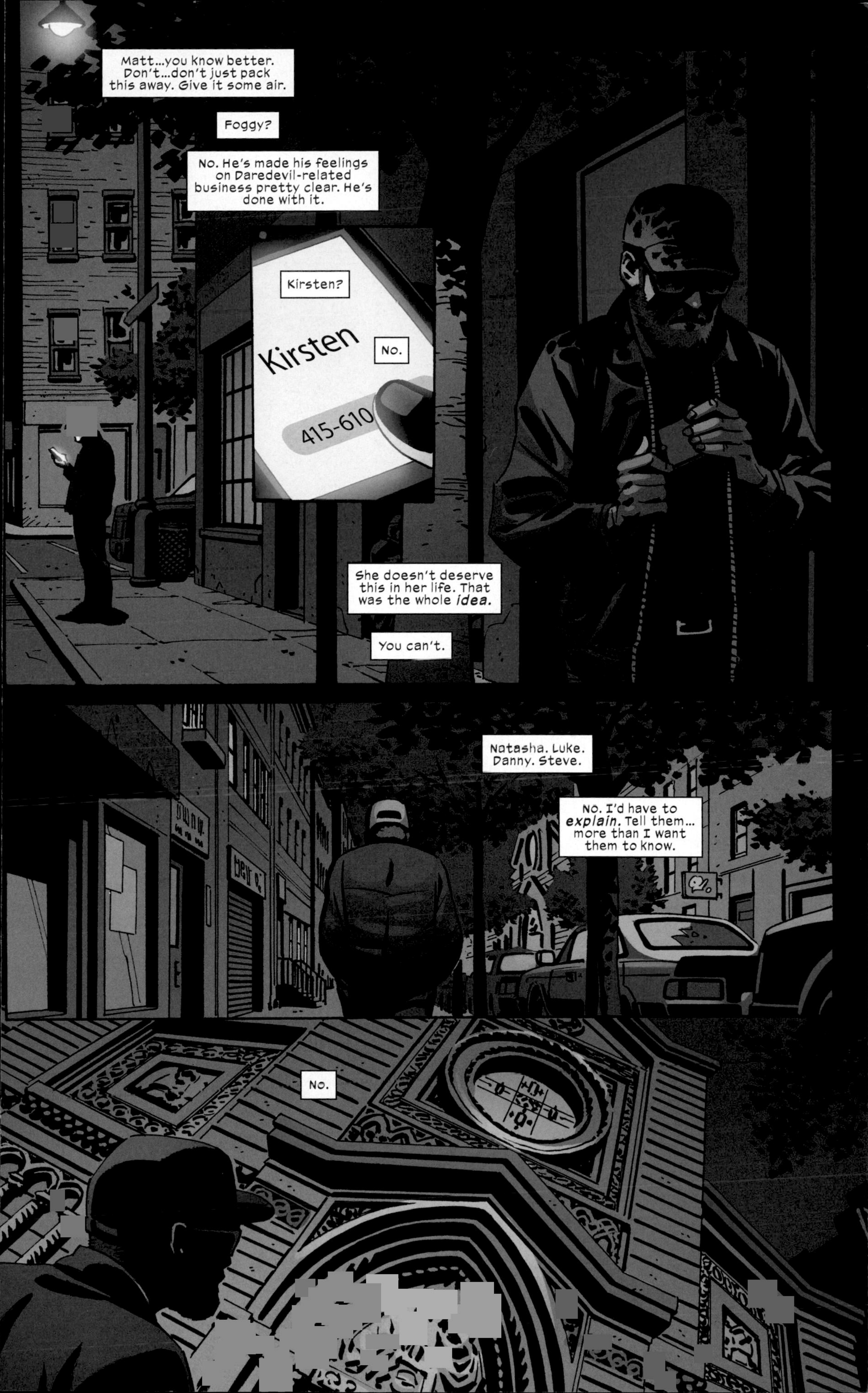
Matt...you know better. Don't...don't just pack this away. Give it some air.
Foggy?
No. He's made his feelings on Daredevil-related business pretty clear. He's done with it.
Kirsten?
Kirsten
No.
415-610
She doesn't deserve this in her life. That was the whole idea.
You can't.
Natasha. Luke. Danny. Steve.
No. I'd have to explain. Tell them... more than I want them to know.
No.

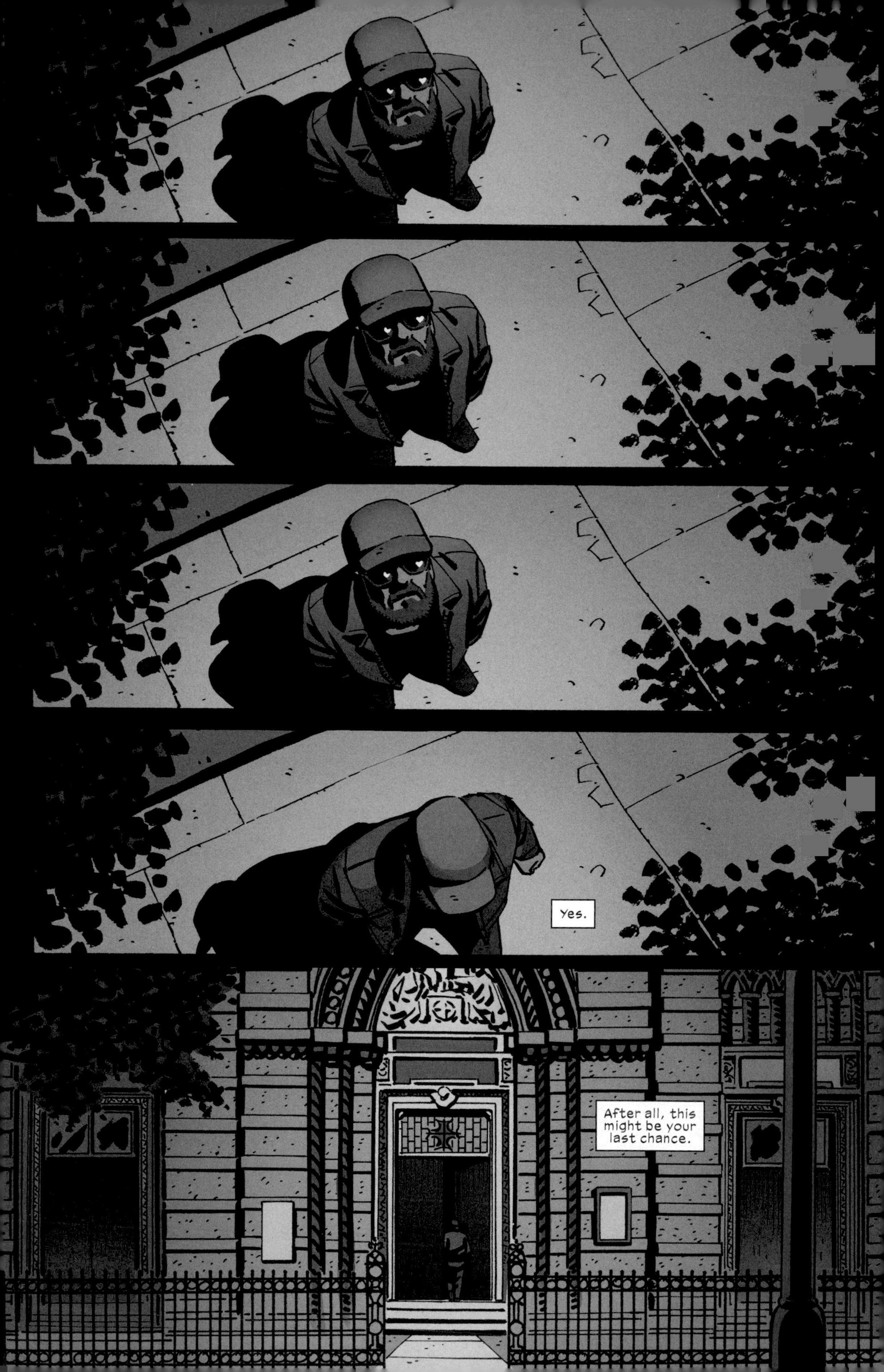
Yes.
After all, this might be your last chance.

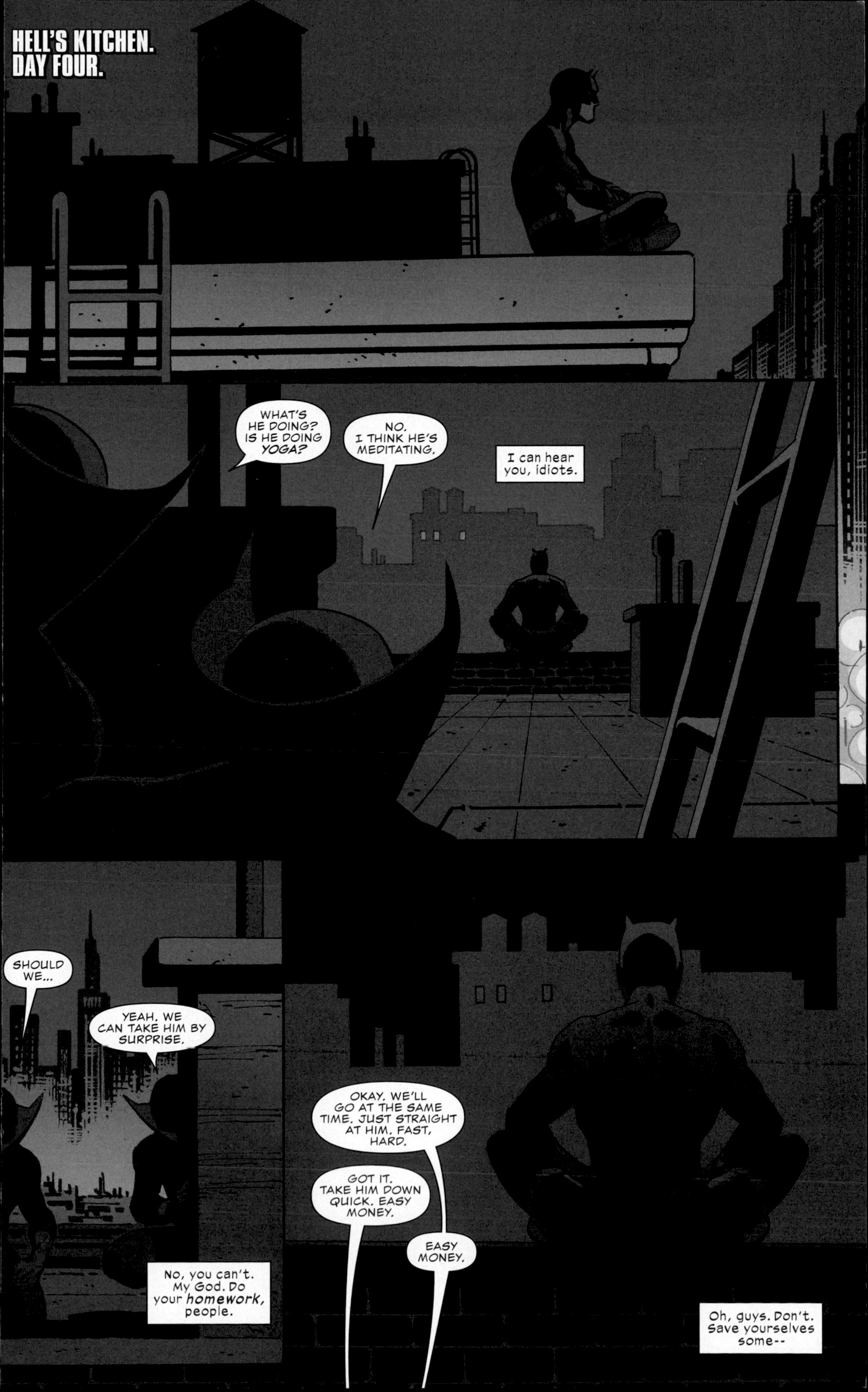
HELL'S KITCHEN. DAY FOUR.
WHAT'S HE DOING? IS HE DOING YOGA?
NO. I THINK HE'S MEDITATING.
I can hear you, idiots.
SHOULD WE...
YEAH. WE CAN TAKE HIM BY SURPRISE.
No, you can't. My God. Do your homework, people.
OKAY. WE'LL GO AT THE SAME TIME. JUST STRAIGHT AT HIM. FAST, HARD.
GOT IT. TAKE HIM DOWN QUICK. EASY MONEY.
EASY MONEY.
Oh, guys. Don't. Save yourselves some--

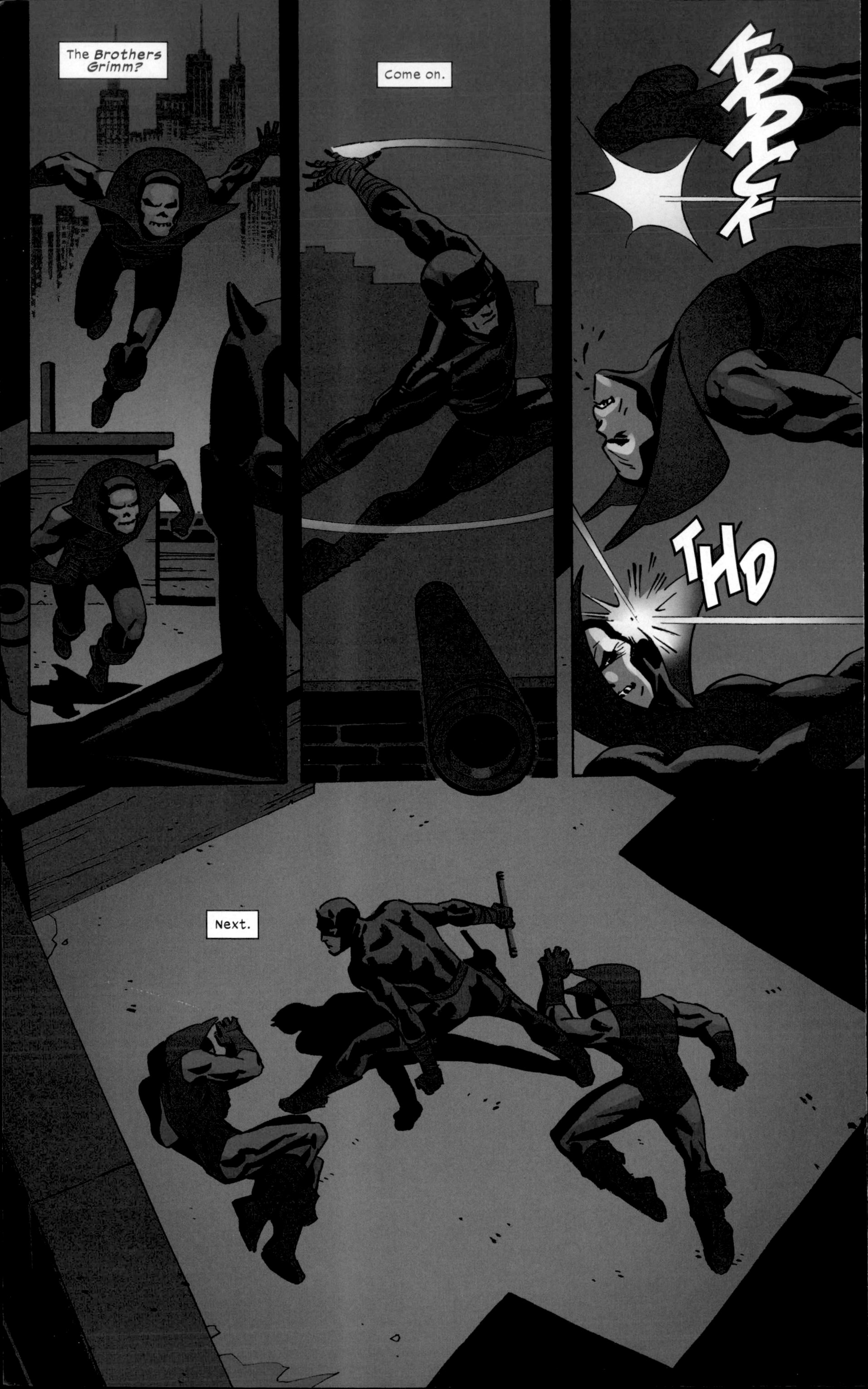
The *Brothers Grimm?*
Come on.
KRACK
THD
Next.

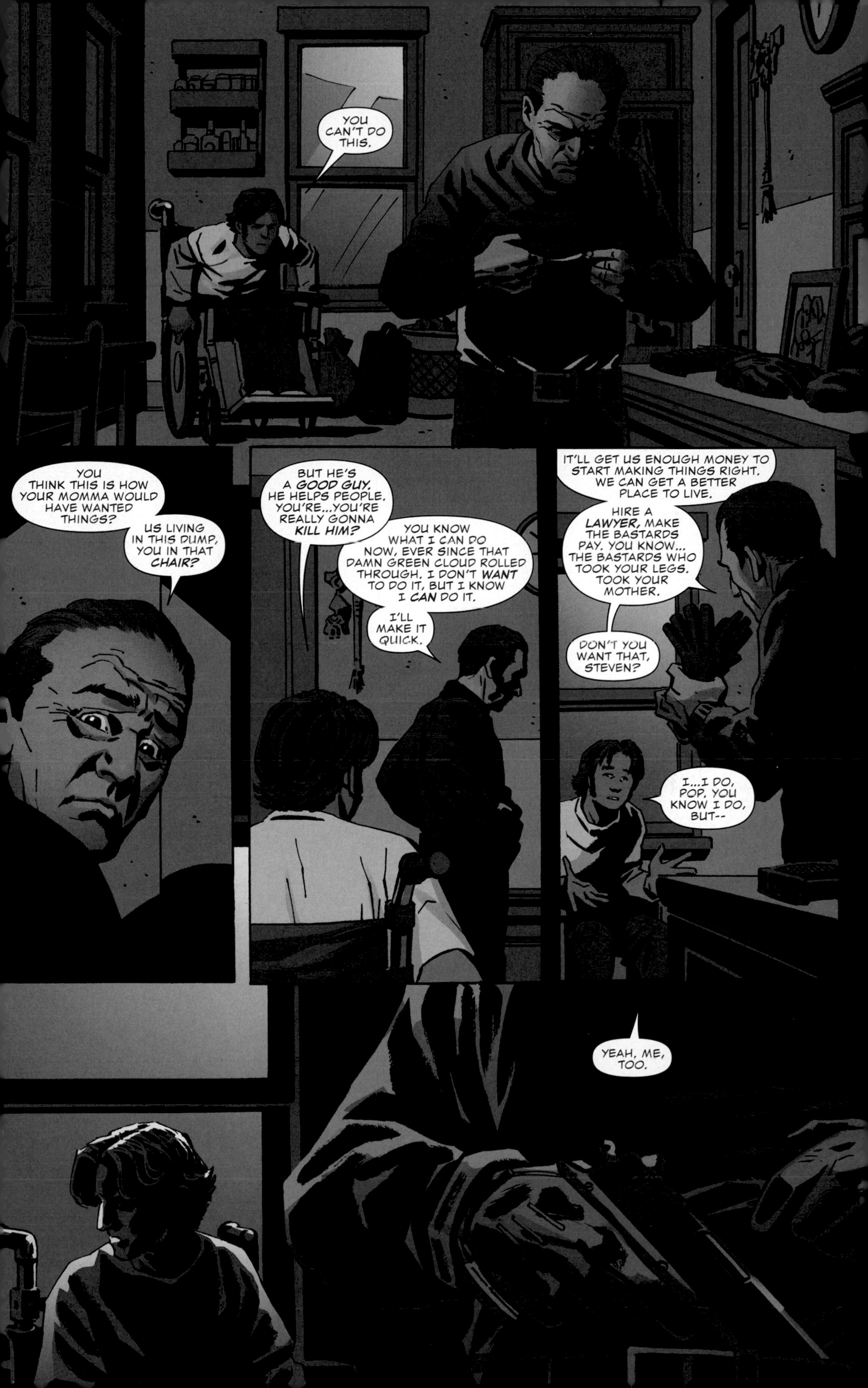
YOU CAN'T DO THIS.
YOU THINK THIS IS HOW YOUR MOMMA WOULD HAVE WANTED THINGS?
US LIVING IN THIS DUMP, YOU IN THAT CHAIR?
BUT HE'S A GOOD GUY. HE HELPS PEOPLE. YOU'RE...YOU'RE REALLY GONNA KILL HIM?
YOU KNOW WHAT I CAN DO NOW, EVER SINCE THAT DAMN GREEN CLOUD ROLLED THROUGH. I DON'T WANT TO DO IT, BUT I KNOW I CAN DO IT.
I'LL MAKE IT QUICK.
IT'LL GET US ENOUGH MONEY TO START MAKING THINGS RIGHT. WE CAN GET A BETTER PLACE TO LIVE.
HIRE A LAWYER, MAKE THE BASTARDS PAY. YOU KNOW... THE BASTARDS WHO TOOK YOUR LEGS. TOOK YOUR MOTHER.
DON'T YOU WANT THAT, STEVEN?
I...I DO, POP, YOU KNOW I DO, BUT--
YEAH, ME, TOO.

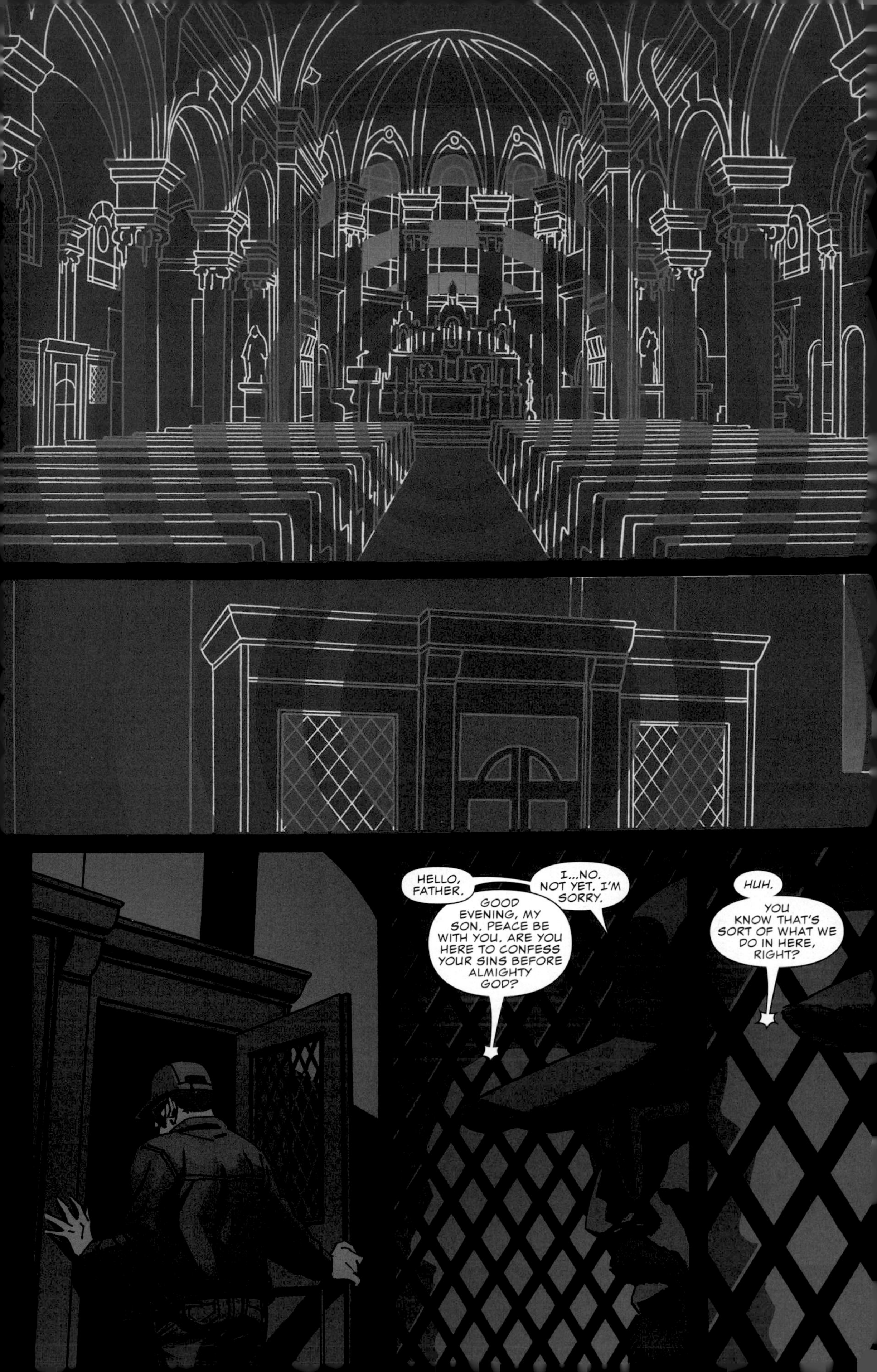
HELLO, FATHER.
GOOD EVENING, MY SON. PEACE BE WITH YOU. ARE YOU HERE TO CONFESS YOUR SINS BEFORE ALMIGHTY GOD?
I...NO. NOT YET. I'M SORRY.
HUH.
YOU KNOW THAT'S SORT OF WHAT WE DO IN HERE, RIGHT?

YES, I'M... JUST...I WAS HOPING PERHAPS WE COULD TALK.

YOU WANT TO *TALK*, HUH?

LOOK, PRIESTS GET ASKED TO PLAY FREE THERAPIST ALL THE TIME, ESPECIALLY IN *THIS* CITY.

BUT I'VE GOT A POLICY.

YOU WANT TO UNBURDEN YOUR SOUL BEFORE THE LORD, SAY A TRUE ACT OF CONTRITION AND BE WASHED CLEAN, THEN SURE, THAT'S WHAT THE BOOTH'S FOR.

BUT YOU JUST WANT TO *TALK*...THEN WE DON'T DO IT IN THE *BOOTH*.

I'LL JUST STEP OUT, AND WAIT A FEW MINUTES. YOU WANT TO JOIN ME, GREAT.

YOU DON'T, I'LL KNOCK ON THE DOOR TWICE, AND THEN I'LL JUST HEAD UP TO THE ALTAR AND DO A LITTLE WORK WITH MY BACK TO THE CHURCH.

YOU CAN SLIP OUT, AND I'LL BE NONE THE WISER.

YOUR CALL, BUT IF YOU DON'T HAVE ANYTHING TO *CONFESS*...

...THEN YOU SHOULDN'T BE WORRIED ABOUT A LITTLE FACE-TO-FACE.

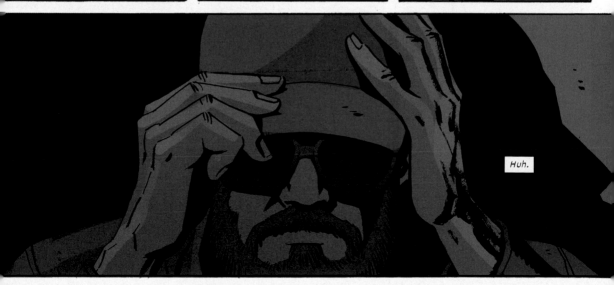

Huh.

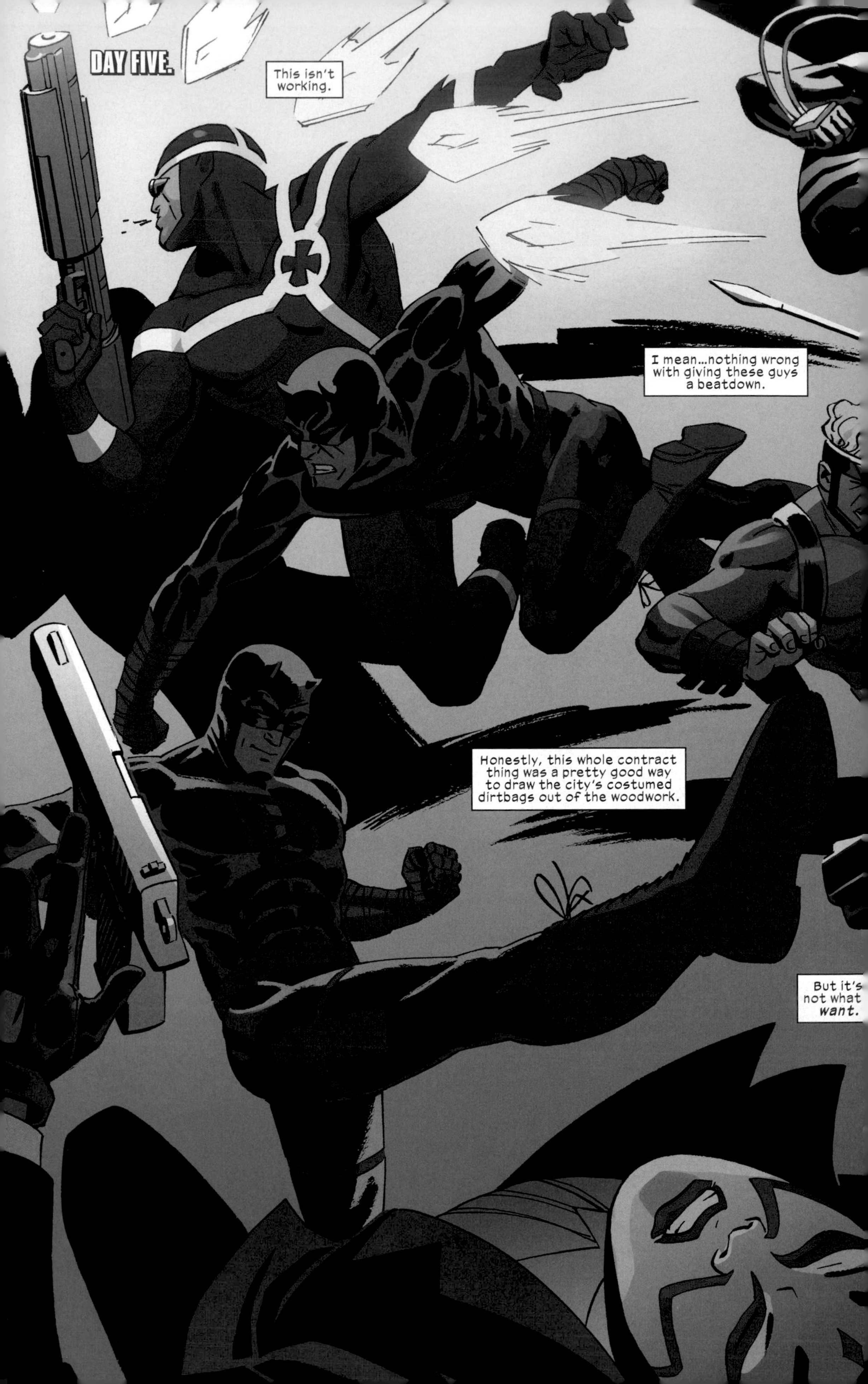
DAY FIVE.
This isn't working.
I mean...nothing wrong with giving these guys a beatdown.
Honestly, this whole contract thing was a pretty good way to draw the city's costumed dirtbags out of the woodwork.
But it's not what want.

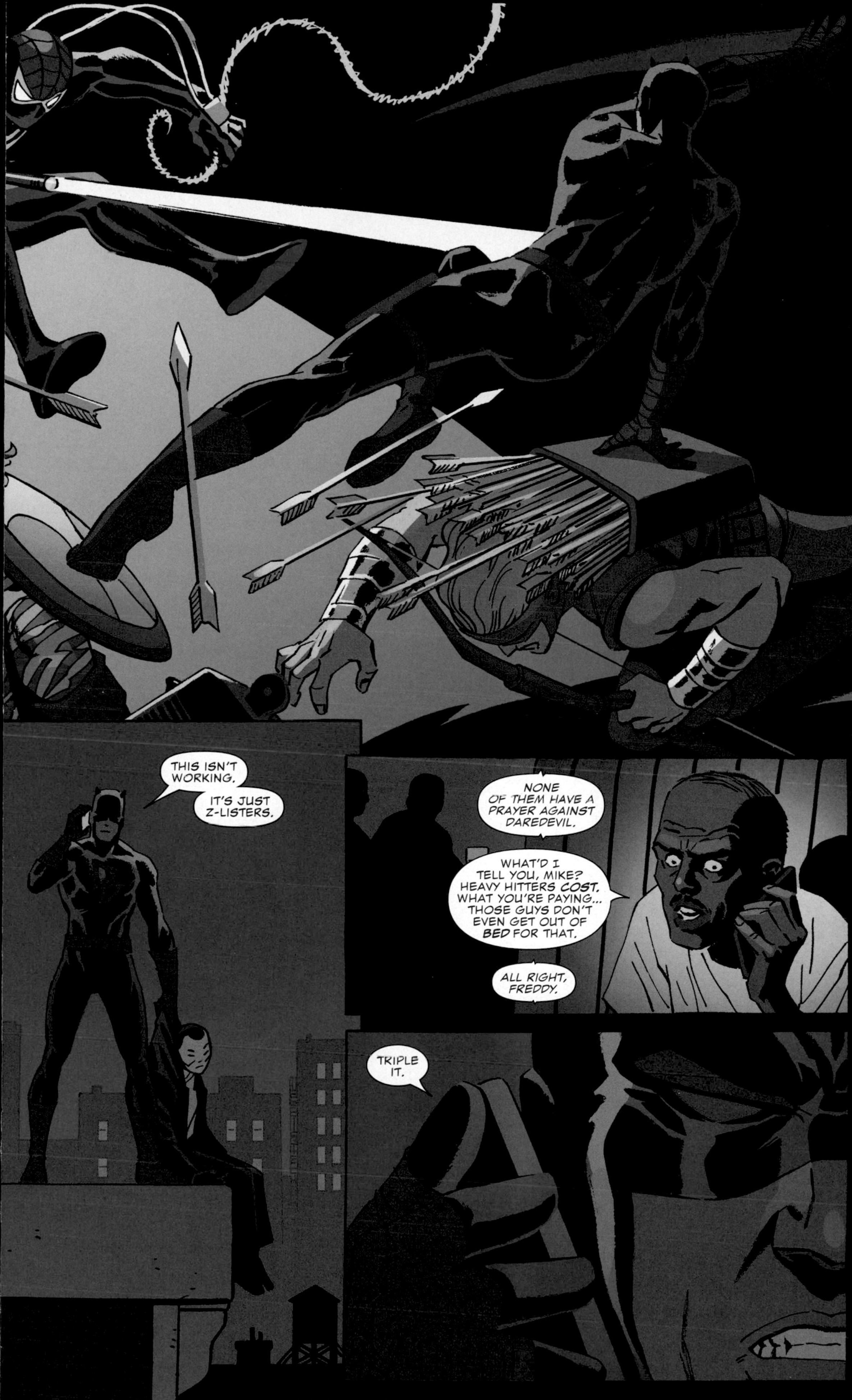
THIS ISN'T WORKING.
IT'S JUST Z-LISTERS.
NONE OF THEM HAVE A PRAYER AGAINST DAREDEVIL.
WHAT'D I TELL YOU, MIKE? HEAVY HITTERS COST. WHAT YOU'RE PAYING... THOSE GUYS DON'T EVEN GET OUT OF BED FOR THAT.
ALL RIGHT, FREDDY.
TRIPLE IT.

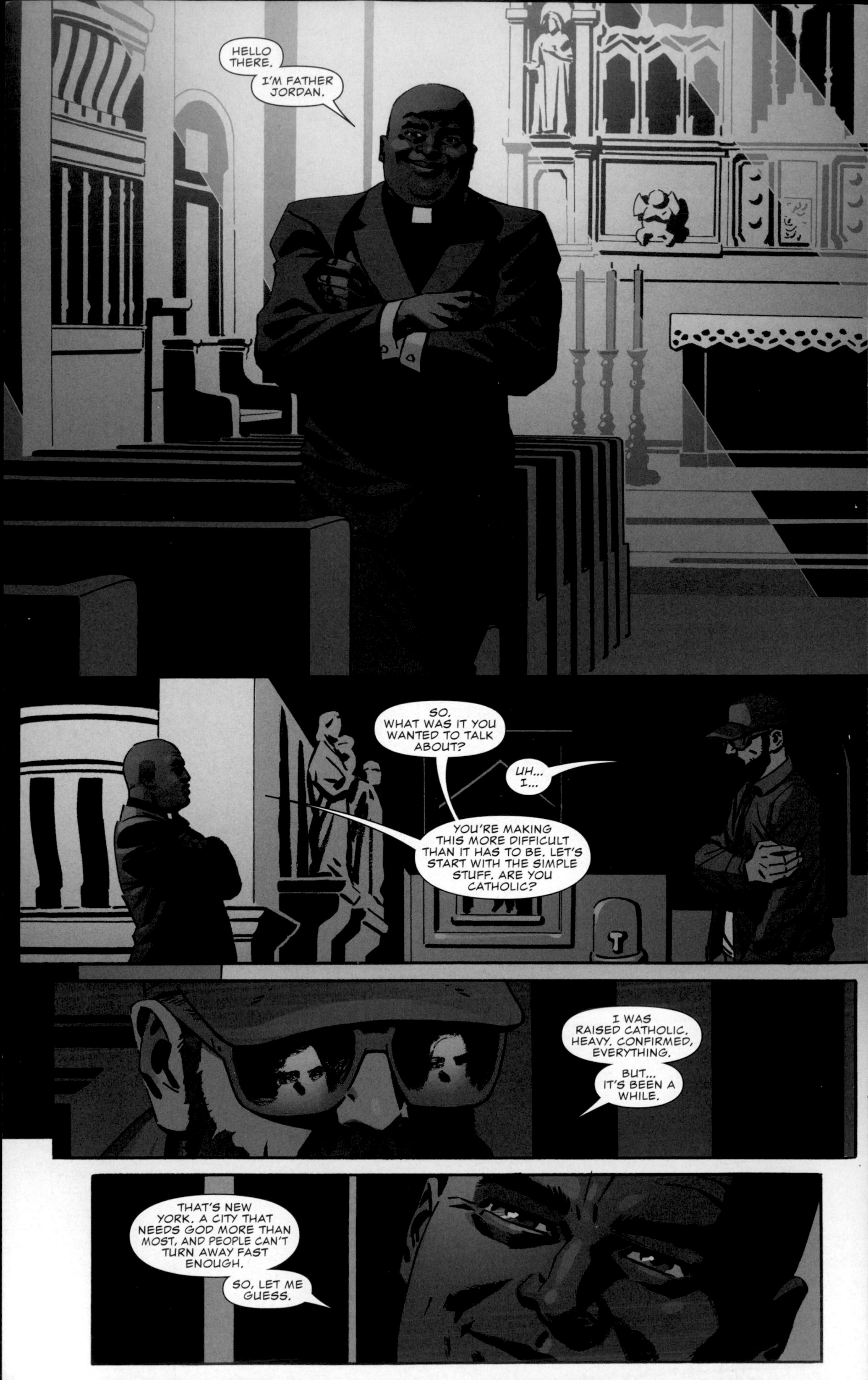
HELLO THERE.
I'M FATHER JORDAN.
SO. WHAT WAS IT YOU WANTED TO TALK ABOUT?
UH... I...
YOU'RE MAKING THIS MORE DIFFICULT THAN IT HAS TO BE. LET'S START WITH THE SIMPLE STUFF. ARE YOU CATHOLIC?
I WAS RAISED CATHOLIC. HEAVY. CONFIRMED, EVERYTHING.
BUT... IT'S BEEN A WHILE.
THAT'S NEW YORK. A CITY THAT NEEDS GOD MORE THAN MOST, AND PEOPLE CAN'T TURN AWAY FAST ENOUGH.
SO, LET ME GUESS.

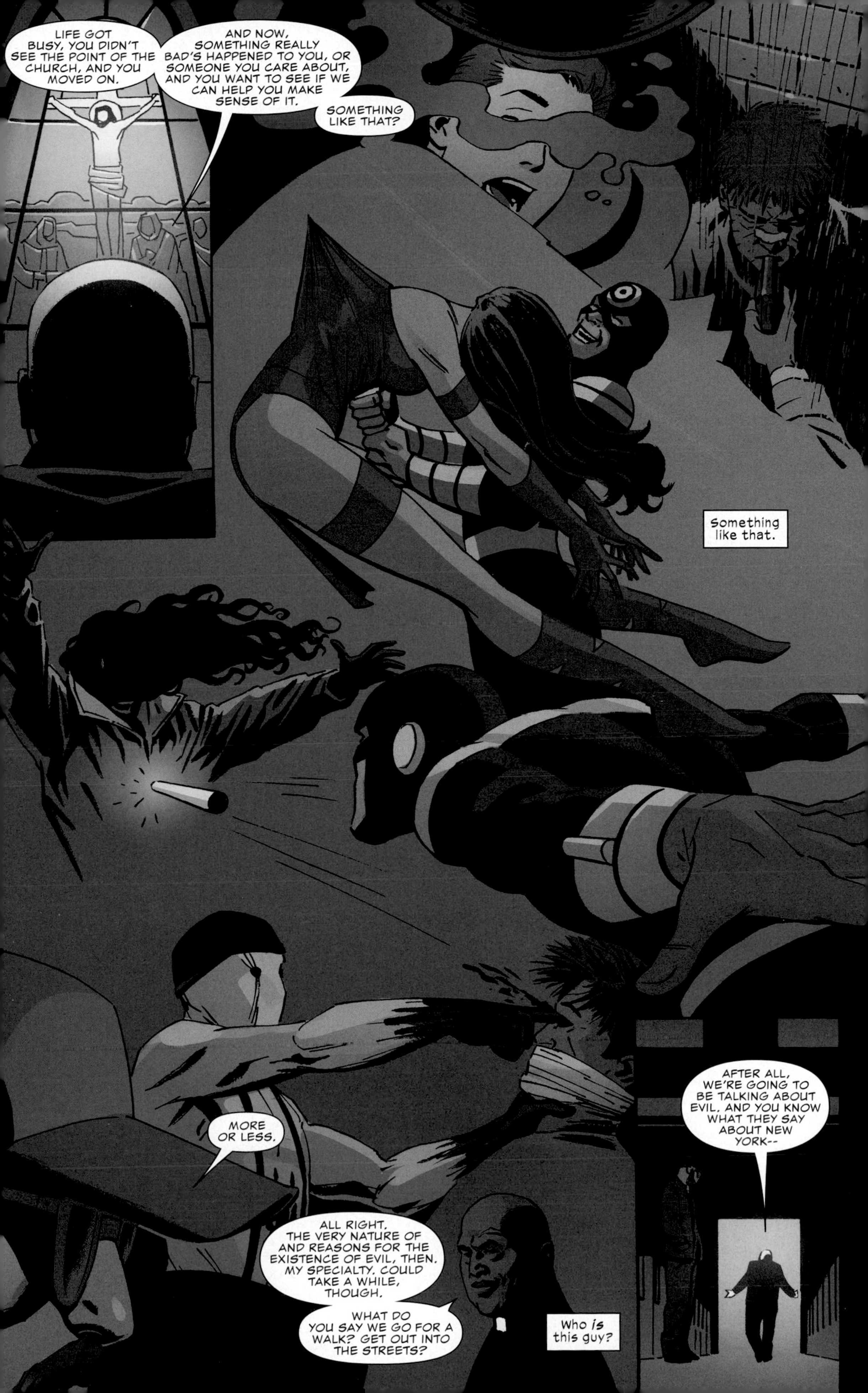
LIFE GOT BUSY, YOU DIDN'T SEE THE POINT OF THE CHURCH, AND YOU MOVED ON.
AND NOW, SOMETHING REALLY BAD'S HAPPENED TO YOU, OR SOMEONE YOU CARE ABOUT, AND YOU WANT TO SEE IF WE CAN HELP YOU MAKE SENSE OF IT.
SOMETHING LIKE THAT?
Something like that.
MORE OR LESS.
AFTER ALL, WE'RE GOING TO BE TALKING ABOUT EVIL, AND YOU KNOW WHAT THEY SAY ABOUT NEW YORK--
ALL RIGHT. THE VERY NATURE OF AND REASONS FOR THE EXISTENCE OF EVIL, THEN. MY SPECIALTY. COULD TAKE A WHILE, THOUGH.
WHAT DO YOU SAY WE GO FOR A WALK? GET OUT INTO THE STREETS?
Who *is* this guy?

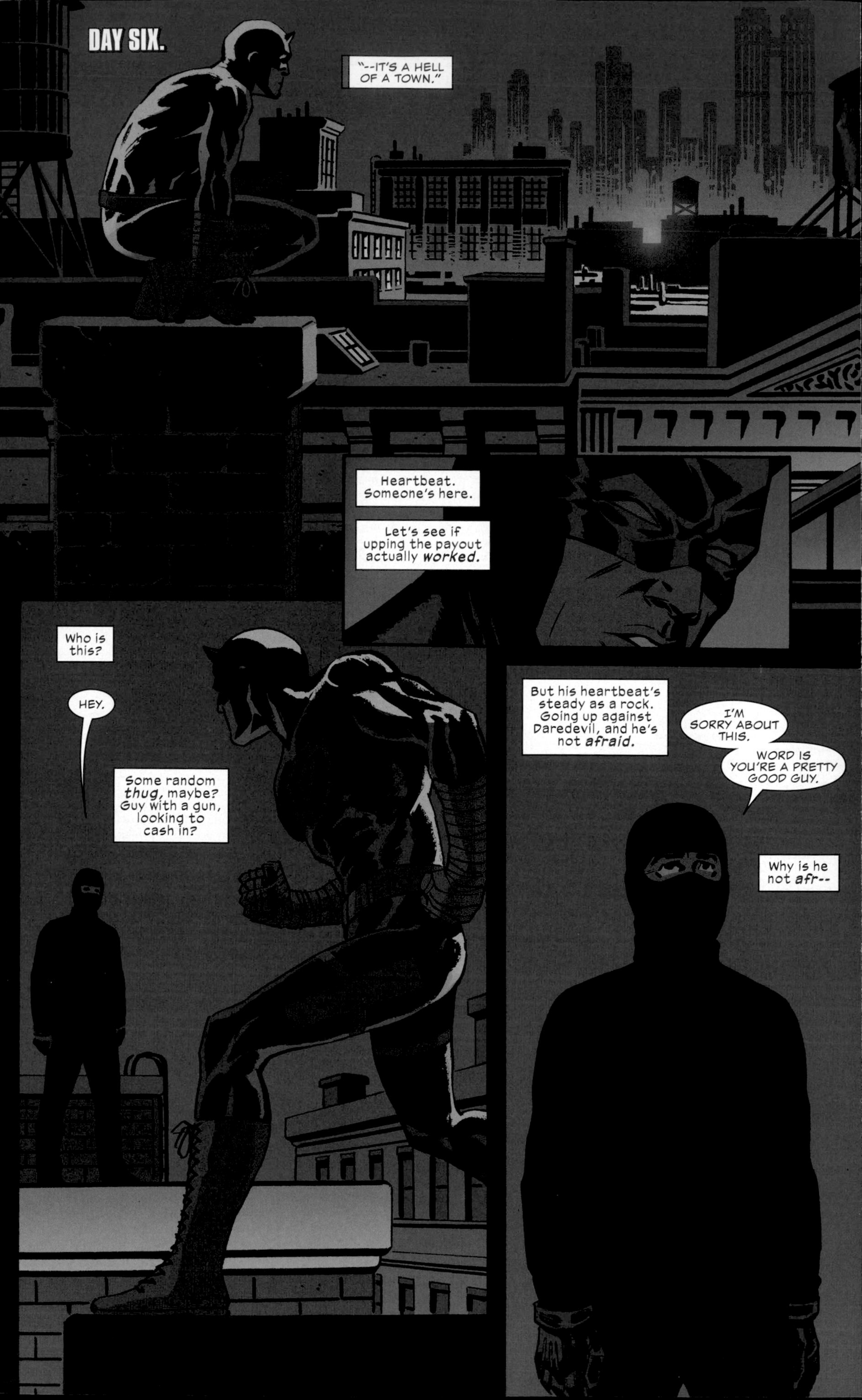
DAY SIX.
"--IT'S A HELL OF A TOWN."
Heartbeat. Someone's here.
Let's see if upping the payout actually *worked.*
Who is this?
HEY.
Some random *thug,* maybe? Guy with a gun, looking to cash in?
But his heartbeat's steady as a rock. Going up against Daredevil, and he's not *afraid.*
I'M SORRY ABOUT THIS.
WORD IS YOU'RE A PRETTY GOOD GUY.
Why is he not *afr--*

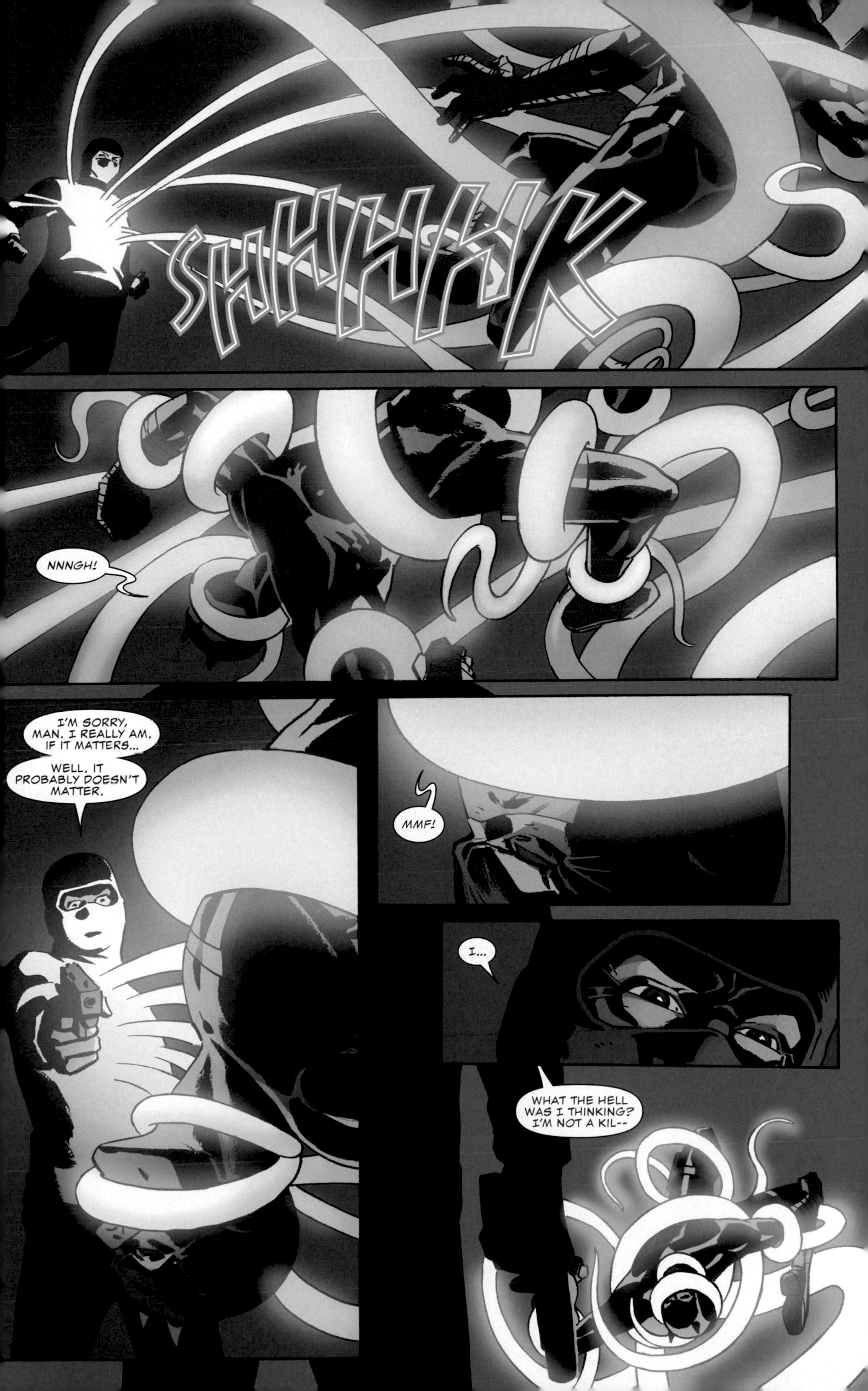
SHHHHHK
NNNGH!
I'M SORRY, MAN. I REALLY AM. IF IT MATTERS...
WELL, IT PROBABLY DOESN'T MATTER.
MMF!
I...
WHAT THE HELL WAS I THINKING? I'M NOT A KIL--

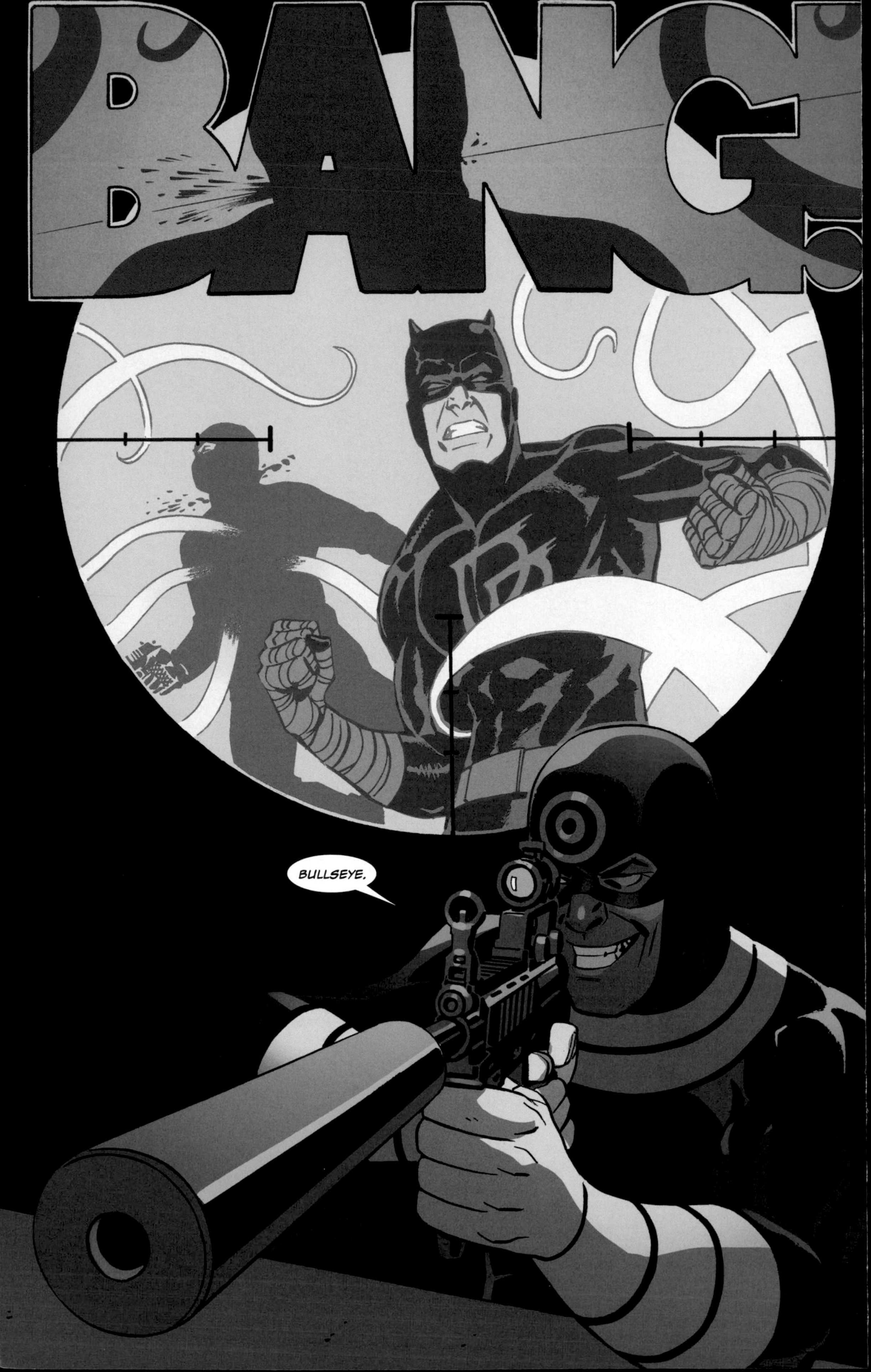
BANG
5
BULLSEYE.

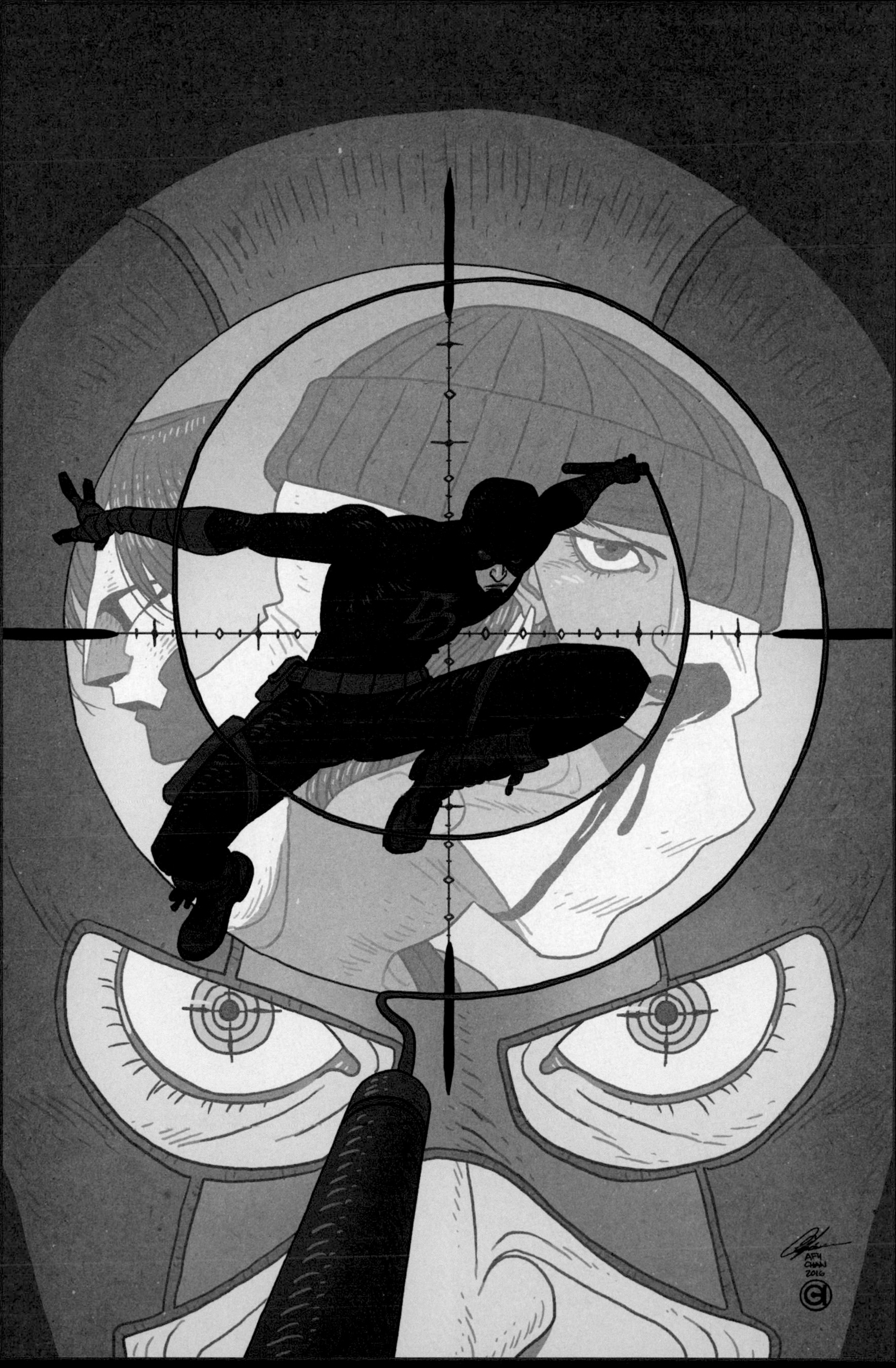
AFU CHAN 2016

AFU CHAN

No. 15 STORY THUS FAR VARIANT

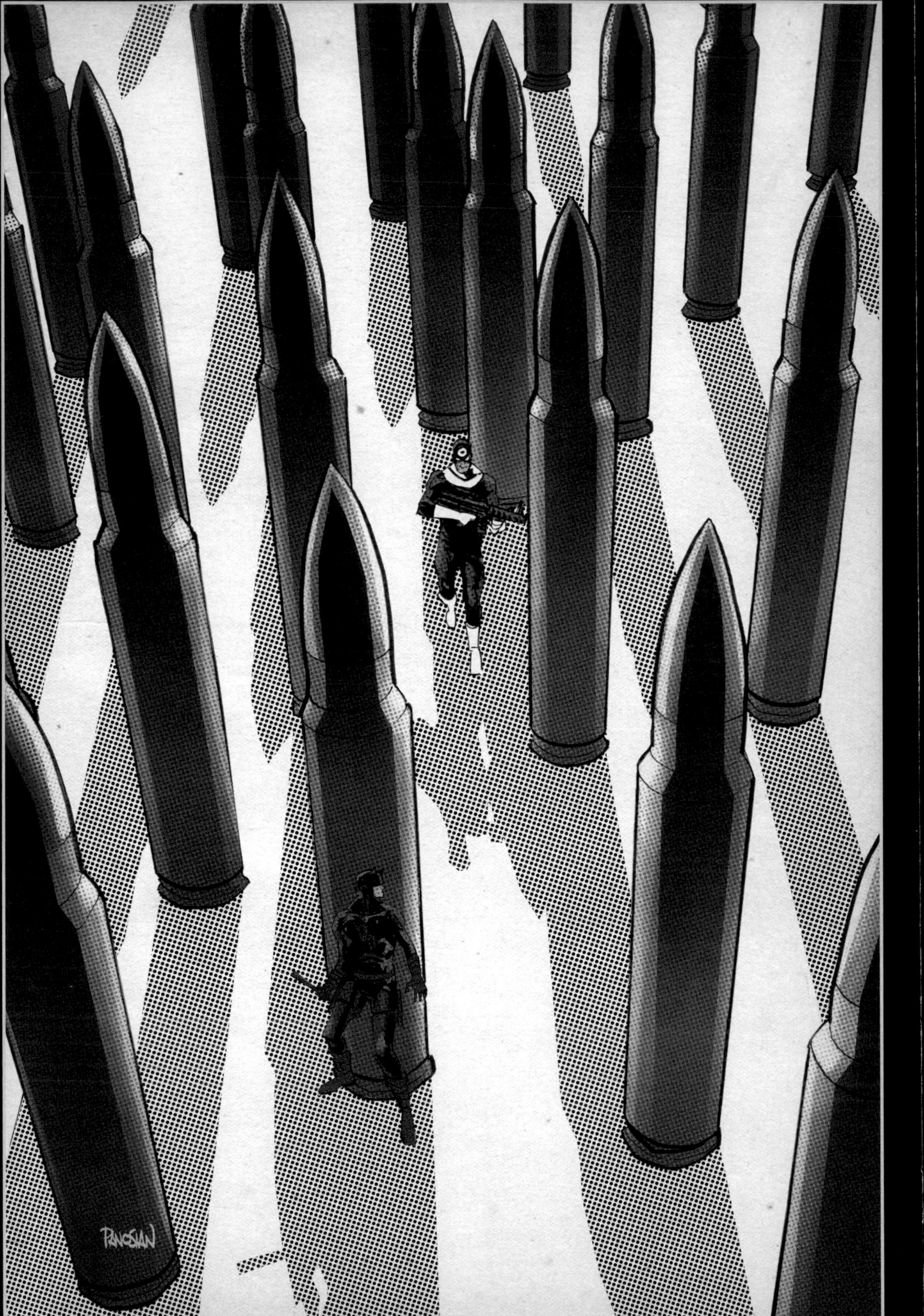
PANOSIAN

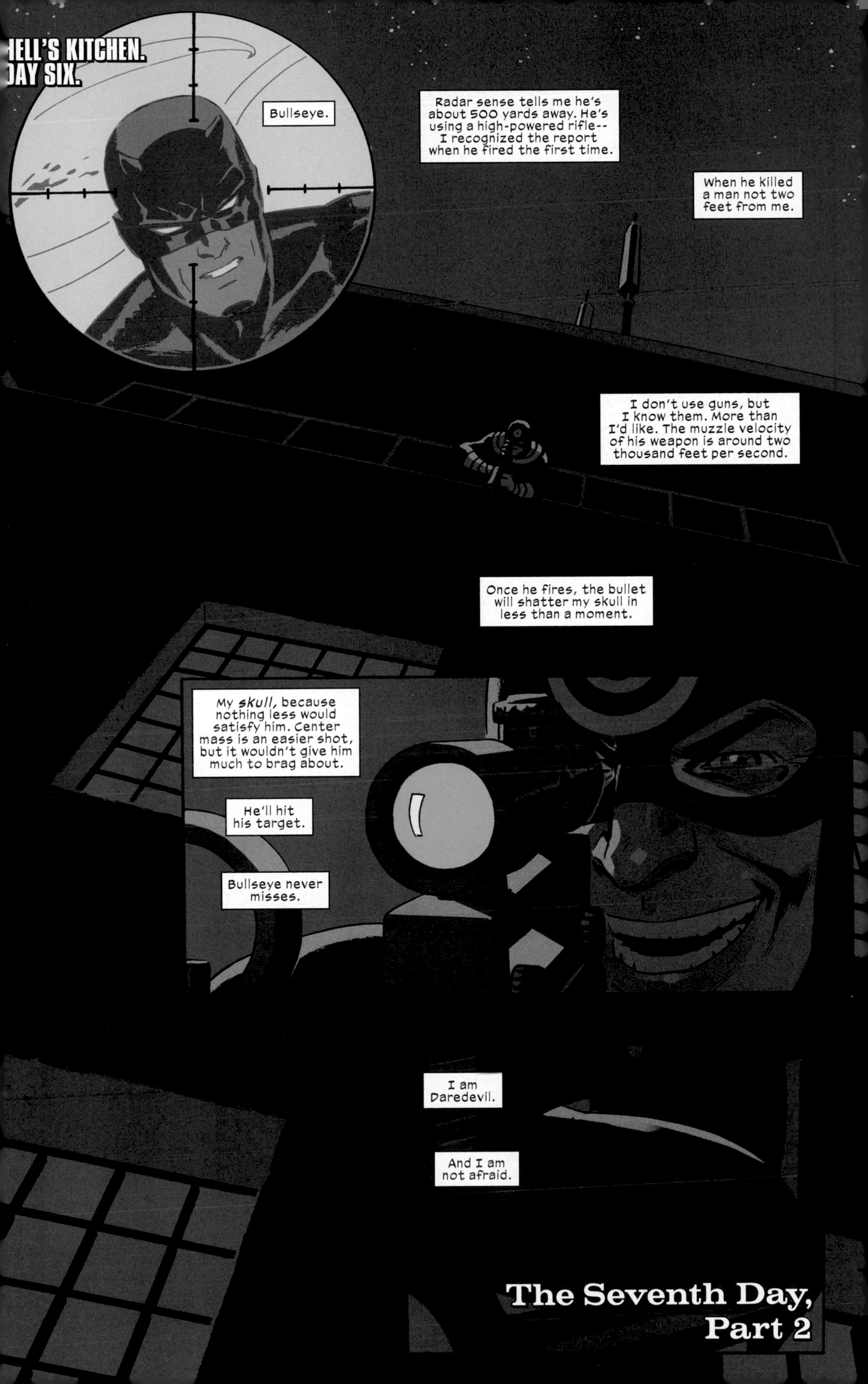
HELL'S KITCHEN.
DAY SIX.
Bullseye.
Radar sense tells me he's about 500 yards away. He's using a high-powered rifle-- I recognized the report when he fired the first time.
When he killed a man not two feet from me.
I don't use guns, but I know them. More than I'd like. The muzzle velocity of his weapon is around two thousand feet per second.
Once he fires, the bullet will shatter my skull in less than a moment.
My skull, because nothing less would satisfy him. Center mass is an easier shot, but it wouldn't give him much to brag about.
He'll hit his target.
Bullseye never misses.
I am Daredevil.
And I am not afraid.
The Seventh Day, Part 2

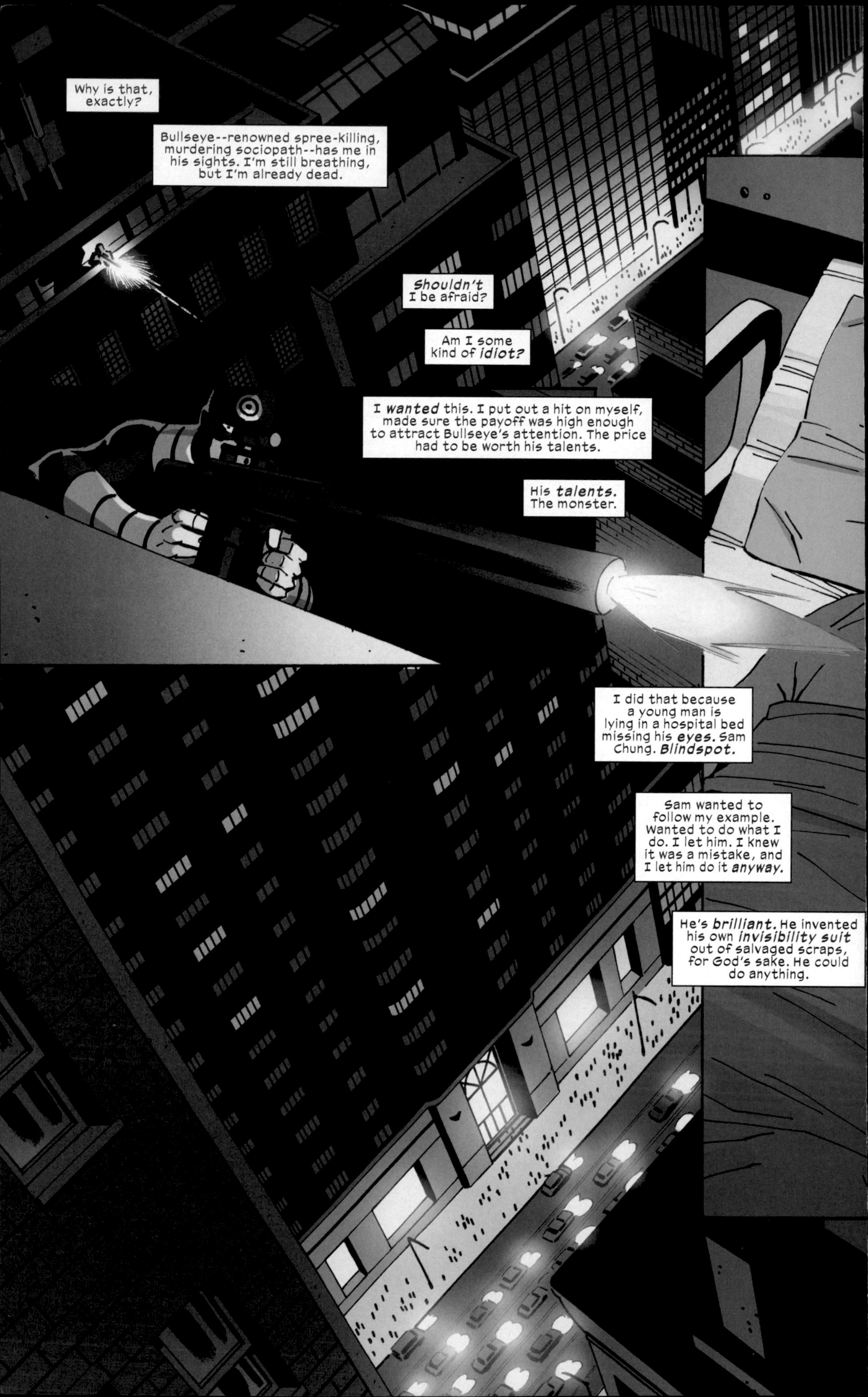
Why is that, exactly?
Bullseye--renowned spree-killing, murdering sociopath--has me in his sights. I'm still breathing, but I'm already dead.
Shouldn't I be afraid?
Am I some kind of *idiot?*
I *wanted* this. I put out a hit on myself, made sure the payoff was high enough to attract Bullseye's attention. The price had to be worth his talents.
His *talents.* The monster.
I did that because a young man is lying in a hospital bed missing his *eyes.* Sam Chung. *Blindspot.*
Sam wanted to follow my example. Wanted to do what I do. I let him. I knew it was a mistake, and I let him do it *anyway.*
He's *brilliant.* He invented his own *invisibility suit* out of salvaged scraps, for God's sake. He could do anything.

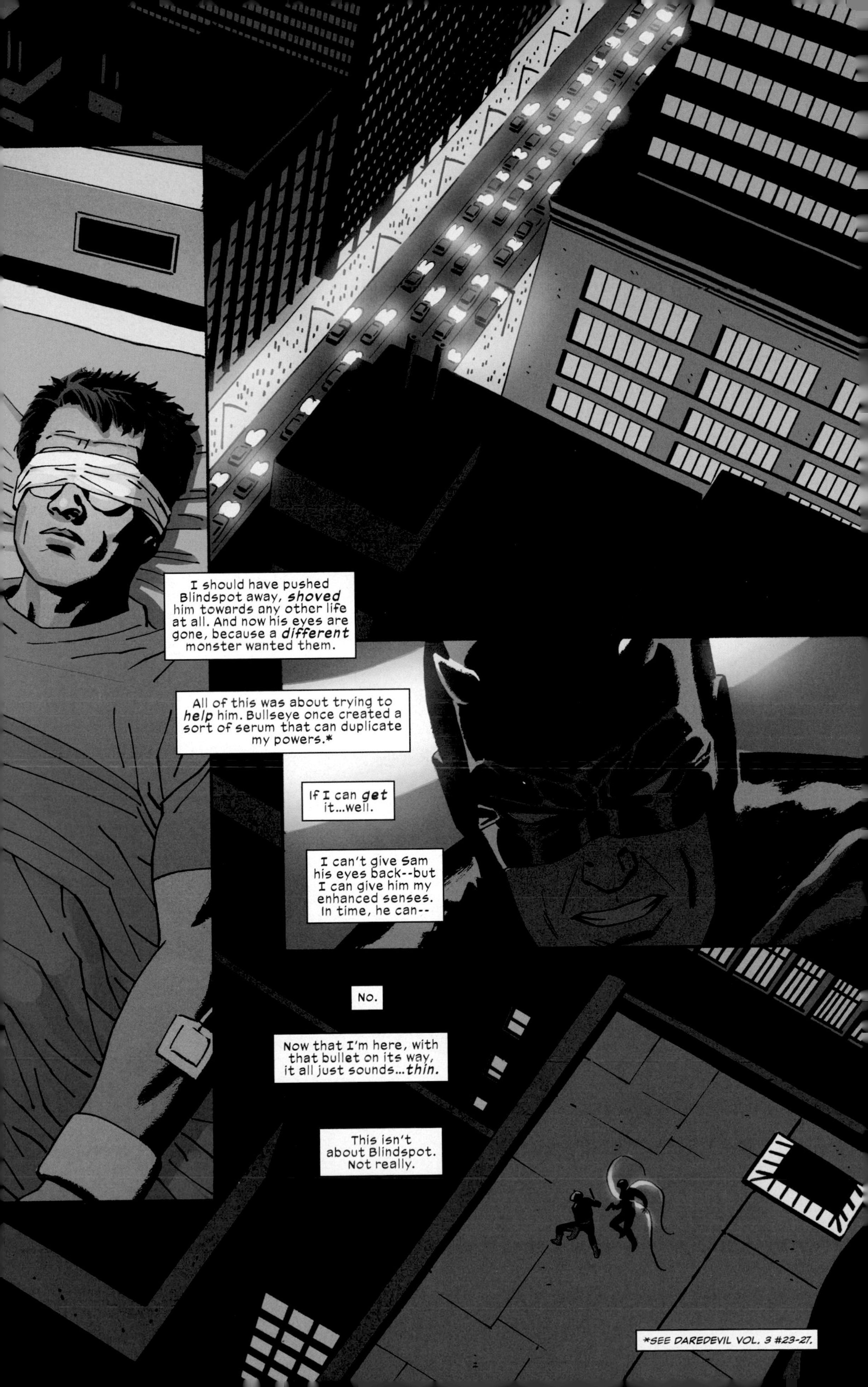
I should have pushed Blindspot away, *shoved* him towards any other life at all. And now his eyes are gone, because a *different* monster wanted them.
All of this was about trying to *help* him. Bullseye once created a sort of serum that can duplicate my powers.*
If I can *get* it...well.
I can't give Sam his eyes back--but I can give him my enhanced senses. In time, he can--
No.
Now that I'm here, with that bullet on its way, it all just sounds...*thin.*
This isn't about Blindspot. Not really.
*SEE DAREDEVIL VOL. 3 #23-27.

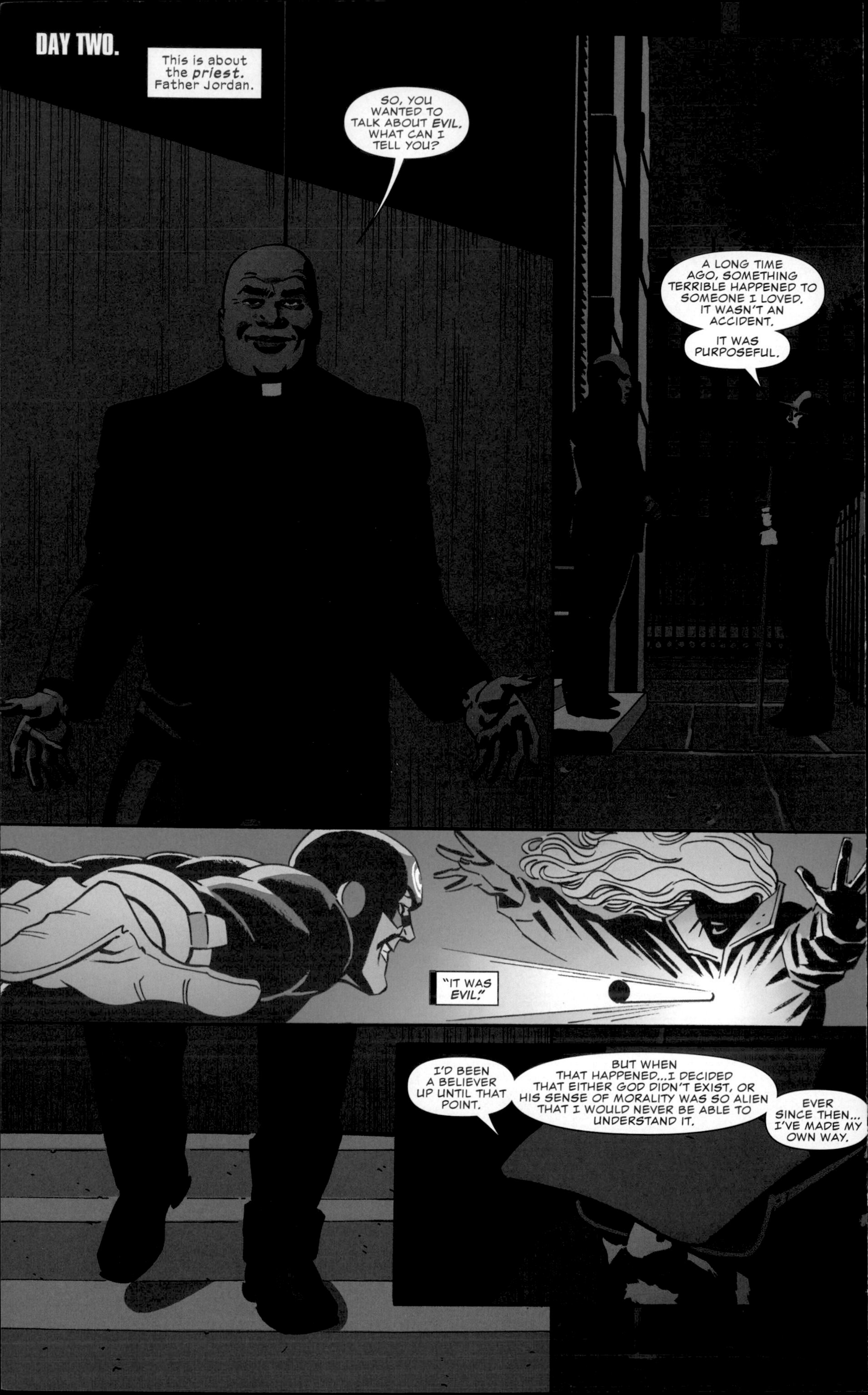
DAY TWO.
This is about the *priest.* Father Jordan.
SO, YOU WANTED TO TALK ABOUT EVIL. WHAT CAN I TELL YOU?
A LONG TIME AGO, SOMETHING TERRIBLE HAPPENED TO SOMEONE I LOVED. IT WASN'T AN ACCIDENT.
IT WAS PURPOSEFUL.
"IT WAS EVIL."
I'D BEEN A BELIEVER UP UNTIL THAT POINT.
BUT WHEN THAT HAPPENED...I DECIDED THAT EITHER GOD DIDN'T EXIST, OR HIS SENSE OF MORALITY WAS SO ALIEN THAT I WOULD NEVER BE ABLE TO UNDERSTAND IT.
EVER SINCE THEN... I'VE MADE MY OWN WAY.

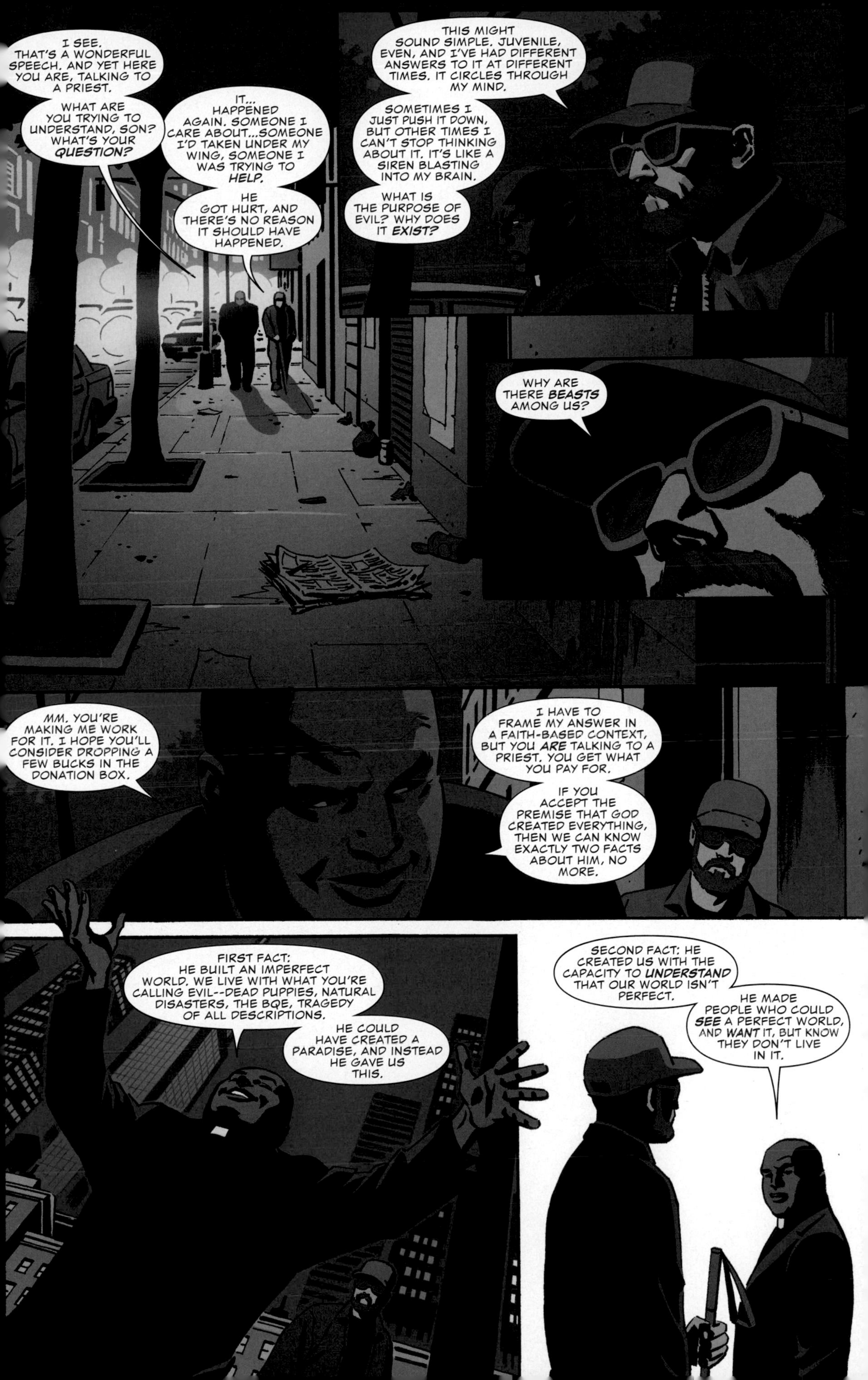
I SEE. THAT'S A WONDERFUL SPEECH. AND YET HERE YOU ARE, TALKING TO A PRIEST.
WHAT ARE YOU TRYING TO UNDERSTAND, SON? WHAT'S YOUR QUESTION?
IT... HAPPENED AGAIN. SOMEONE I CARE ABOUT...SOMEONE I'D TAKEN UNDER MY WING, SOMEONE I WAS TRYING TO HELP.
HE GOT HURT, AND THERE'S NO REASON IT SHOULD HAVE HAPPENED.
THIS MIGHT SOUND SIMPLE. JUVENILE, EVEN, AND I'VE HAD DIFFERENT ANSWERS TO IT AT DIFFERENT TIMES. IT CIRCLES THROUGH MY MIND.
SOMETIMES I JUST PUSH IT DOWN, BUT OTHER TIMES I CAN'T STOP THINKING ABOUT IT. IT'S LIKE A SIREN BLASTING INTO MY BRAIN.
WHAT IS THE PURPOSE OF EVIL? WHY DOES IT EXIST?
WHY ARE THERE BEASTS AMONG US?
MM. YOU'RE MAKING ME WORK FOR IT. I HOPE YOU'LL CONSIDER DROPPING A FEW BUCKS IN THE DONATION BOX.
I HAVE TO FRAME MY ANSWER IN A FAITH-BASED CONTEXT, BUT YOU ARE TALKING TO A PRIEST. YOU GET WHAT YOU PAY FOR.
IF YOU ACCEPT THE PREMISE THAT GOD CREATED EVERYTHING, THEN WE CAN KNOW EXACTLY TWO FACTS ABOUT HIM, NO MORE.
FIRST FACT: HE BUILT AN IMPERFECT WORLD. WE LIVE WITH WHAT YOU'RE CALLING EVIL--DEAD PUPPIES, NATURAL DISASTERS, THE BQE, TRAGEDY OF ALL DESCRIPTIONS.
HE COULD HAVE CREATED A PARADISE, AND INSTEAD HE GAVE US THIS.
SECOND FACT: HE CREATED US WITH THE CAPACITY TO UNDERSTAND THAT OUR WORLD ISN'T PERFECT.
HE MADE PEOPLE WHO COULD SEE A PERFECT WORLD, AND WANT IT, BUT KNOW THEY DON'T LIVE IN IT.

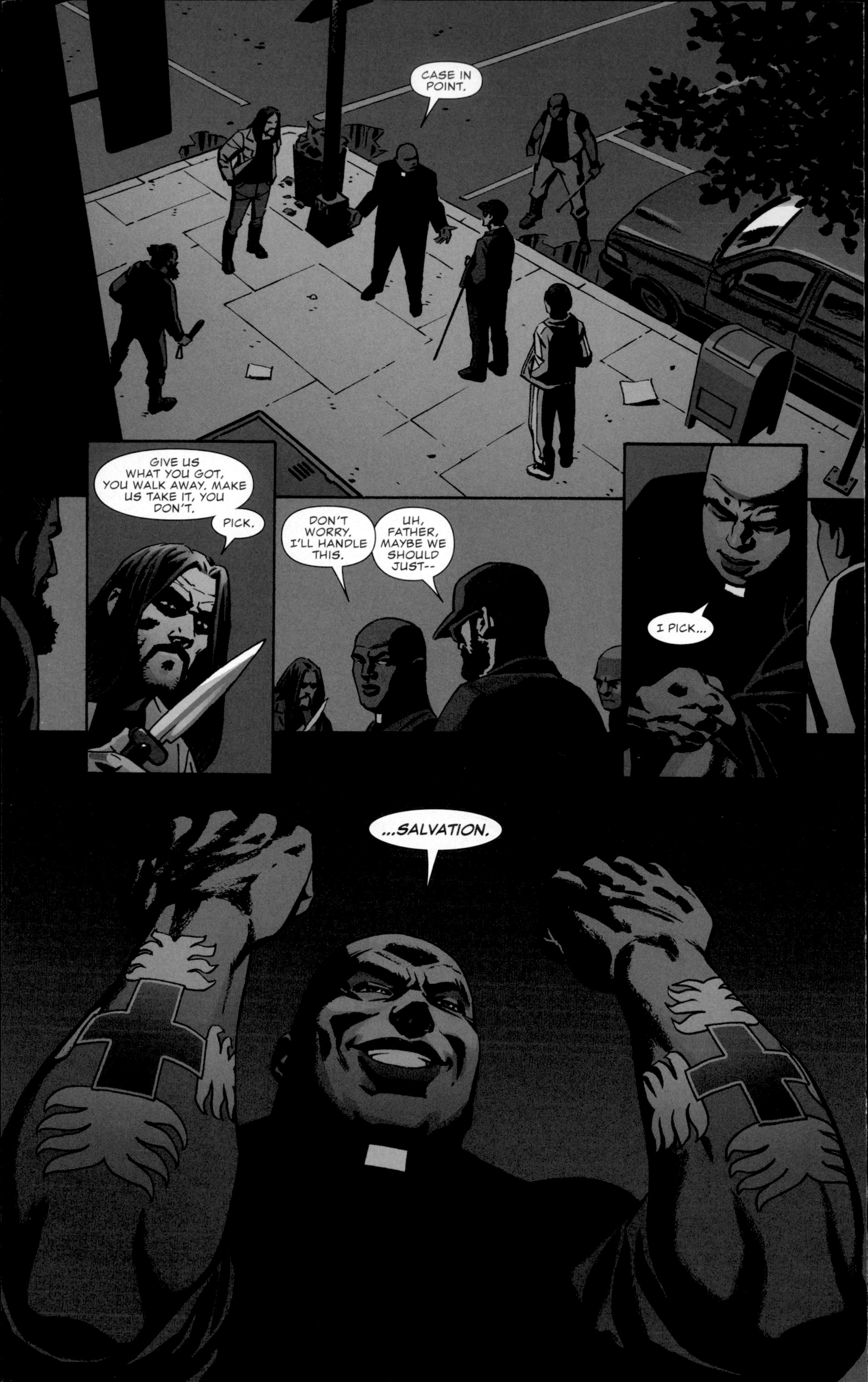
CASE IN POINT.
GIVE US WHAT YOU GOT, YOU WALK AWAY. MAKE US TAKE IT, YOU DON'T.
PICK.
DON'T WORRY. I'LL HANDLE THIS.
UH, FATHER, MAYBE WE SHOULD JUST--
I PICK...
...SALVATION.

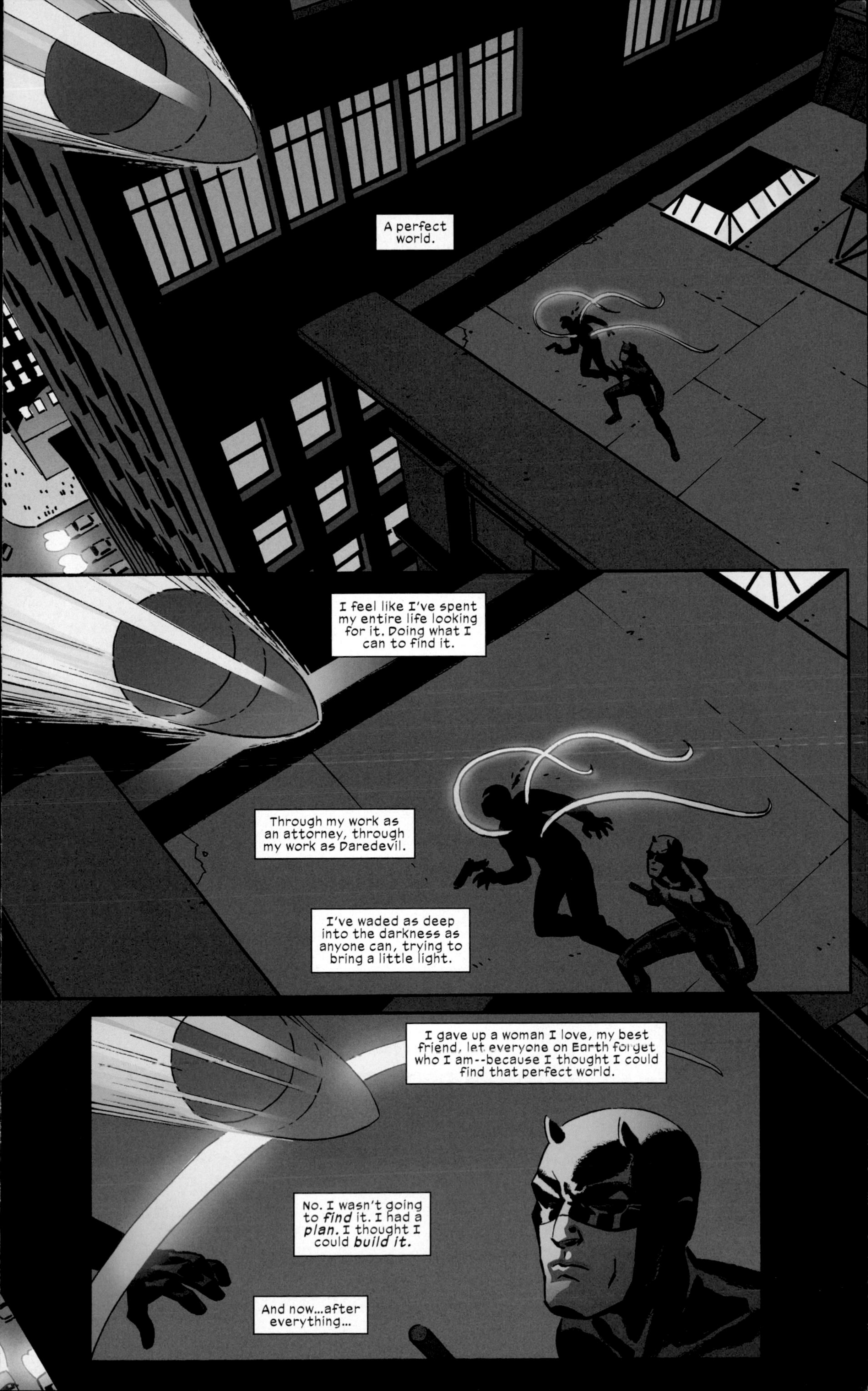
A perfect world.
I feel like I've spent my entire life looking for it. Doing what I can to find it.
Through my work as an attorney, through my work as Daredevil.
I've waded as deep into the darkness as anyone can, trying to bring a little light.
I gave up a woman I love, my best friend, let everyone on Earth forget who I am--because I thought I could find that perfect world.
No. I wasn't going to *find* it. I had a *plan*. I thought I could *build it*.
And now...after everything...

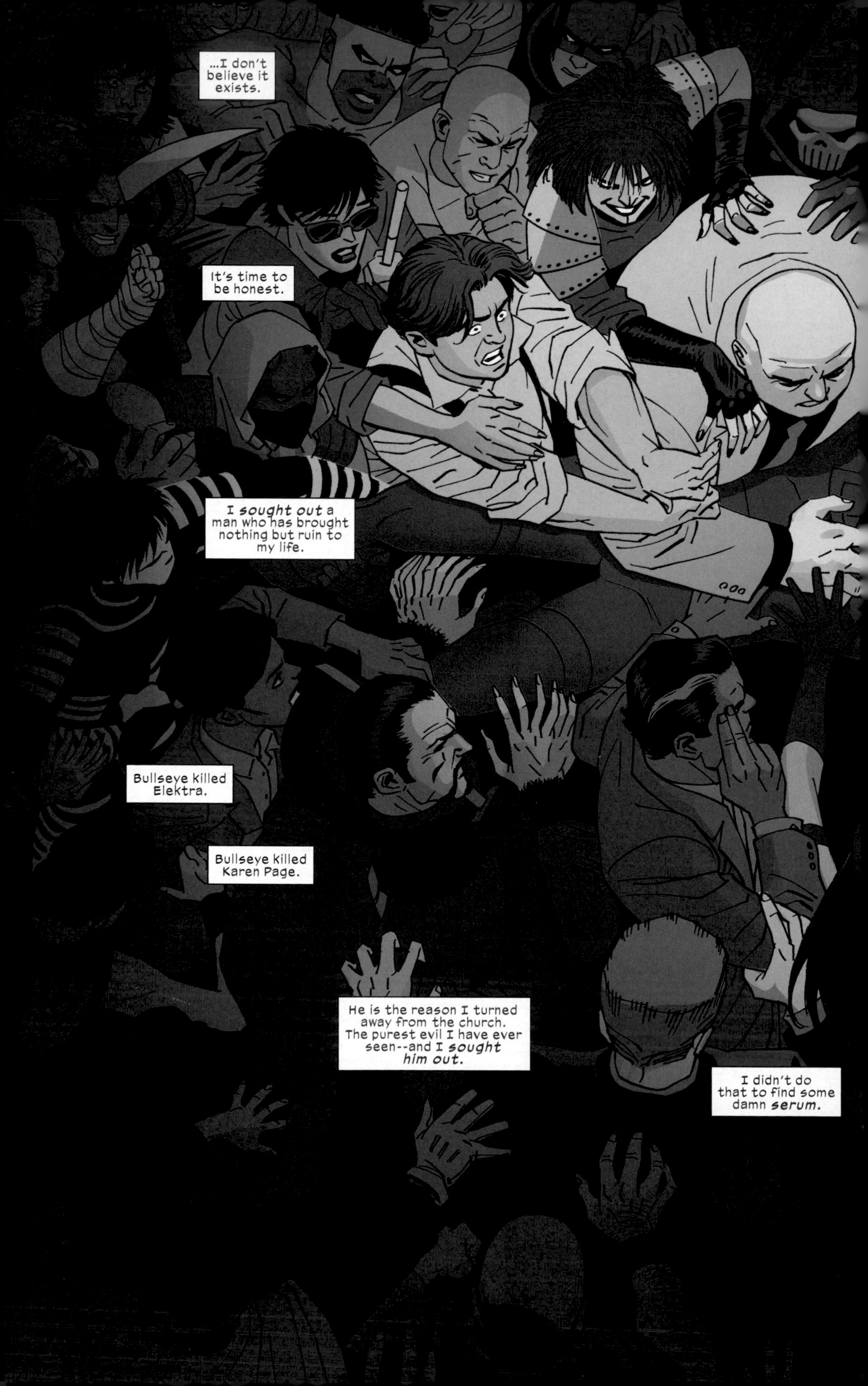
...I don't believe it exists.
It's time to be honest.
I *sought out* a man who has brought nothing but ruin to my life.
Bullseye killed Elektra.
Bullseye killed Karen Page.
He is the reason I turned away from the church. The purest evil I have ever seen--and I *sought him out.*
I didn't do that to find some damn *serum.*

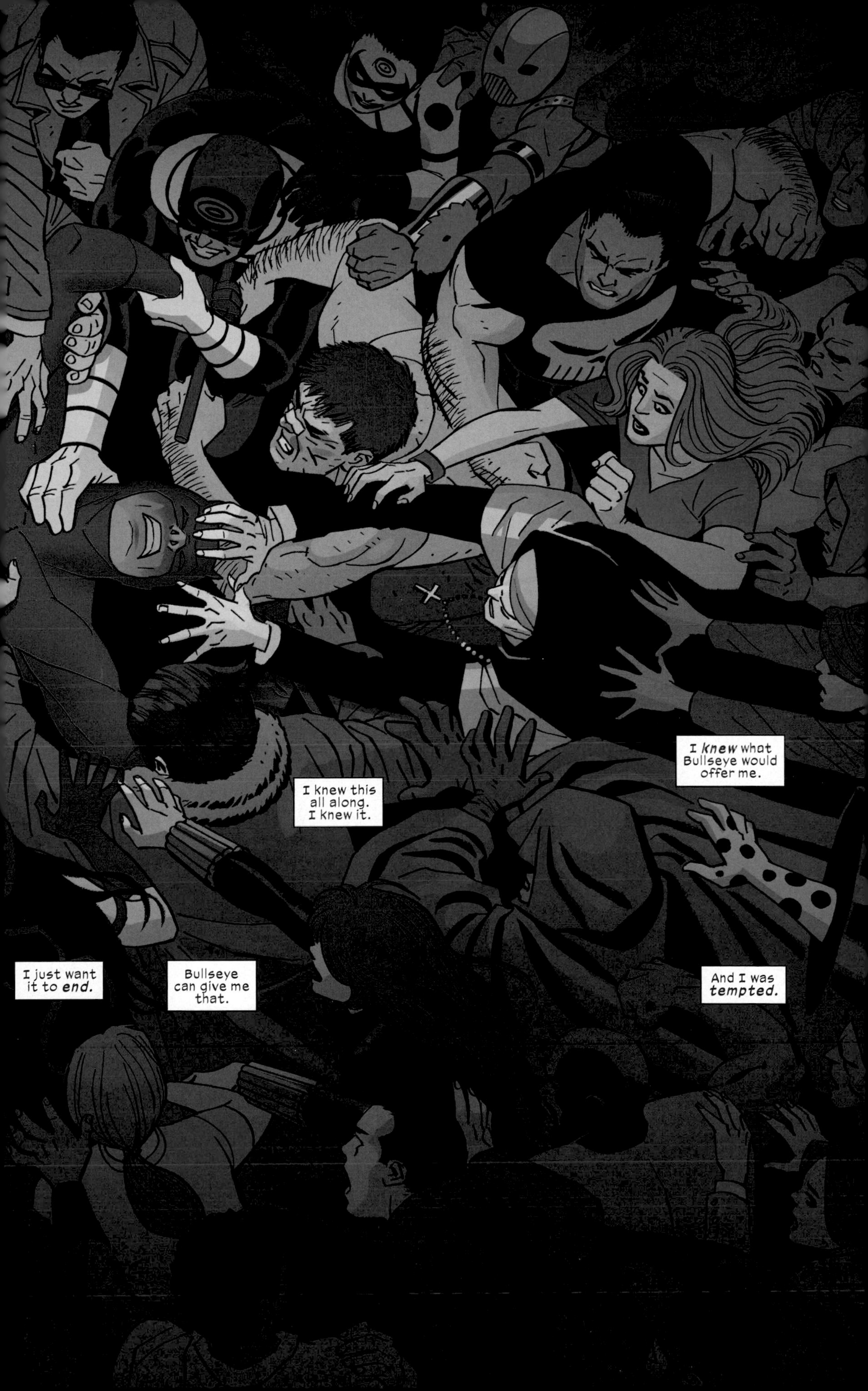
I knew this all along. I knew it.
I *knew* what Bullseye would offer me.
I just want it to *end.*
Bullseye can give me that.
And I was *tempted.*

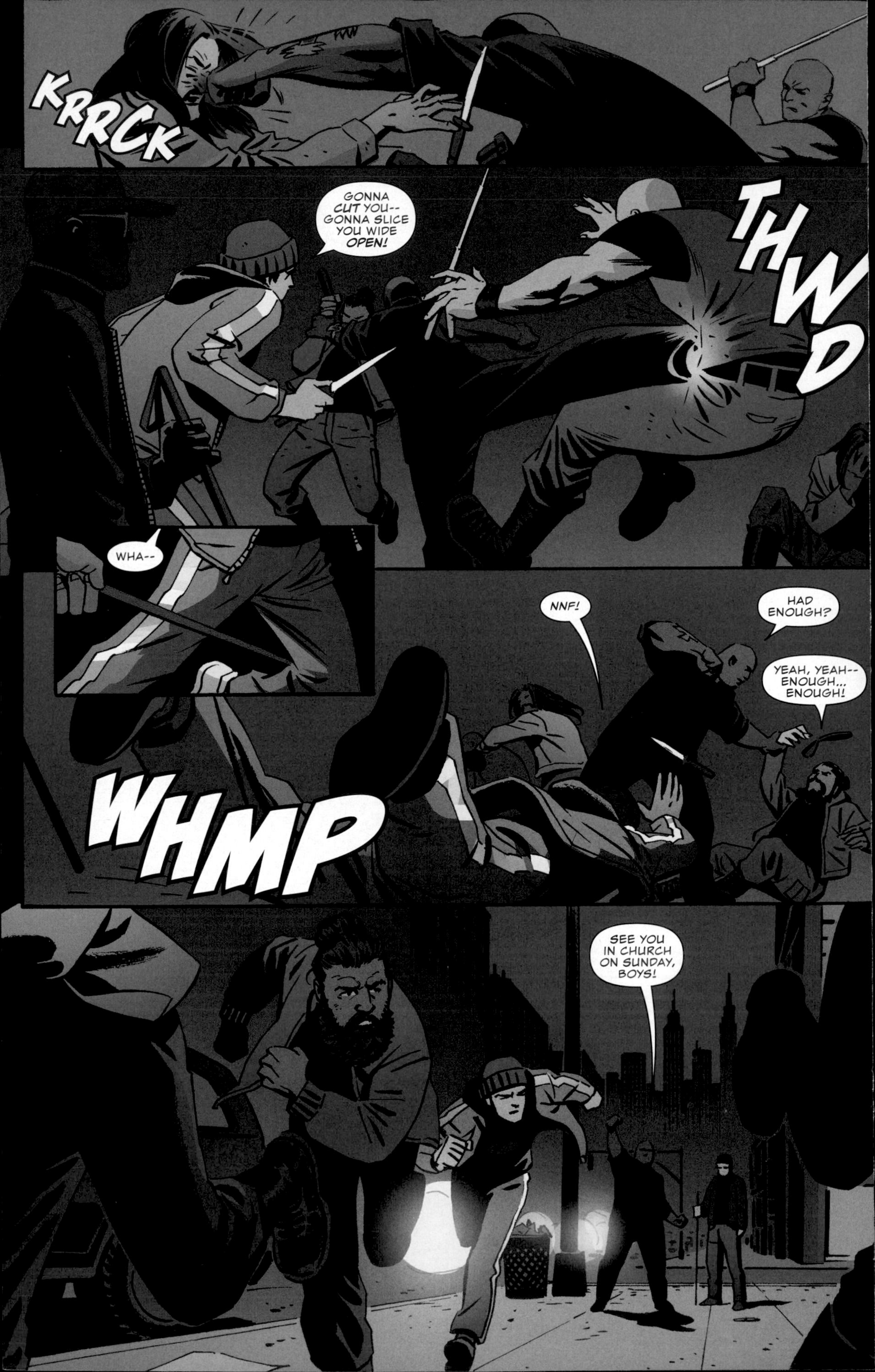
KRRCK
GONNA CUT YOU-- GONNA SLICE YOU WIDE OPEN!
THWD
WHA--
NNF!
HAD ENOUGH?
YEAH, YEAH-- ENOUGH... ENOUGH!
WHMP
SEE YOU IN CHURCH ON SUNDAY, BOYS!

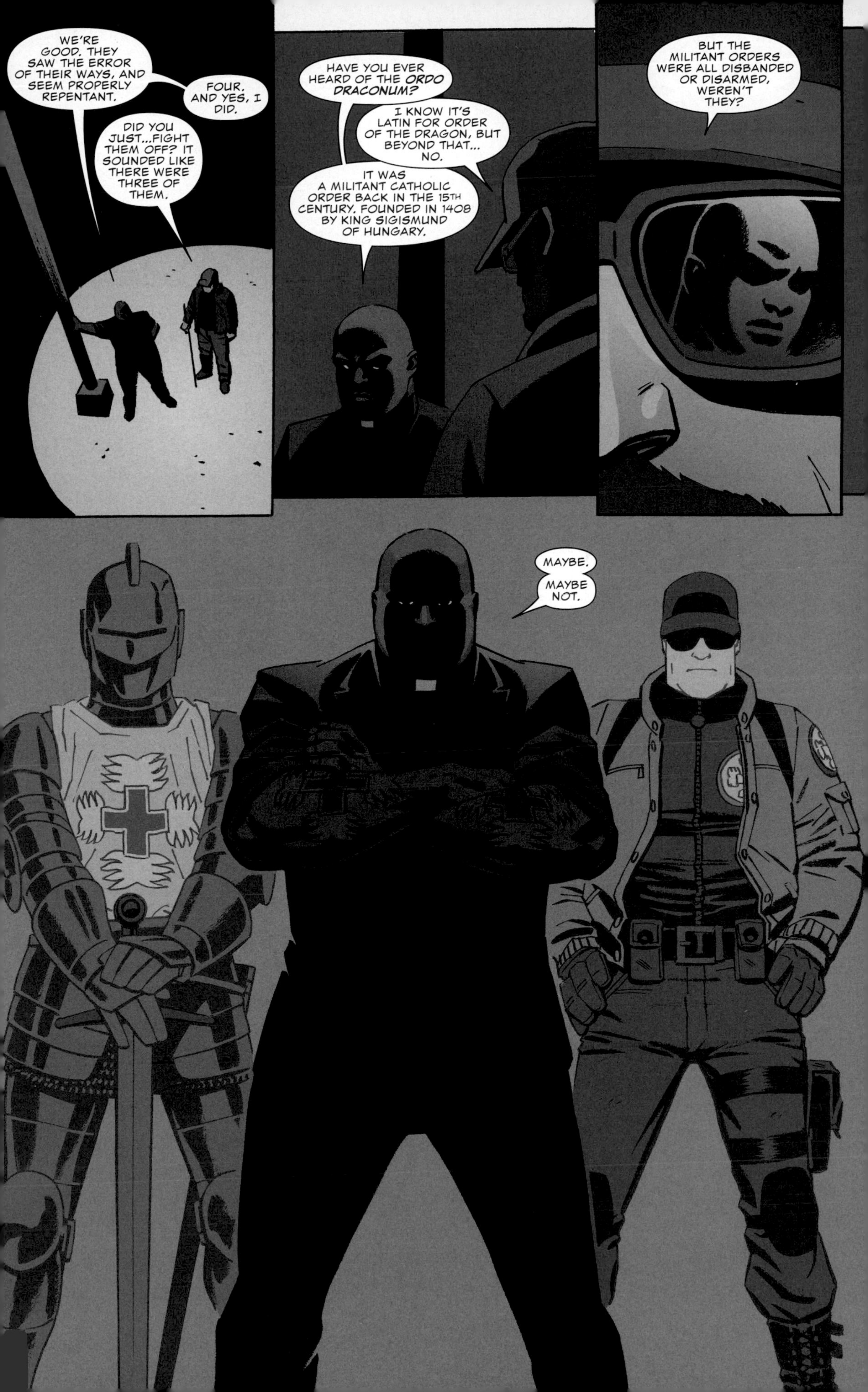
WE'RE GOOD. THEY SAW THE ERROR OF THEIR WAYS, AND SEEM PROPERLY REPENTANT.
DID YOU JUST...FIGHT THEM OFF? IT SOUNDED LIKE THERE WERE THREE OF THEM.
FOUR. AND YES, I DID.
HAVE YOU EVER HEARD OF THE *ORDO DRACONUM?*
I KNOW IT'S LATIN FOR ORDER OF THE DRAGON, BUT BEYOND THAT... NO.
IT WAS A MILITANT CATHOLIC ORDER BACK IN THE 15TH CENTURY. FOUNDED IN 1408 BY KING SIGISMUND OF HUNGARY.
BUT THE MILITANT ORDERS WERE ALL DISBANDED OR DISARMED, WEREN'T THEY?
MAYBE.
MAYBE NOT.

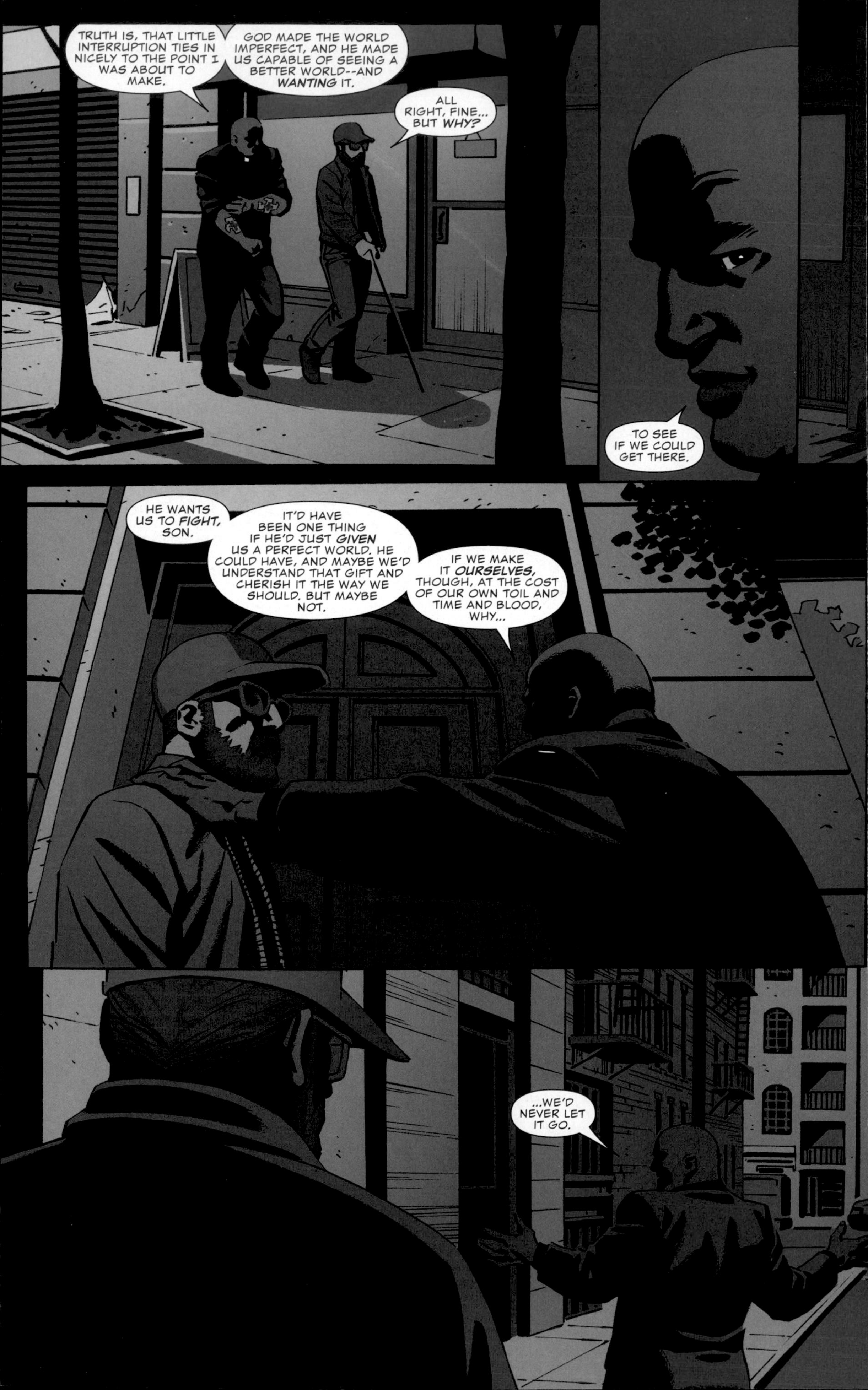
TRUTH IS, THAT LITTLE INTERRUPTION TIES IN NICELY TO THE POINT I WAS ABOUT TO MAKE.
GOD MADE THE WORLD IMPERFECT, AND HE MADE US CAPABLE OF SEEING A BETTER WORLD--AND WANTING IT.
ALL RIGHT, FINE... BUT WHY?
TO SEE IF WE COULD GET THERE.
HE WANTS US TO FIGHT, SON.
IT'D HAVE BEEN ONE THING IF HE'D JUST GIVEN US A PERFECT WORLD. HE COULD HAVE, AND MAYBE WE'D UNDERSTAND THAT GIFT AND CHERISH IT THE WAY WE SHOULD. BUT MAYBE NOT.
IF WE MAKE IT OURSELVES, THOUGH, AT THE COST OF OUR OWN TOIL AND TIME AND BLOOD, WHY...
...WE'D NEVER LET IT GO.

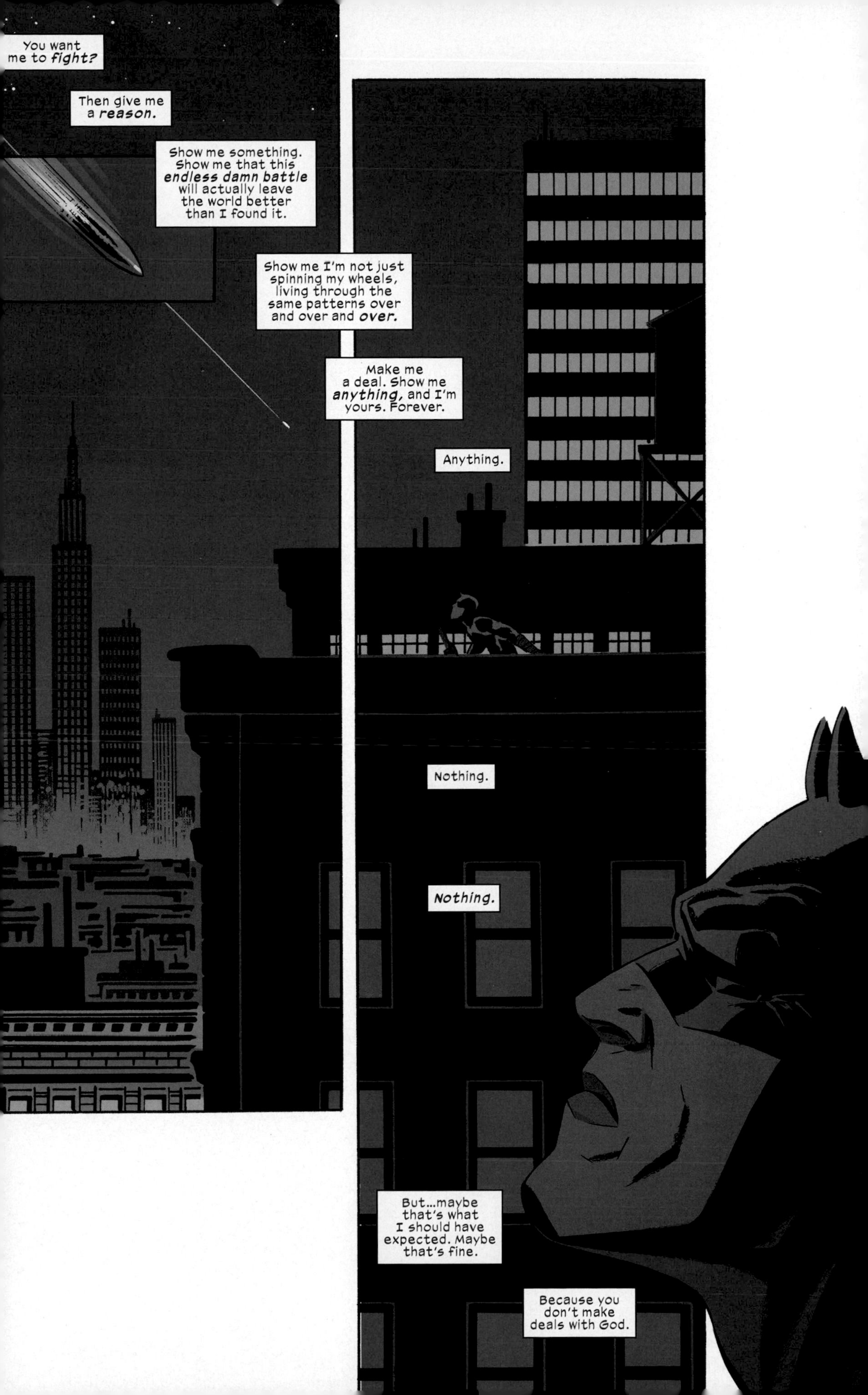
You want me to *fight?*
Then give me a *reason.*
Show me something. Show me that this *endless damn battle* will actually leave the world better than I found it.
Show me I'm not just spinning my wheels, living through the same patterns over and over and *over.*
Make me a deal. Show me *anything,* and I'm yours. Forever.
Anything.
Nothing.
Nothing.
But...maybe that's what I should have expected. Maybe that's fine.
Because you don't make deals with God.

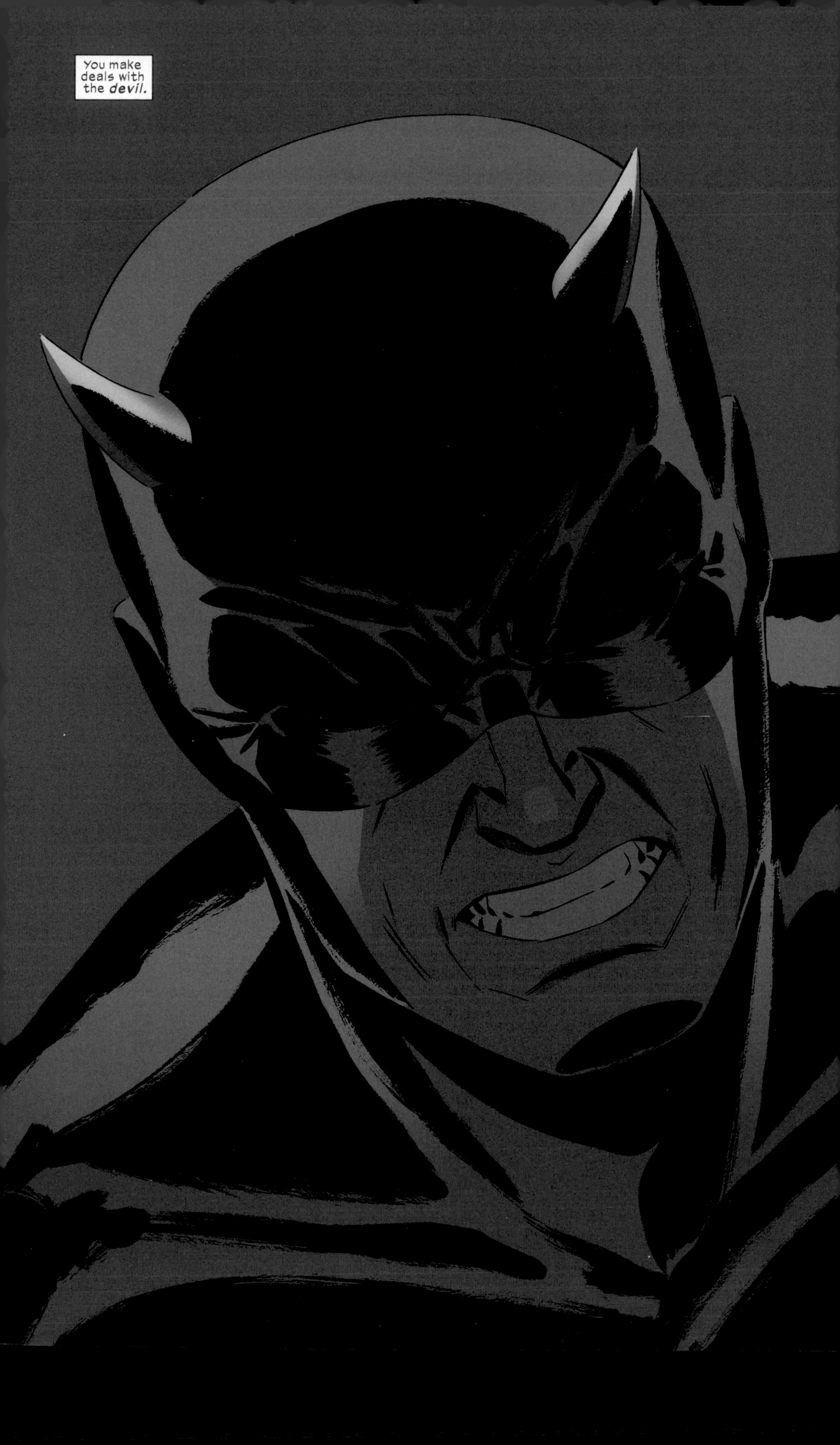
You make deals with the *devil.*

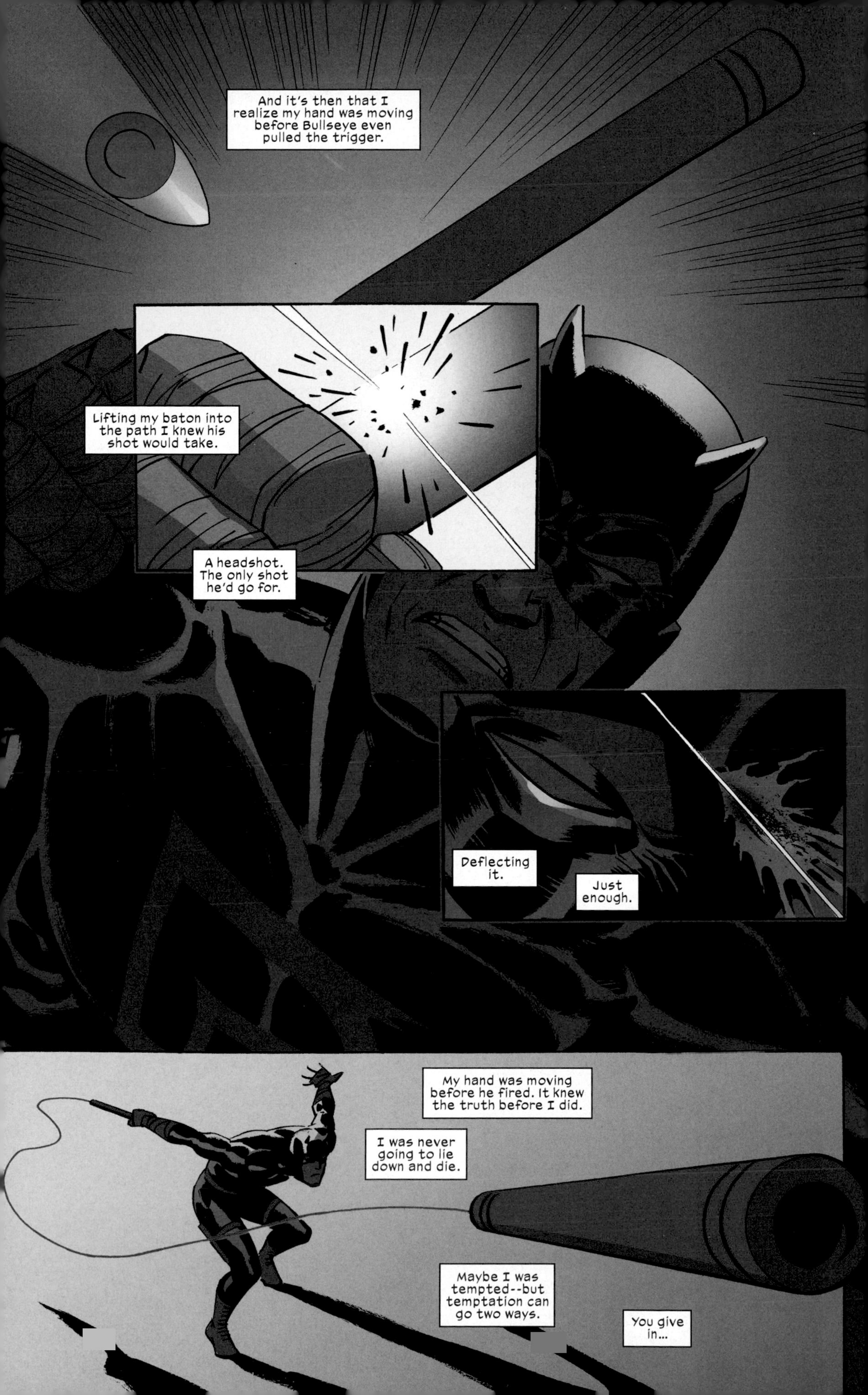
And it's then that I realize my hand was moving before Bullseye even pulled the trigger.
Lifting my baton into the path I knew his shot would take.
A headshot. The only shot he'd go for.
Deflecting it.
Just enough.
My hand was moving before he fired. It knew the truth before I did.
I was never going to lie down and die.
Maybe I was tempted--but temptation can go two ways.
You give in...

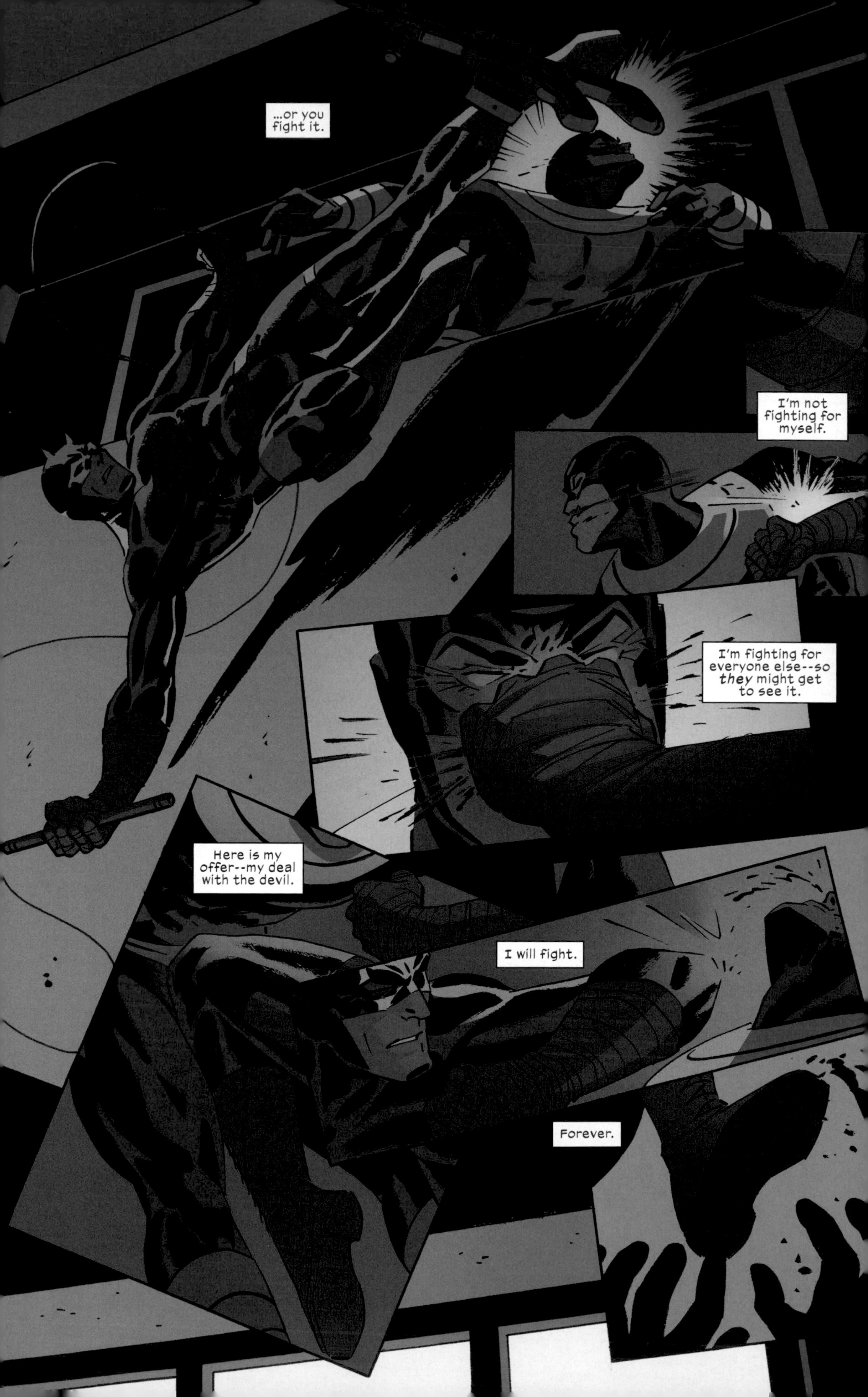
...or you fight it.
I'm not fighting for myself.
I'm fighting for everyone else--so *they* might get to see it.
Here is my offer--my deal with the devil.
I will fight.
Forever.

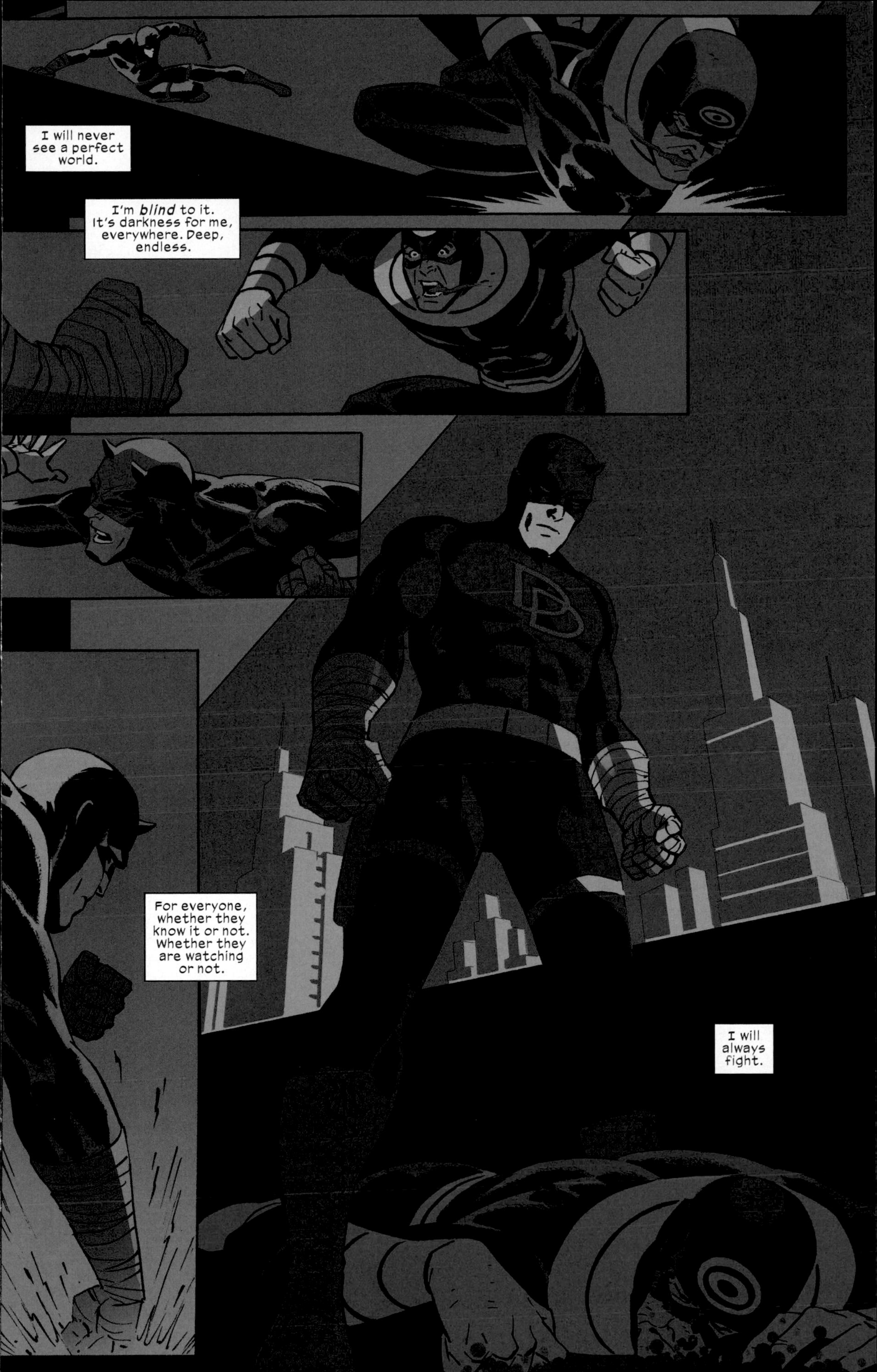
I will never see a perfect world.
I'm *blind* to it. It's darkness for me, everywhere. Deep, endless.
For everyone, whether they know it or not. Whether they are watching or not.
I will always fight.

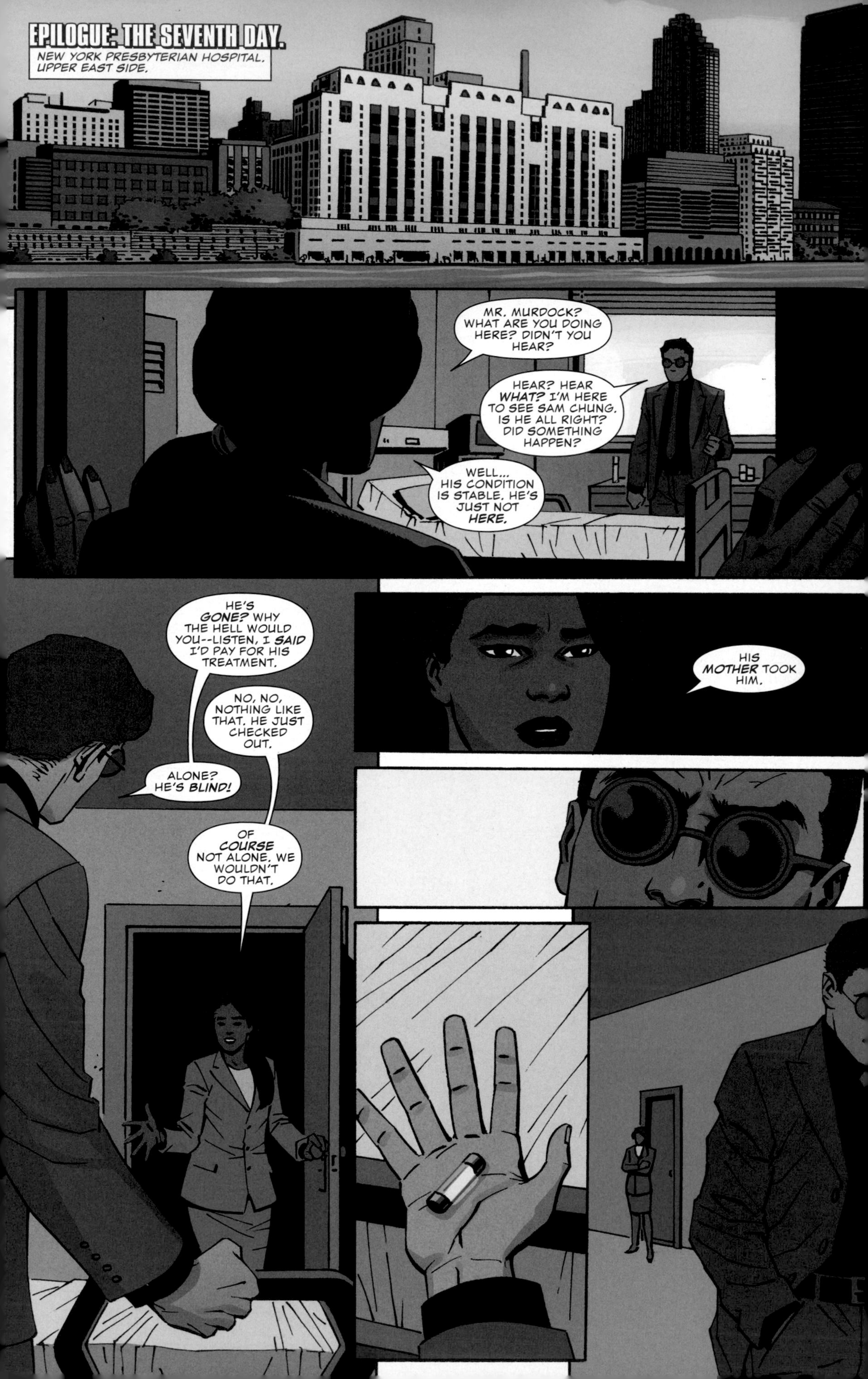
EPILOGUE: THE SEVENTH DAY.
NEW YORK PRESBYTERIAN HOSPITAL, UPPER EAST SIDE.
MR. MURDOCK? WHAT ARE YOU DOING HERE? DIDN'T YOU HEAR?
HEAR? HEAR WHAT? I'M HERE TO SEE SAM CHUNG. IS HE ALL RIGHT? DID SOMETHING HAPPEN?
WELL... HIS CONDITION IS STABLE. HE'S JUST NOT HERE.
HE'S GONE? WHY THE HELL WOULD YOU--LISTEN, I SAID I'D PAY FOR HIS TREATMENT.
NO, NO, NOTHING LIKE THAT. HE JUST CHECKED OUT.
ALONE? HE'S BLIND!
OF COURSE NOT ALONE. WE WOULDN'T DO THAT.
HIS MOTHER TOOK HIM.

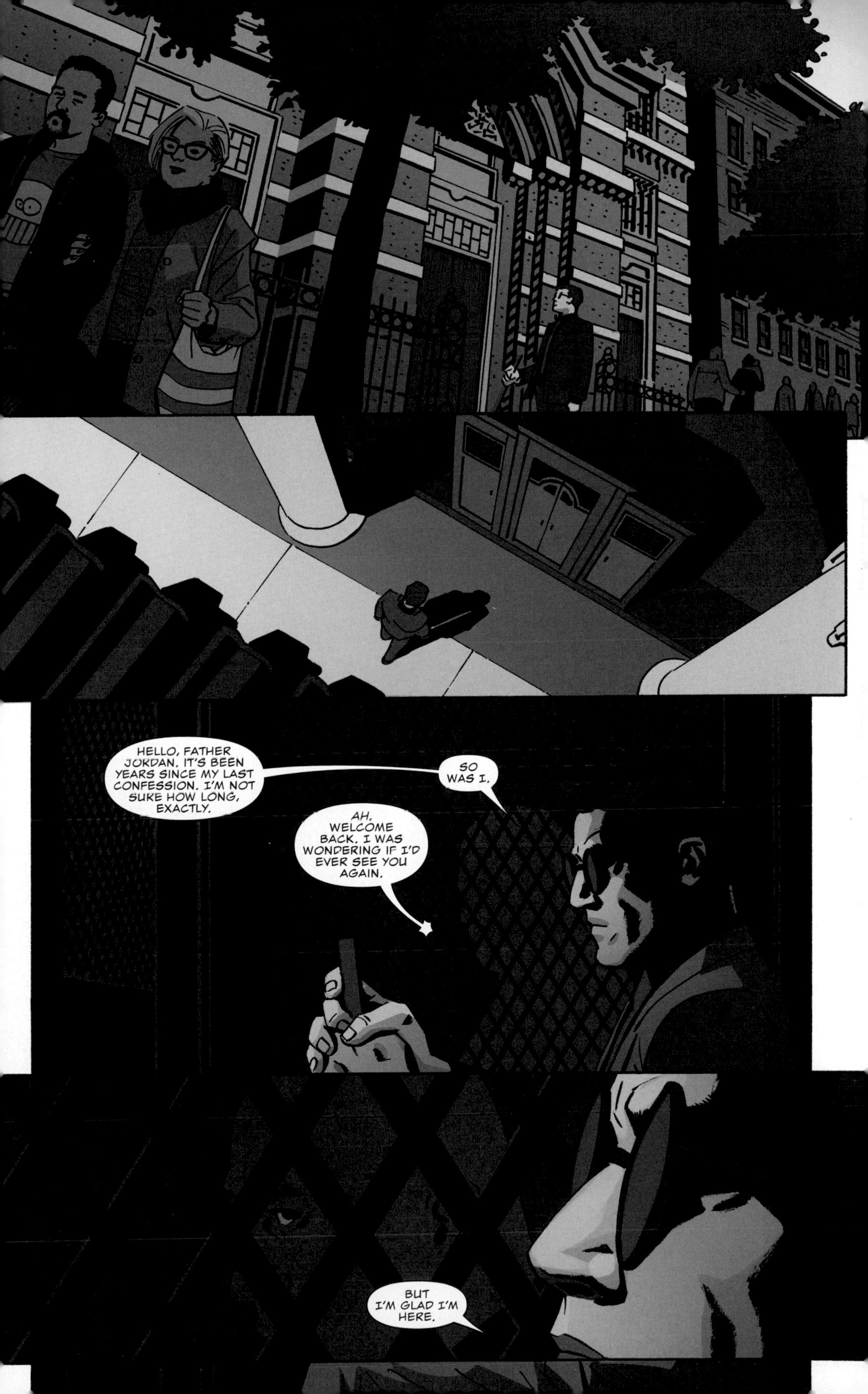
HELLO, FATHER JORDAN. IT'S BEEN YEARS SINCE MY LAST CONFESSION. I'M NOT SURE HOW LONG, EXACTLY.
SO WAS I.
AH, WELCOME BACK. I WAS WONDERING IF I'D EVER SEE YOU AGAIN.
BUT I'M GLAD I'M HERE.

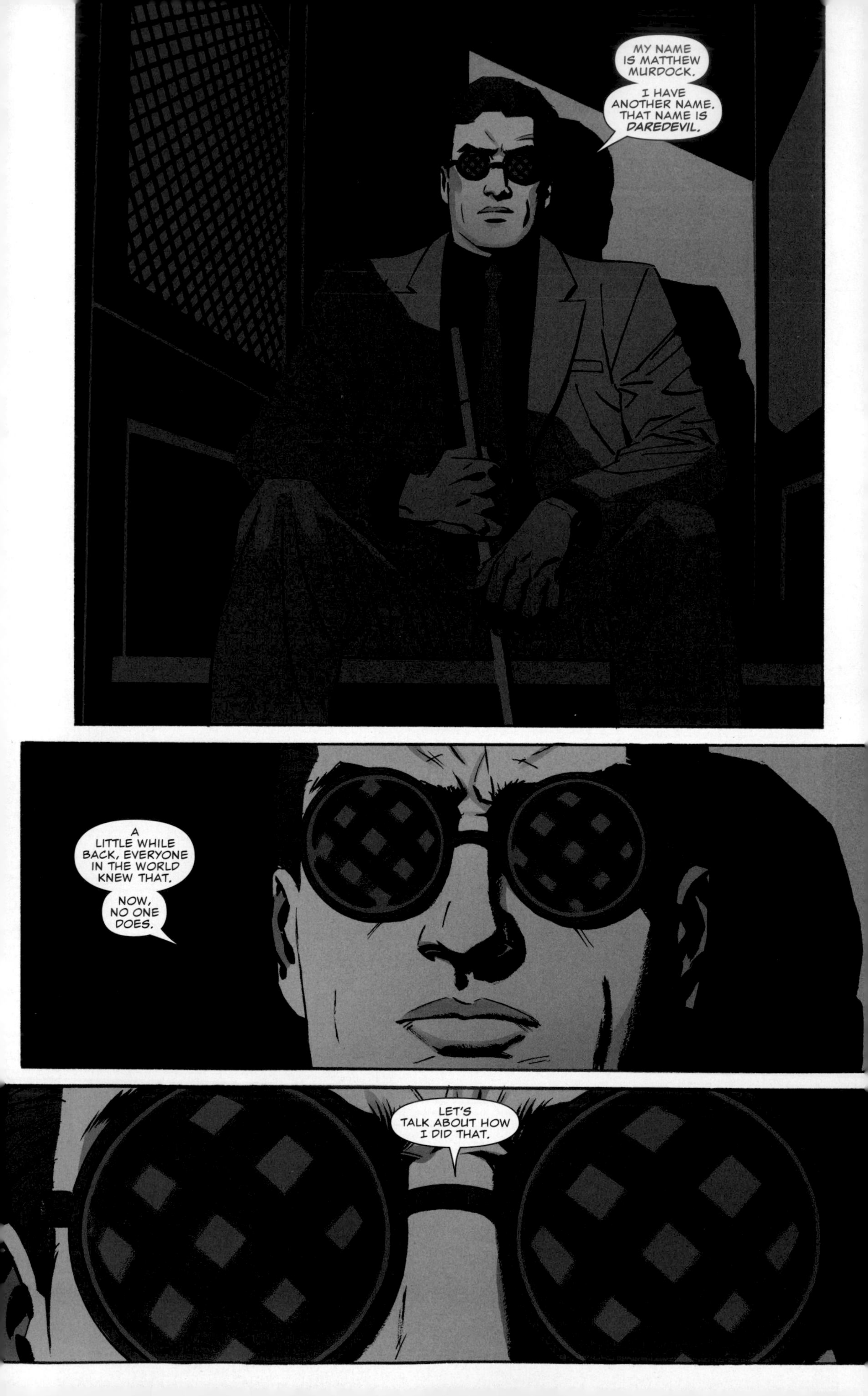
MY NAME IS MATTHEW MURDOCK.
I HAVE ANOTHER NAME. THAT NAME IS DAREDEVIL.
A LITTLE WHILE BACK, EVERYONE IN THE WORLD KNEW THAT.
NOW, NO ONE DOES.
LET'S TALK ABOUT HOW I DID THAT.

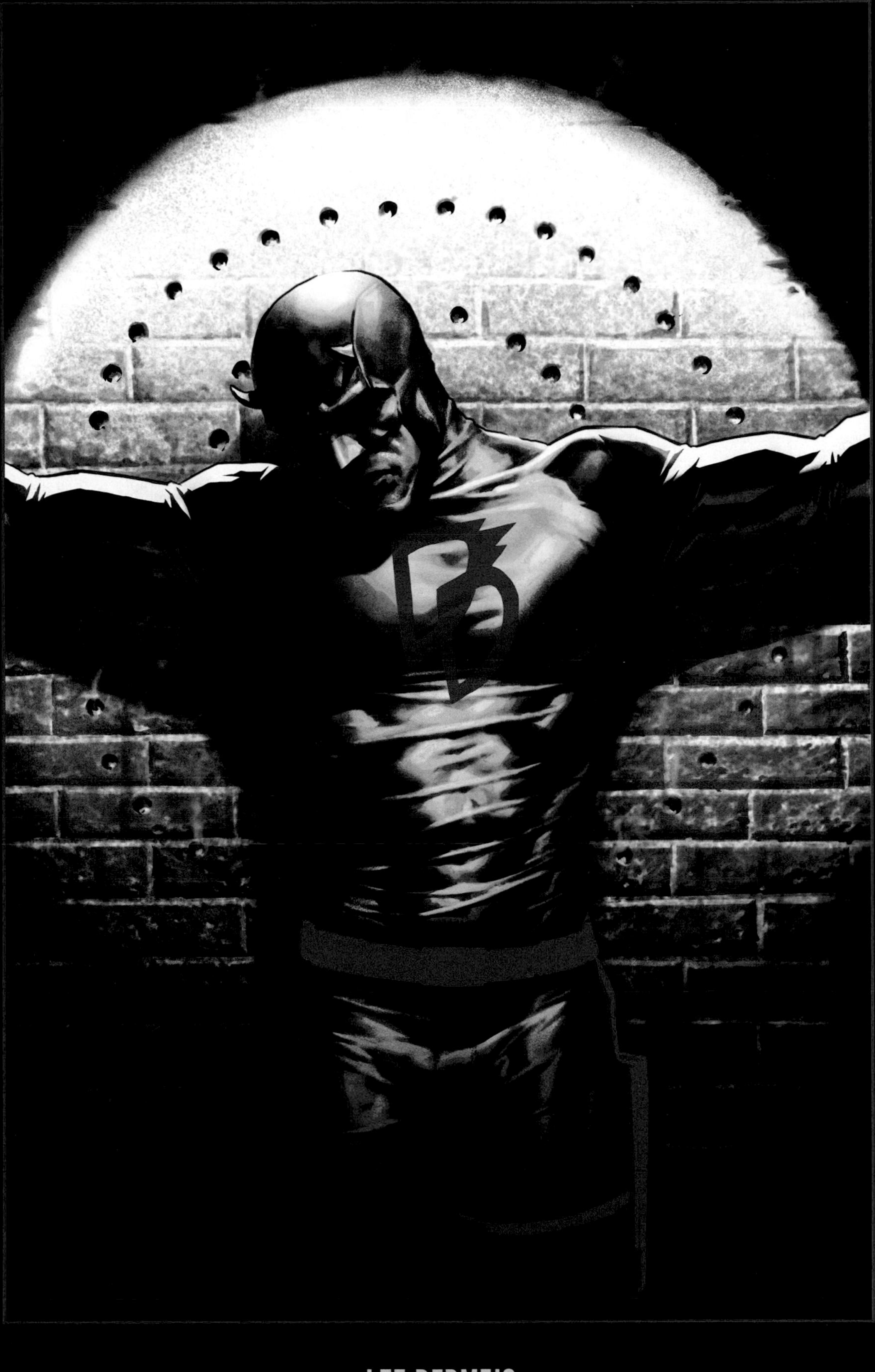

LEE BERMEJO
No. 15 VARIANT

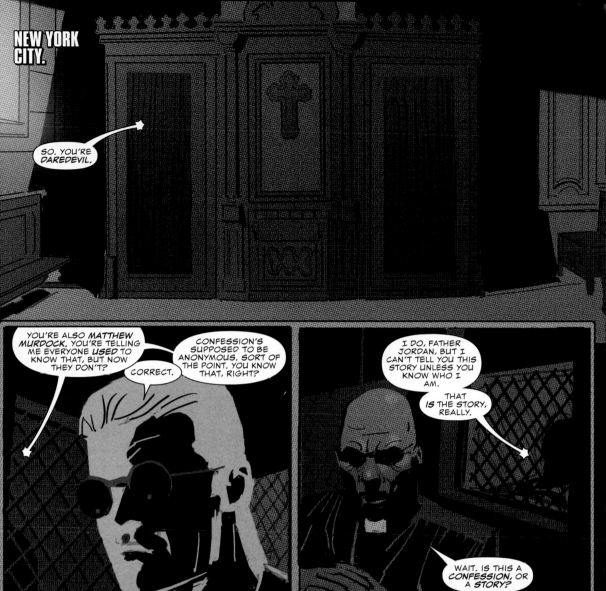

SO. YOU'RE DAREDEVIL.

YOU'RE ALSO *MATTHEW MURDOCK,* YOU'RE TELLING ME EVERYONE *USED* TO KNOW THAT, BUT NOW THEY DON'T?

CORRECT.

CONFESSION'S SUPPOSED TO BE ANONYMOUS, SORT OF THE POINT. YOU KNOW THAT, RIGHT?

I DO, FATHER JORDAN, BUT I CAN'T TELL YOU THIS STORY UNLESS YOU KNOW WHO I AM.

THAT *IS* THE STORY, REALLY.

WAIT. IS THIS A *CONFESSION,* OR A *STORY?*

BOTH.

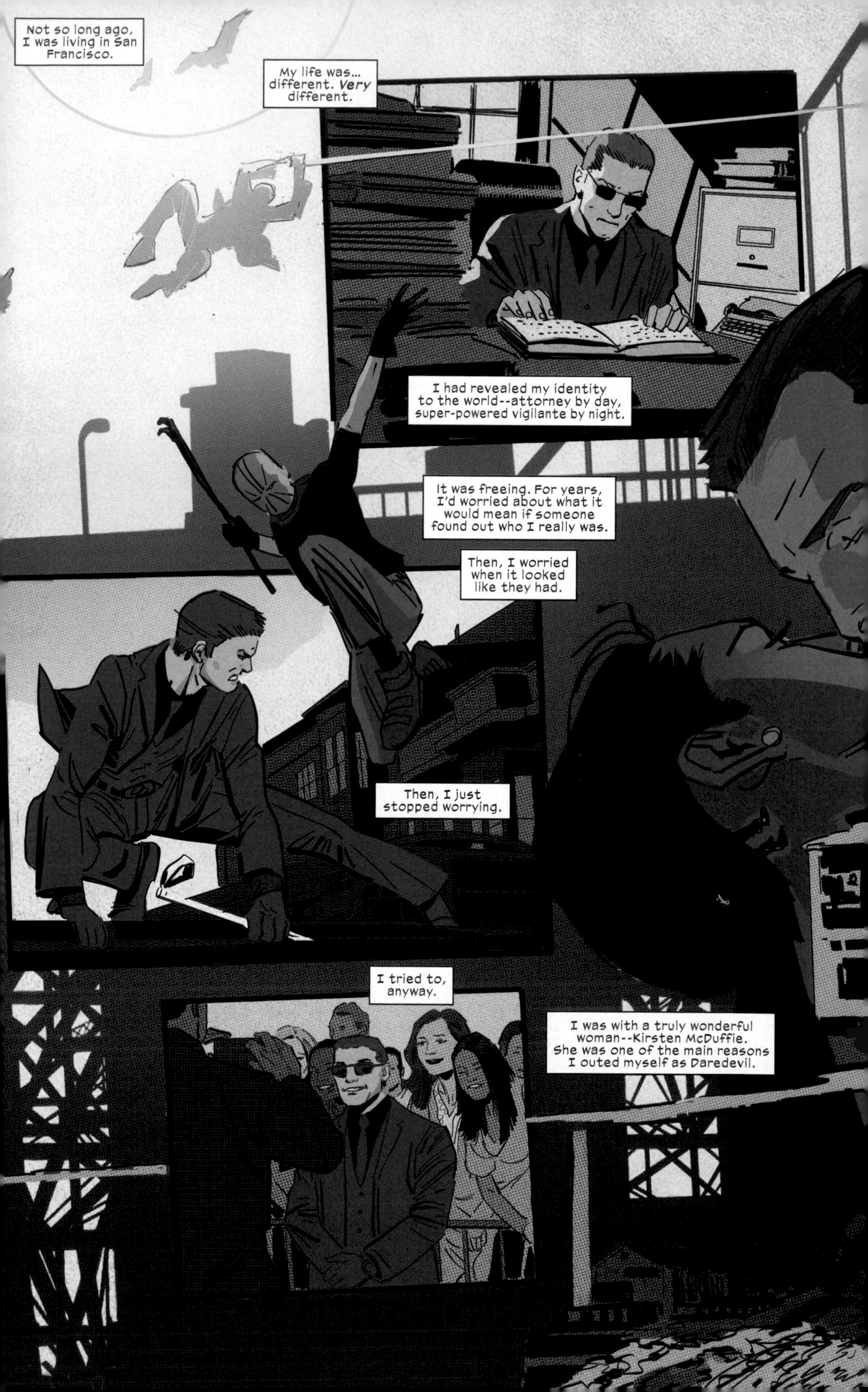
Not so long ago, I was living in San Francisco.
My life was... different. *Very* different.
I had revealed my identity to the world--attorney by day, super-powered vigilante by night.
It was freeing. For years, I'd worried about what it would mean if someone found out who I really was.
Then, I worried when it looked like they had.
Then, I just stopped worrying.
I tried to, anyway.
I was with a truly wonderful woman--Kirsten McDuffie. She was one of the main reasons I outed myself as Daredevil.

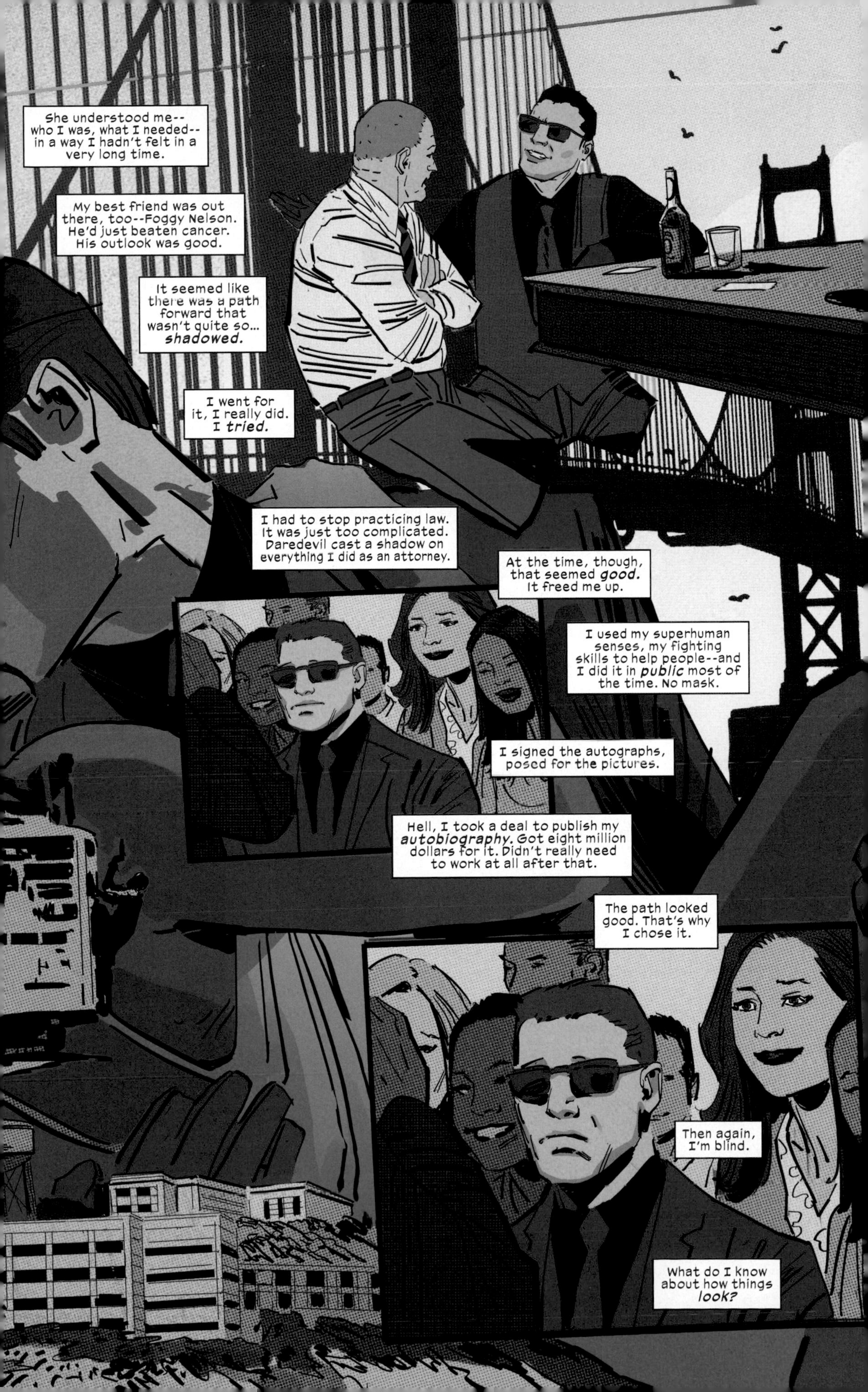
She understood me--who I was, what I needed--in a way I hadn't felt in a very long time.
My best friend was out there, too--Foggy Nelson. He'd just beaten cancer. His outlook was good.
It seemed like there was a path forward that wasn't quite so... *shadowed.*
I went for it, I really did. I *tried.*
I had to stop practicing law. It was just too complicated. Daredevil cast a shadow on everything I did as an attorney.
At the time, though, that seemed *good.* It freed me up.
I used my superhuman senses, my fighting skills to help people--and I did it in *public* most of the time. No mask.
I signed the autographs, posed for the pictures.
Hell, I took a deal to publish my *autobiography.* Got eight million dollars for it. Didn't really need to work at all after that.
The path looked good. That's why I chose it.
Then again, I'm blind.
What do I know about how things *look?*

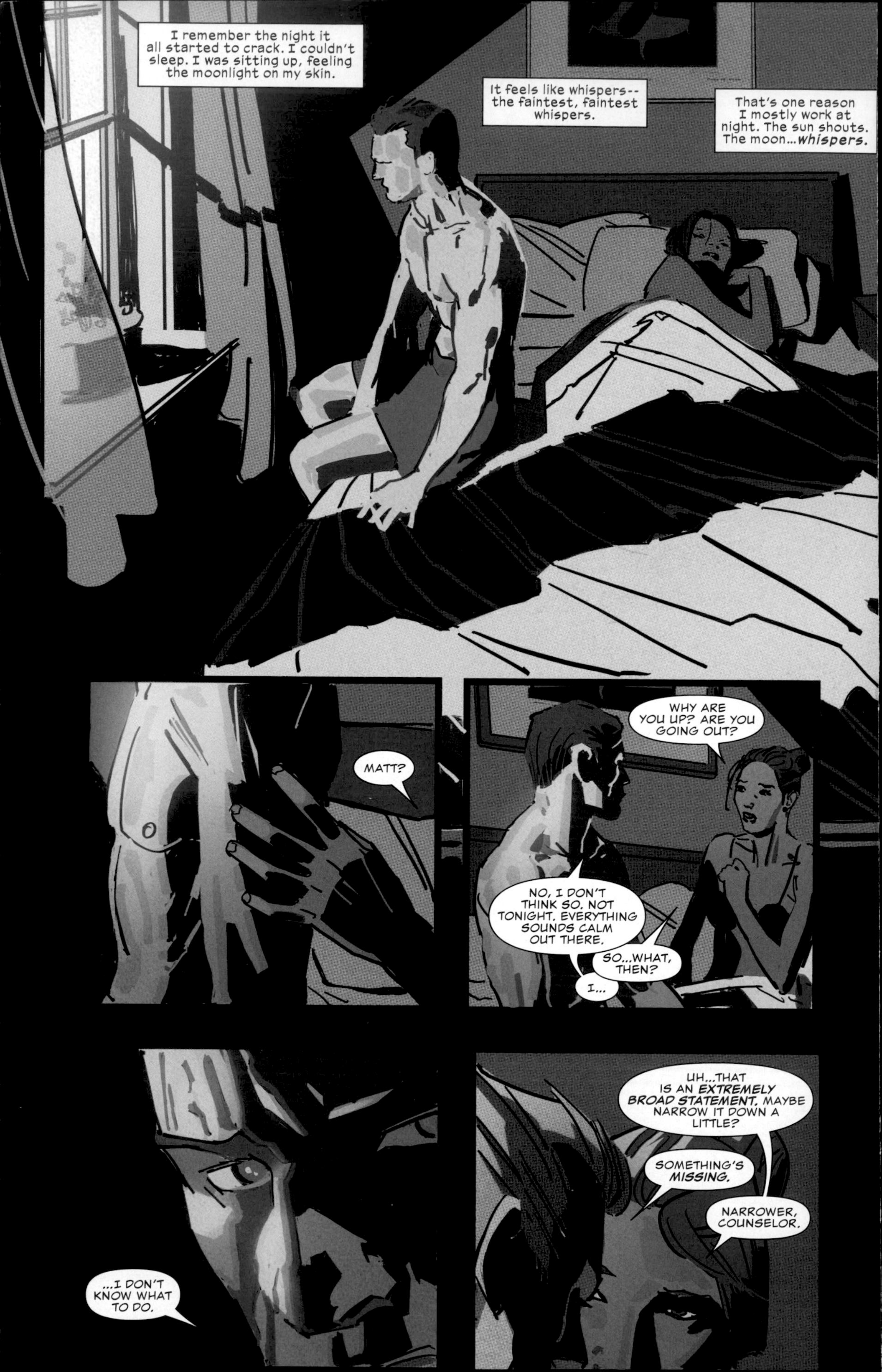

I remember the night it all started to crack. I couldn't sleep. I was sitting up, feeling the moonlight on my skin.
It feels like whispers-- the faintest, faintest whispers.
That's one reason I mostly work at night. The sun shouts. The moon...*whispers.*
MATT?
WHY ARE YOU UP? ARE YOU GOING OUT?
NO, I DON'T THINK SO. NOT TONIGHT. EVERYTHING SOUNDS CALM OUT THERE.
SO...WHAT, THEN?
I...
...I DON'T KNOW WHAT TO DO.
UH...THAT IS AN ***EXTREMELY BROAD STATEMENT.*** MAYBE NARROW IT DOWN A LITTLE?
SOMETHING'S ***MISSING.***
NARROWER, COUNSELOR.

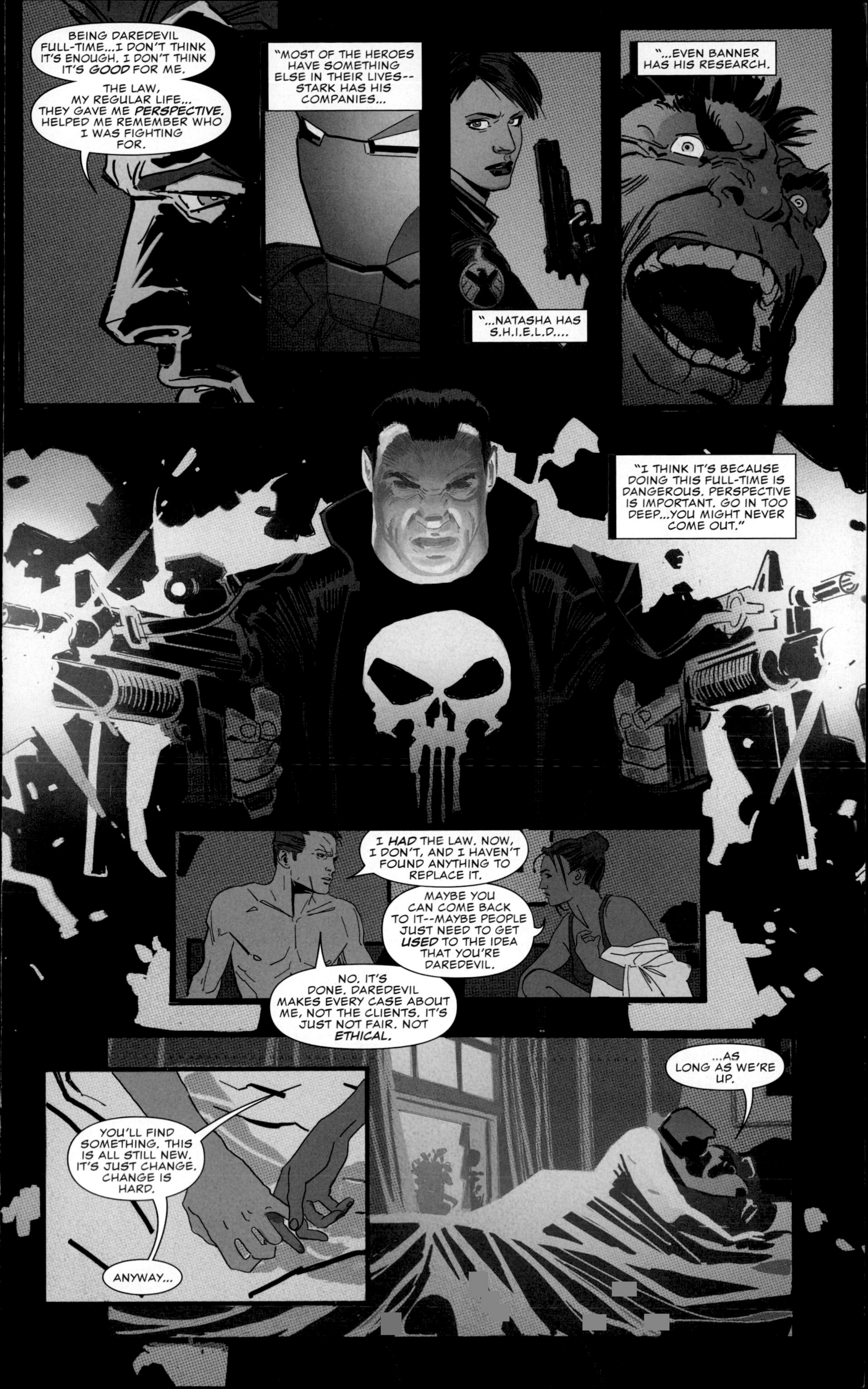
BEING DAREDEVIL FULL-TIME...I DON'T THINK IT'S ENOUGH. I DON'T THINK IT'S GOOD FOR ME.
THE LAW, MY REGULAR LIFE... THEY GAVE ME PERSPECTIVE. HELPED ME REMEMBER WHO I WAS FIGHTING FOR.
"MOST OF THE HEROES HAVE SOMETHING ELSE IN THEIR LIVES-- STARK HAS HIS COMPANIES...
"...NATASHA HAS S.H.I.E.L.D....
"...EVEN BANNER HAS HIS RESEARCH.
"I THINK IT'S BECAUSE DOING THIS FULL-TIME IS DANGEROUS. PERSPECTIVE IS IMPORTANT. GO IN TOO DEEP...YOU MIGHT NEVER COME OUT."
I HAD THE LAW. NOW, I DON'T, AND I HAVEN'T FOUND ANYTHING TO REPLACE IT.
MAYBE YOU CAN COME BACK TO IT--MAYBE PEOPLE JUST NEED TO GET USED TO THE IDEA THAT YOU'RE DAREDEVIL.
NO. IT'S DONE. DAREDEVIL MAKES EVERY CASE ABOUT ME, NOT THE CLIENTS. IT'S JUST NOT FAIR. NOT ETHICAL.
YOU'LL FIND SOMETHING. THIS IS ALL STILL NEW. IT'S JUST CHANGE. CHANGE IS HARD.
ANYWAY...
...AS LONG AS WE'RE UP.

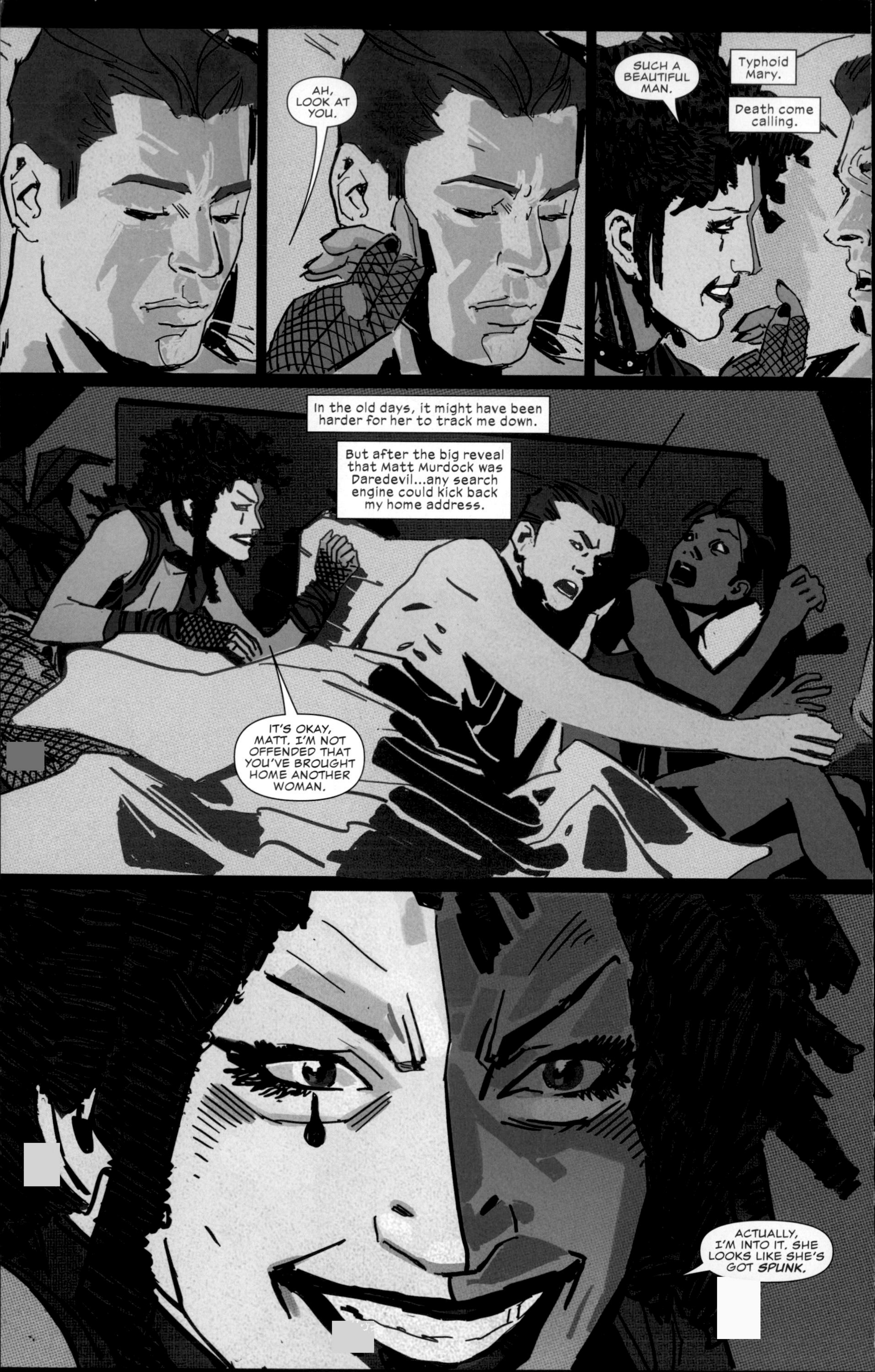
AH, LOOK AT YOU.
SUCH A BEAUTIFUL MAN.
Typhoid Mary.
Death come calling.
In the old days, it might have been harder for her to track me down.
But after the big reveal that Matt Murdock was Daredevil...any search engine could kick back my home address.
IT'S OKAY, MATT. I'M NOT OFFENDED THAT YOU'VE BROUGHT HOME ANOTHER WOMAN.
ACTUALLY, I'M INTO IT. SHE LOOKS LIKE SHE'S GOT SPUNK.

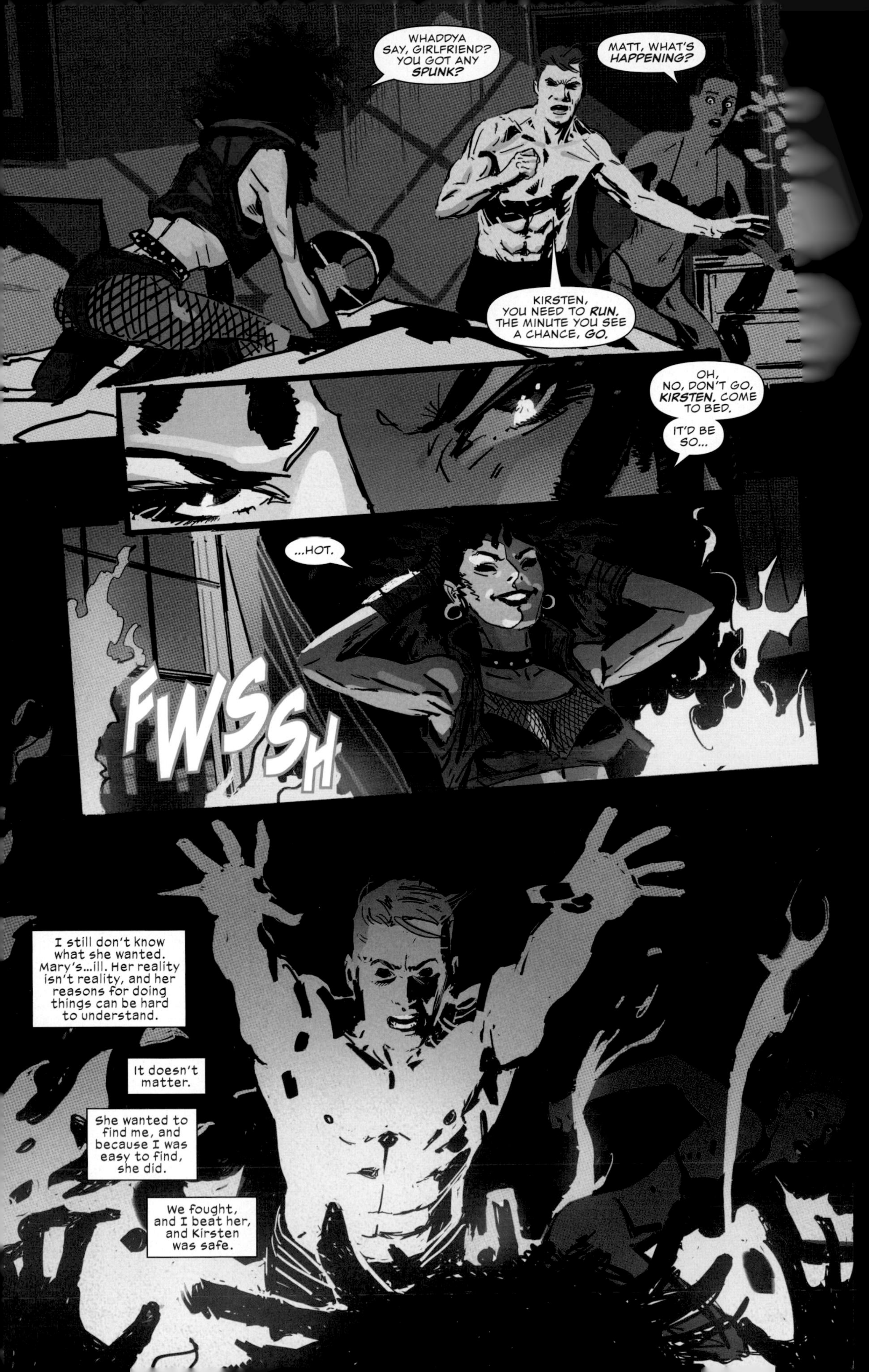
WHADDYA SAY, GIRLFRIEND? YOU GOT ANY SPUNK?
MATT, WHAT'S HAPPENING?
KIRSTEN, YOU NEED TO RUN. THE MINUTE YOU SEE A CHANCE, GO.
OH, NO, DON'T GO, KIRSTEN. COME TO BED.
IT'D BE SO...
...HOT.
FWSSH
I still don't know what she wanted. Mary's...ill. Her reality isn't reality, and her reasons for doing things can be hard to understand.
It doesn't matter.
She wanted to find me, and because I was easy to find, she did.
We fought, and I beat her, and Kirsten was safe.

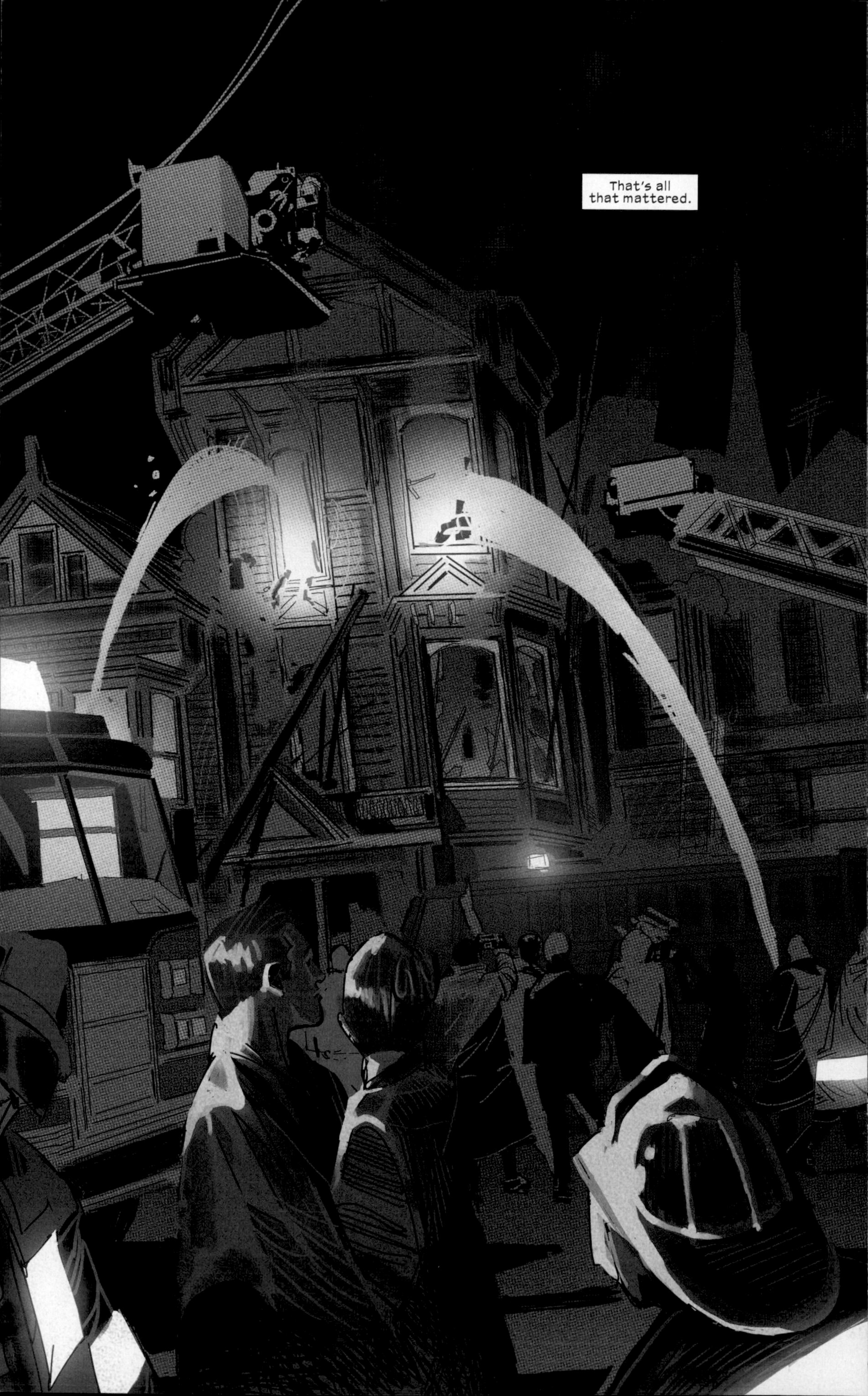
That's all that mattered.

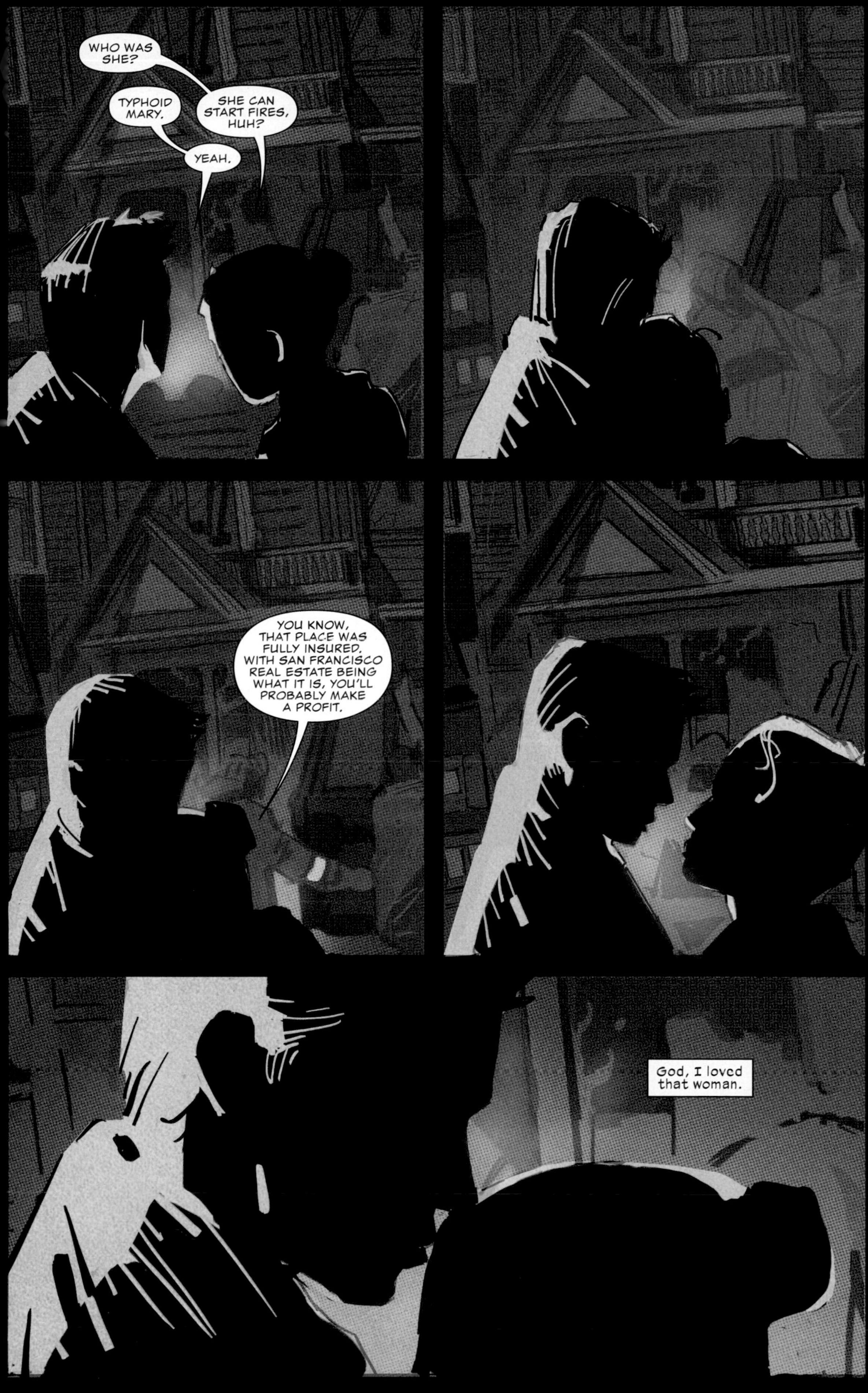
WHO WAS SHE?
TYPHOID MARY.
SHE CAN START FIRES, HUH?
YEAH.
YOU KNOW, THAT PLACE WAS FULLY INSURED. WITH SAN FRANCISCO REAL ESTATE BEING WHAT IT IS, YOU'LL PROBABLY MAKE A PROFIT.
God, I loved that woman.

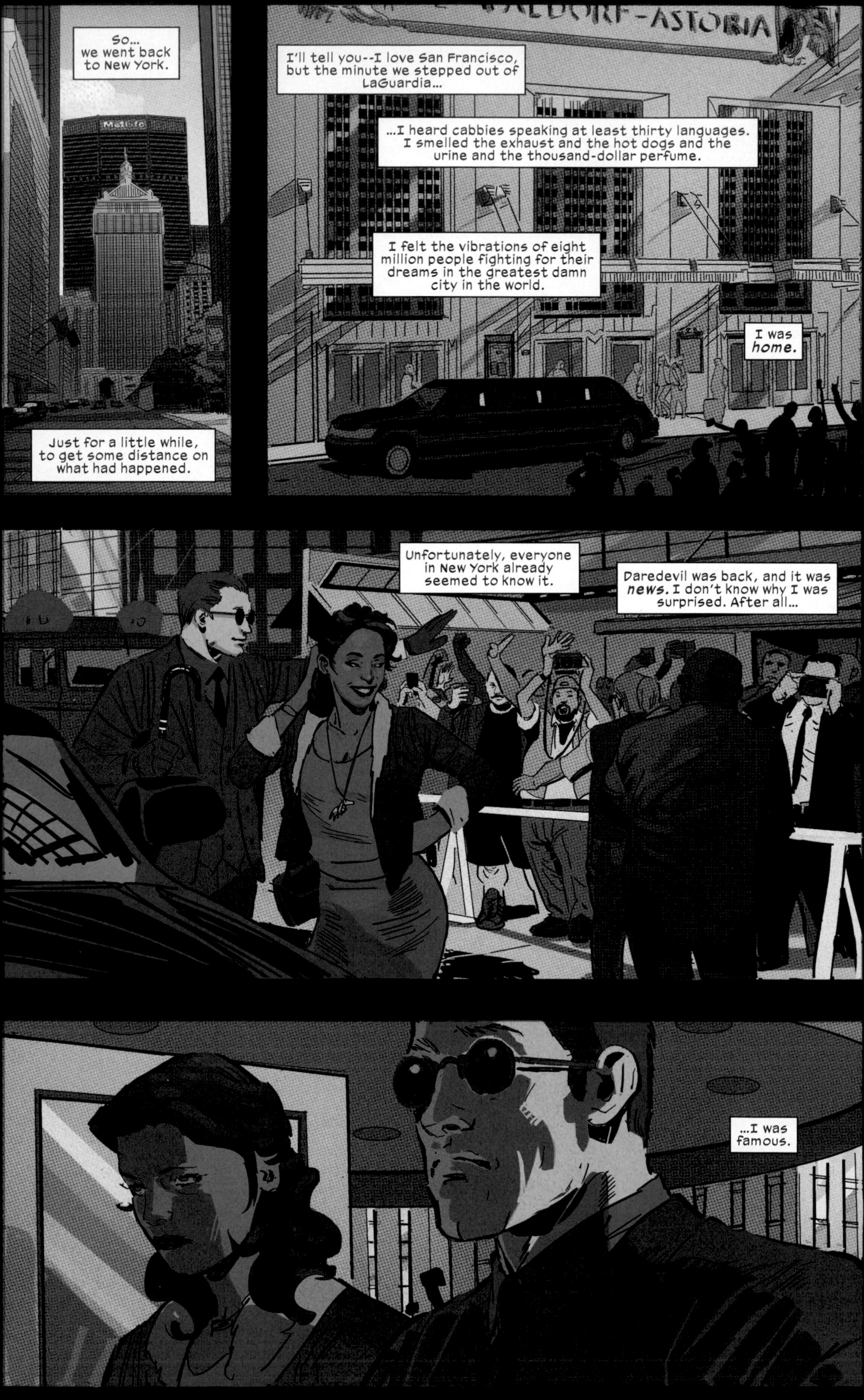

So... we went back to New York.
Just for a little while, to get some distance on what had happened.
WALDORF-ASTORIA
I'll tell you--I love San Francisco, but the minute we stepped out of LaGuardia...
...I heard cabbies speaking at least thirty languages. I smelled the exhaust and the hot dogs and the urine and the thousand-dollar perfume.
I felt the vibrations of eight million people fighting for their dreams in the greatest damn city in the world.
I was *home.*
Unfortunately, everyone in New York already seemed to know it.
Daredevil was back, and it was *news.* I don't know why I was surprised. After all...
...I was famous.

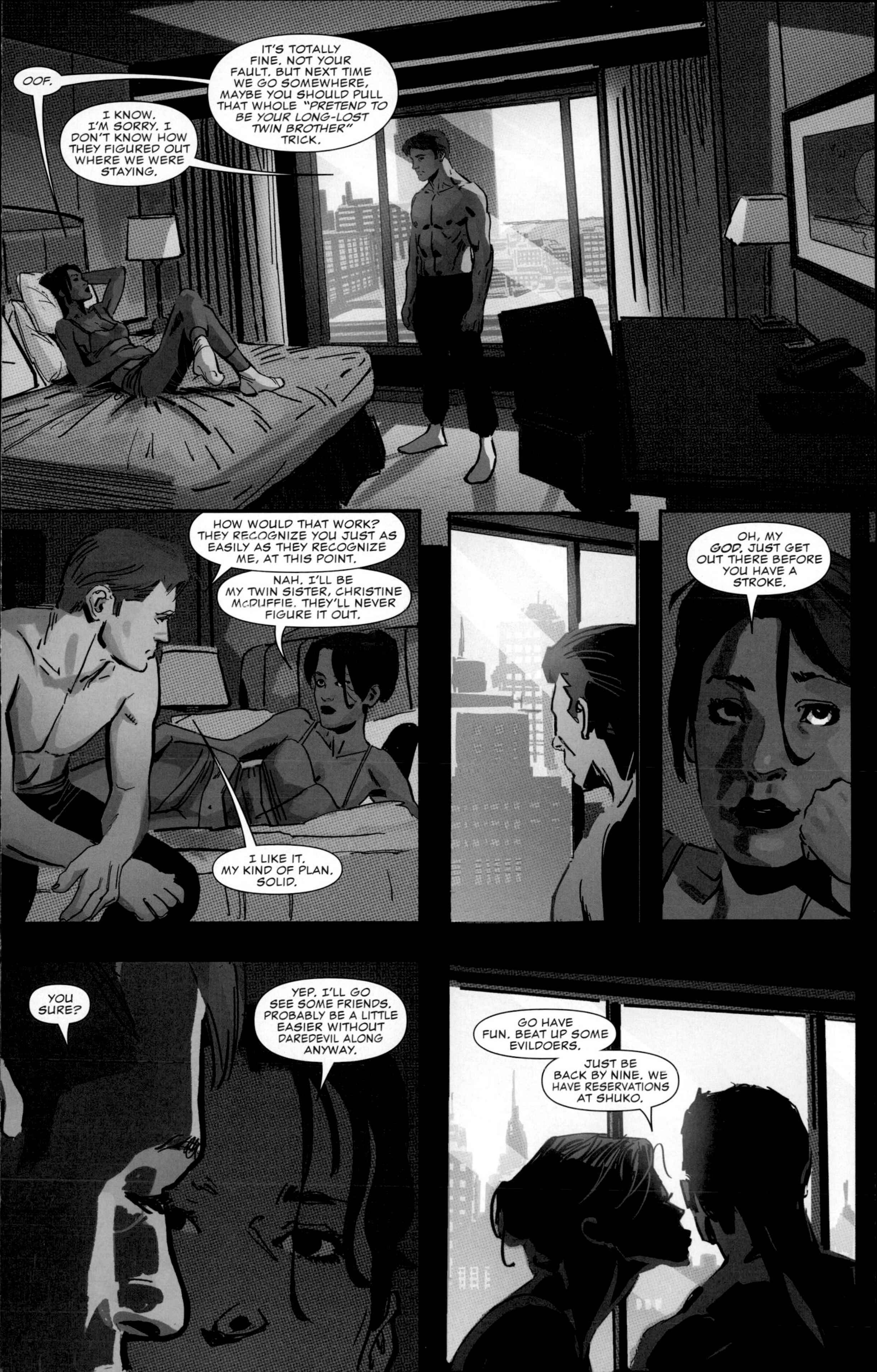
OOF.
IT'S TOTALLY FINE. NOT YOUR FAULT. BUT NEXT TIME WE GO SOMEWHERE, MAYBE YOU SHOULD PULL THAT WHOLE "PRETEND TO BE YOUR LONG-LOST TWIN BROTHER" TRICK.
I KNOW. I'M SORRY. I DON'T KNOW HOW THEY FIGURED OUT WHERE WE WERE STAYING.
HOW WOULD THAT WORK? THEY RECOGNIZE YOU JUST AS EASILY AS THEY RECOGNIZE ME, AT THIS POINT.
NAH. I'LL BE MY TWIN SISTER, CHRISTINE McDUFFIE. THEY'LL NEVER FIGURE IT OUT.
I LIKE IT. MY KIND OF PLAN. SOLID.
OH, MY GOD. JUST GET OUT THERE BEFORE YOU HAVE A STROKE.
YOU SURE?
YEP. I'LL GO SEE SOME FRIENDS. PROBABLY BE A LITTLE EASIER WITHOUT DAREDEVIL ALONG ANYWAY.
GO HAVE FUN. BEAT UP SOME EVILDOERS.
JUST BE BACK BY NINE. WE HAVE RESERVATIONS AT SHUKO.

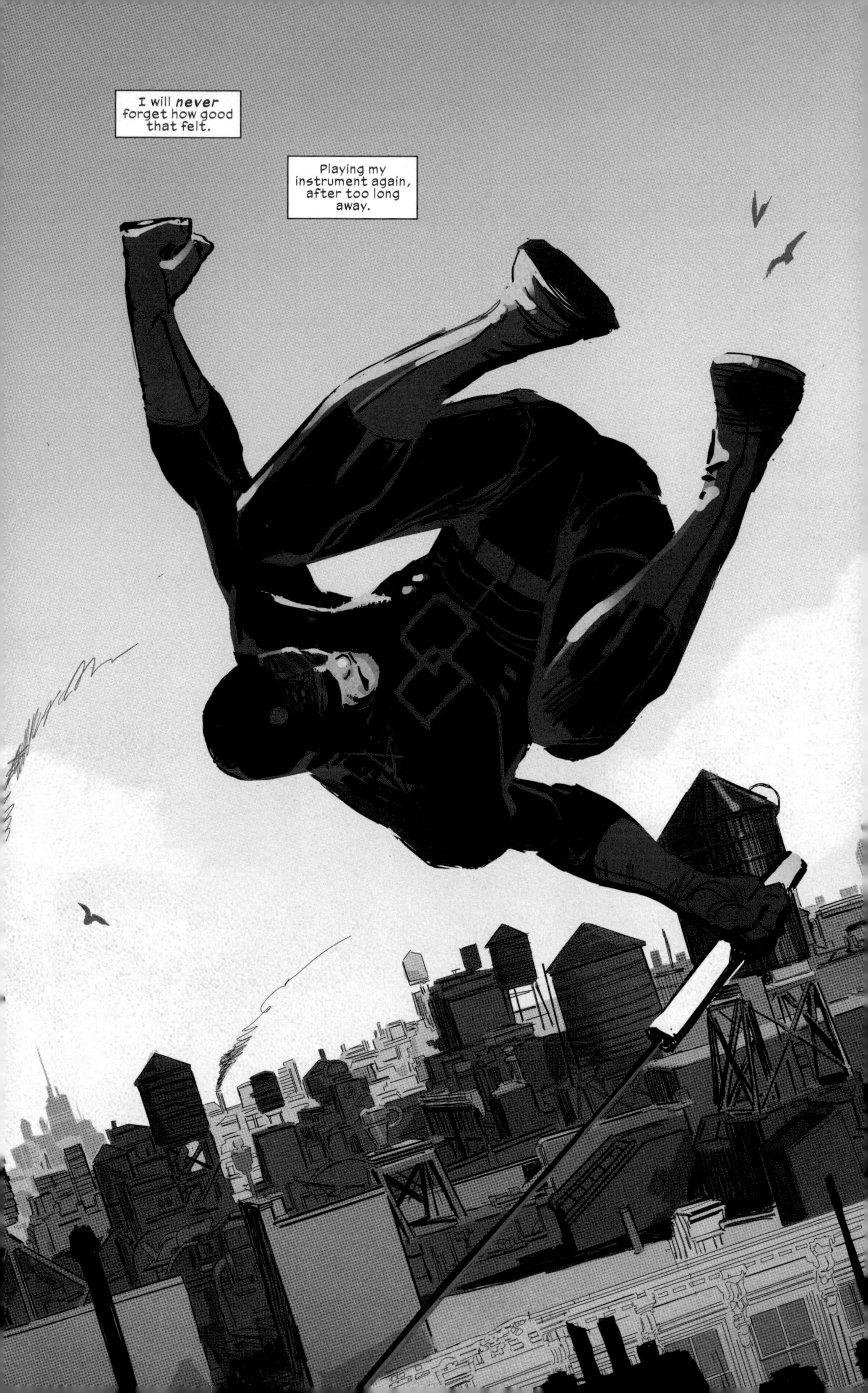
I will *never* forget how good that felt.
Playing my instrument again, after too long away.

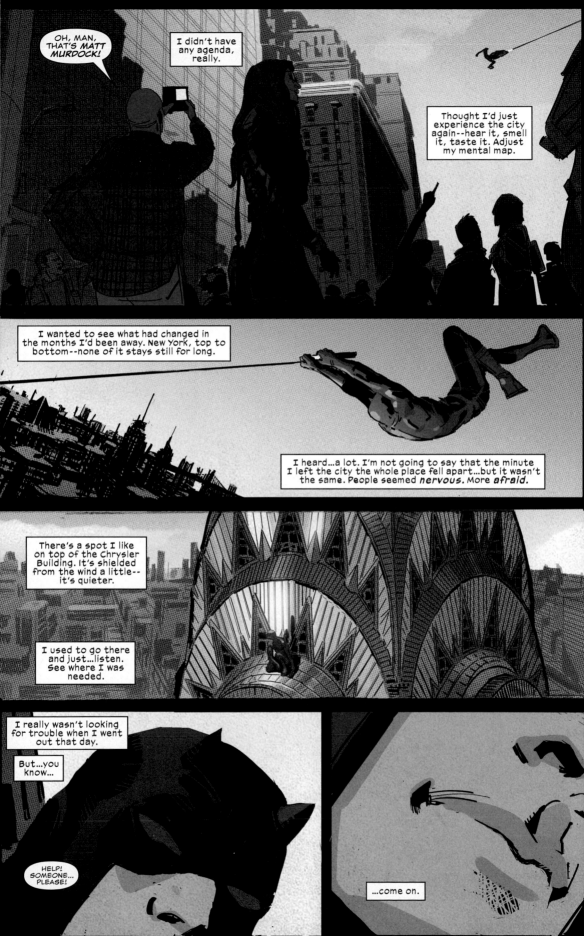

OH, MAN, THAT'S *MATT MURDOCK!*

I didn't have any agenda, really.

Thought I'd just experience the city again--hear it, smell it, taste it. Adjust my mental map.

I wanted to see what had changed in the months I'd been away. New York, top to bottom--none of it stays still for long.

I heard...a lot. I'm not going to say that the minute I left the city the whole place fell apart...but it wasn't the same. People seemed *nervous.* More *afraid.*

There's a spot I like on top of the Chrysler Building. It's shielded from the wind a little-- it's quieter.

I used to go there and just...listen. See where I was needed.

I really wasn't looking for trouble when I went out that day.

But...you know...

HELP! SOMEONE... PLEASE!

...come on.

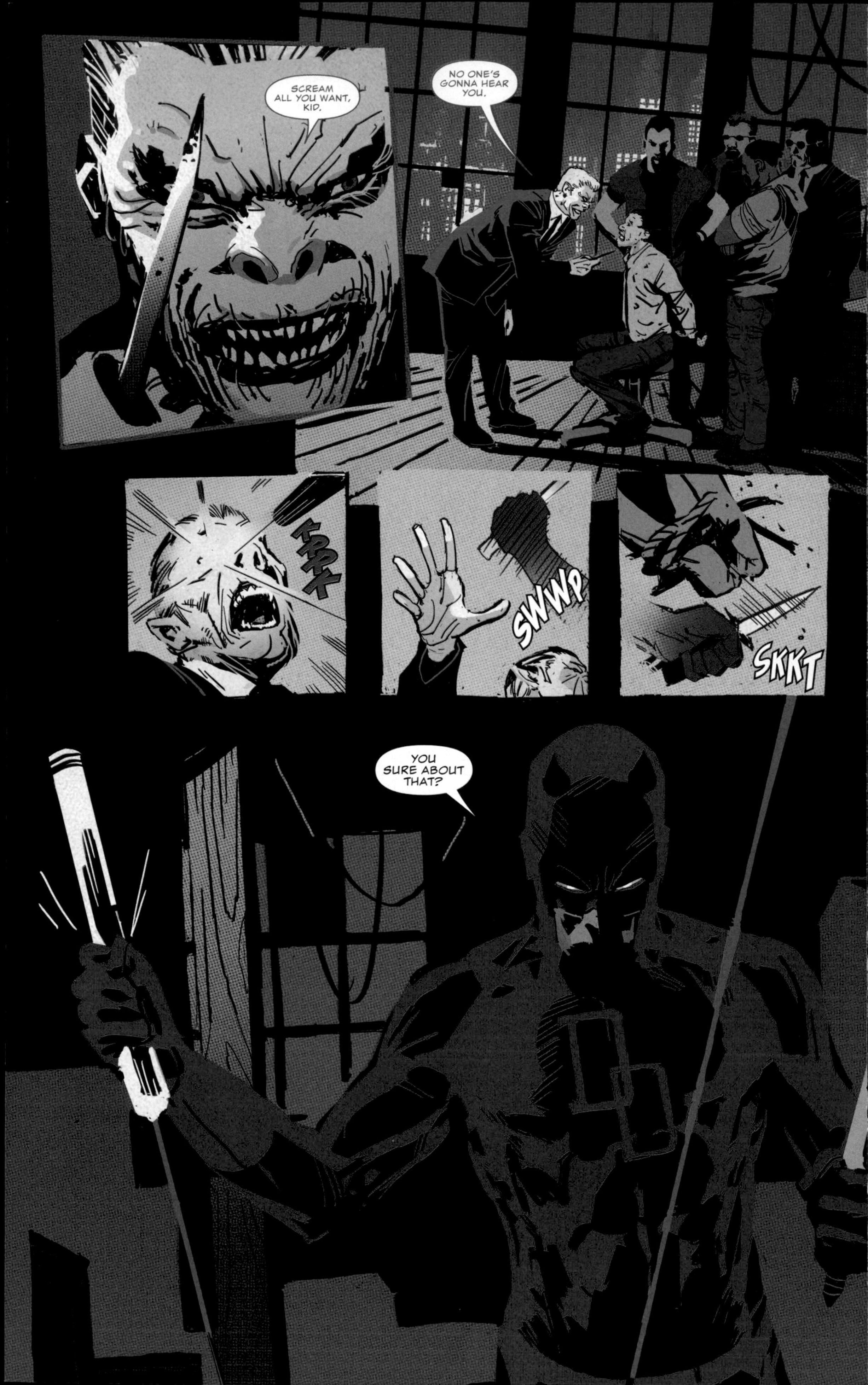
SCREAM ALL YOU WANT, KID.
NO ONE'S GONNA HEAR YOU.
KRRK
SWWP
SKKT
YOU SURE ABOUT THAT?

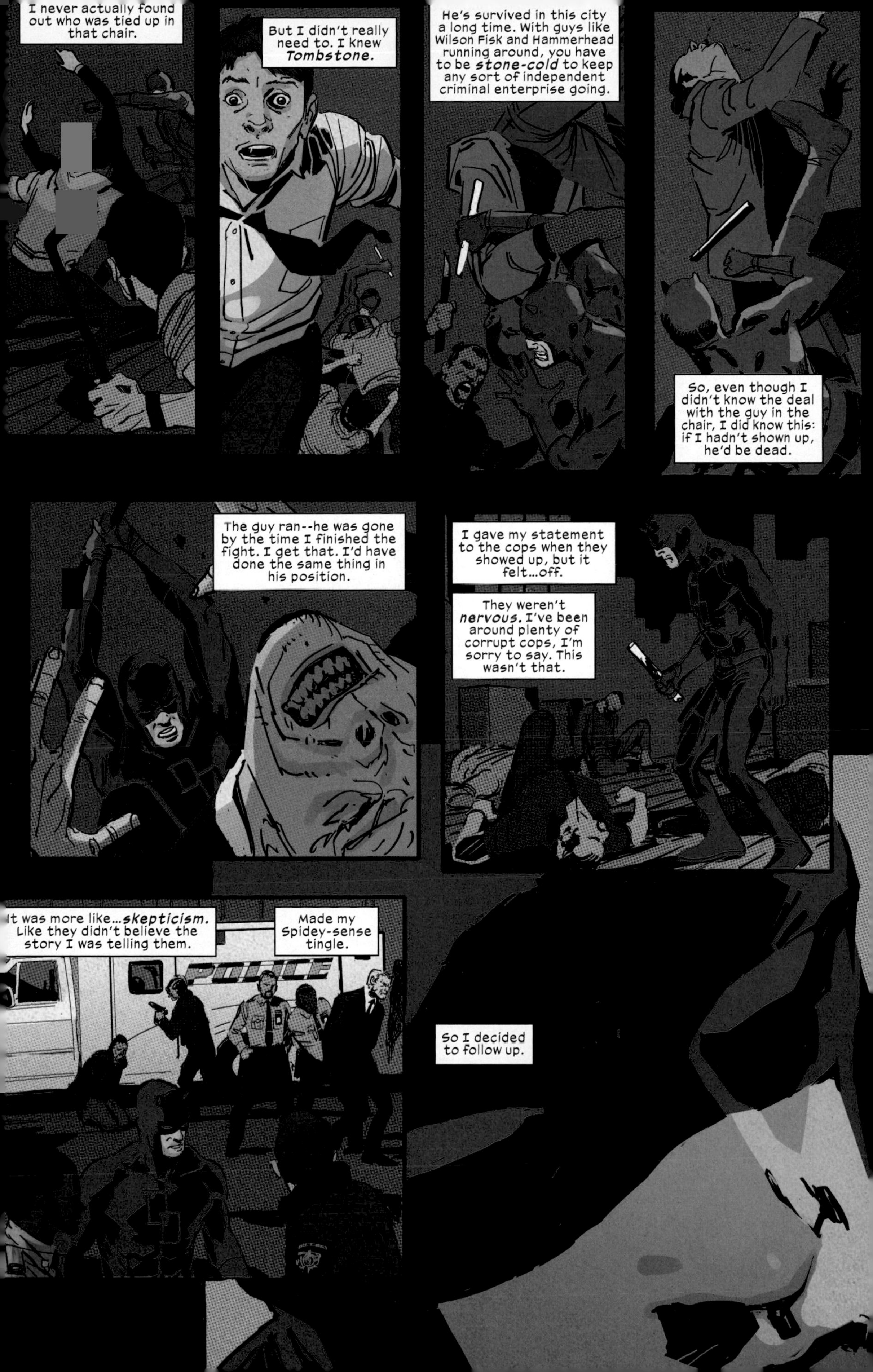
I never actually found out who was tied up in that chair.
But I didn't really need to. I knew *Tombstone.*
He's survived in this city a long time. With guys like Wilson Fisk and Hammerhead running around, you have to be *stone-cold* to keep any sort of independent criminal enterprise going.
So, even though I didn't know the deal with the guy in the chair, I did know this: if I hadn't shown up, he'd be dead.
The guy ran--he was gone by the time I finished the fight. I get that. I'd have done the same thing in his position.
I gave my statement to the cops when they showed up, but it felt...off.
They weren't *nervous.* I've been around plenty of corrupt cops, I'm sorry to say. This wasn't that.
It was more like...*skepticism.* Like they didn't believe the story I was telling them.
Made my Spidey-sense tingle.
POLICE
So I decided to follow up.

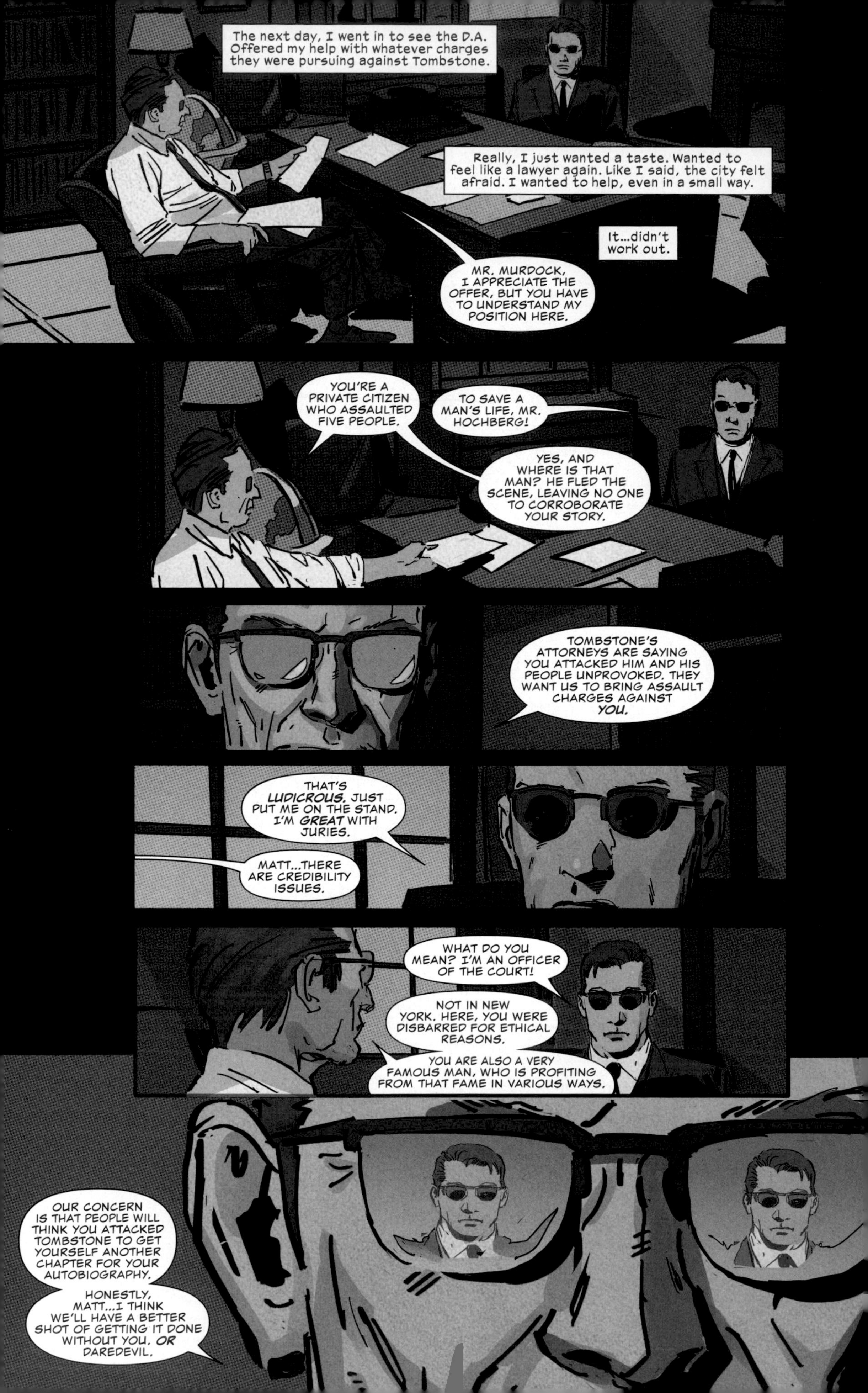
The next day, I went in to see the D.A. Offered my help with whatever charges they were pursuing against Tombstone.
Really, I just wanted a taste. Wanted to feel like a lawyer again. Like I said, the city felt afraid. I wanted to help, even in a small way.
It...didn't work out.
MR. MURDOCK, I APPRECIATE THE OFFER, BUT YOU HAVE TO UNDERSTAND MY POSITION HERE.
YOU'RE A PRIVATE CITIZEN WHO ASSAULTED FIVE PEOPLE.
TO SAVE A MAN'S LIFE, MR. HOCHBERG!
YES, AND WHERE IS THAT MAN? HE FLED THE SCENE, LEAVING NO ONE TO CORROBORATE YOUR STORY.
TOMBSTONE'S ATTORNEYS ARE SAYING YOU ATTACKED HIM AND HIS PEOPLE UNPROVOKED. THEY WANT US TO BRING ASSAULT CHARGES AGAINST *YOU.*
THAT'S ***LUDICROUS.*** JUST PUT ME ON THE STAND. I'M ***GREAT*** WITH JURIES.
MATT...THERE ARE CREDIBILITY ISSUES.
WHAT DO YOU MEAN? I'M AN OFFICER OF THE COURT!
NOT IN NEW YORK. HERE, YOU WERE DISBARRED FOR ETHICAL REASONS.
YOU ARE ALSO A VERY FAMOUS MAN, WHO IS PROFITING FROM THAT FAME IN VARIOUS WAYS.
OUR CONCERN IS THAT PEOPLE WILL THINK YOU ATTACKED TOMBSTONE TO GET YOURSELF ANOTHER CHAPTER FOR YOUR AUTOBIOGRAPHY.
HONESTLY, MATT...I THINK WE'LL HAVE A BETTER SHOT OF GETTING IT DONE WITHOUT YOU. *OR* DAREDEVIL.

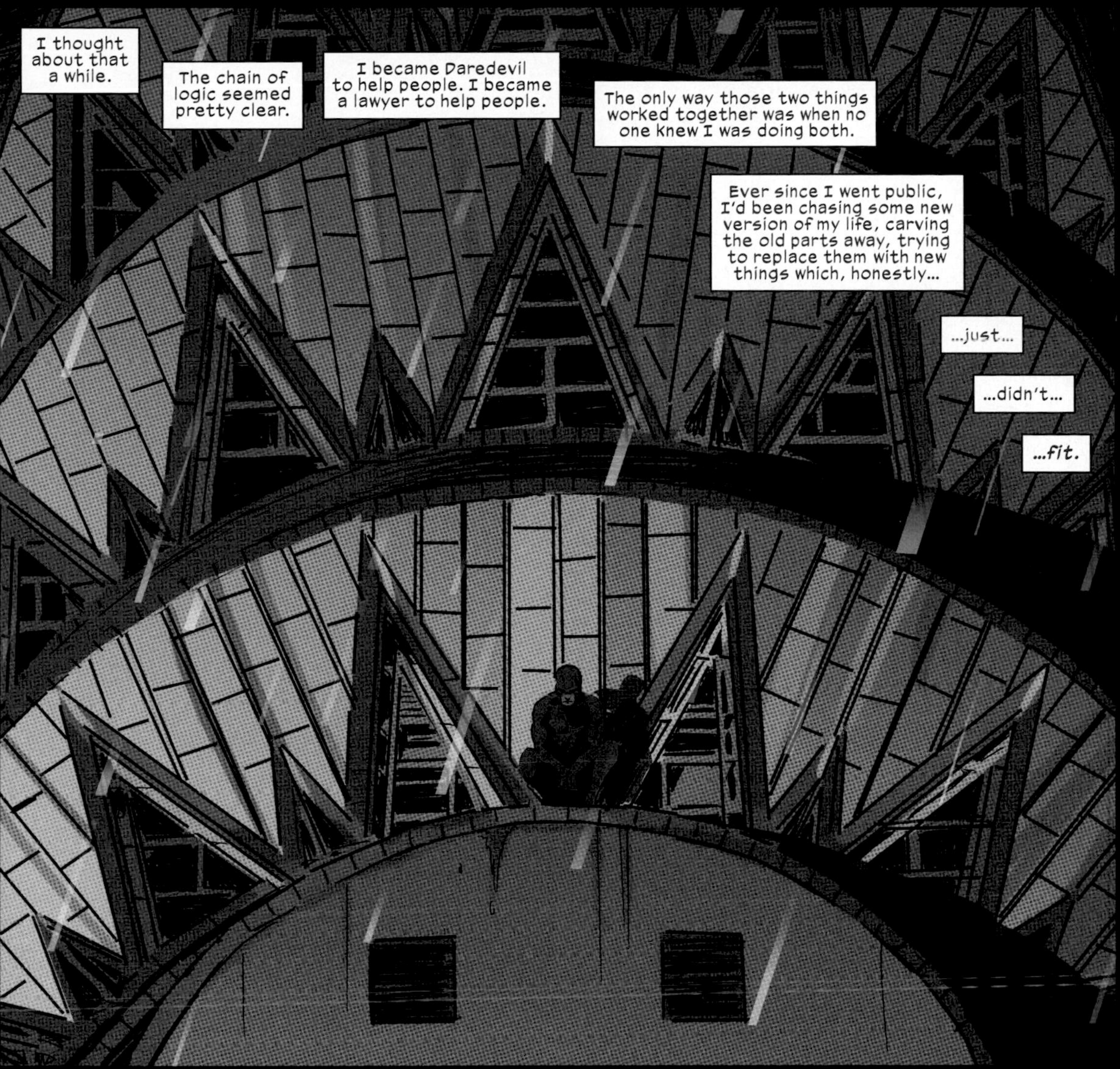
I thought about that a while.
The chain of logic seemed pretty clear.
I became Daredevil to help people. I became a lawyer to help people.
The only way those two things worked together was when no one knew I was doing both.
Ever since I went public, I'd been chasing some new version of my life, carving the old parts away, trying to replace them with new things which, honestly...
...just...
...didn't...
...*fit*.

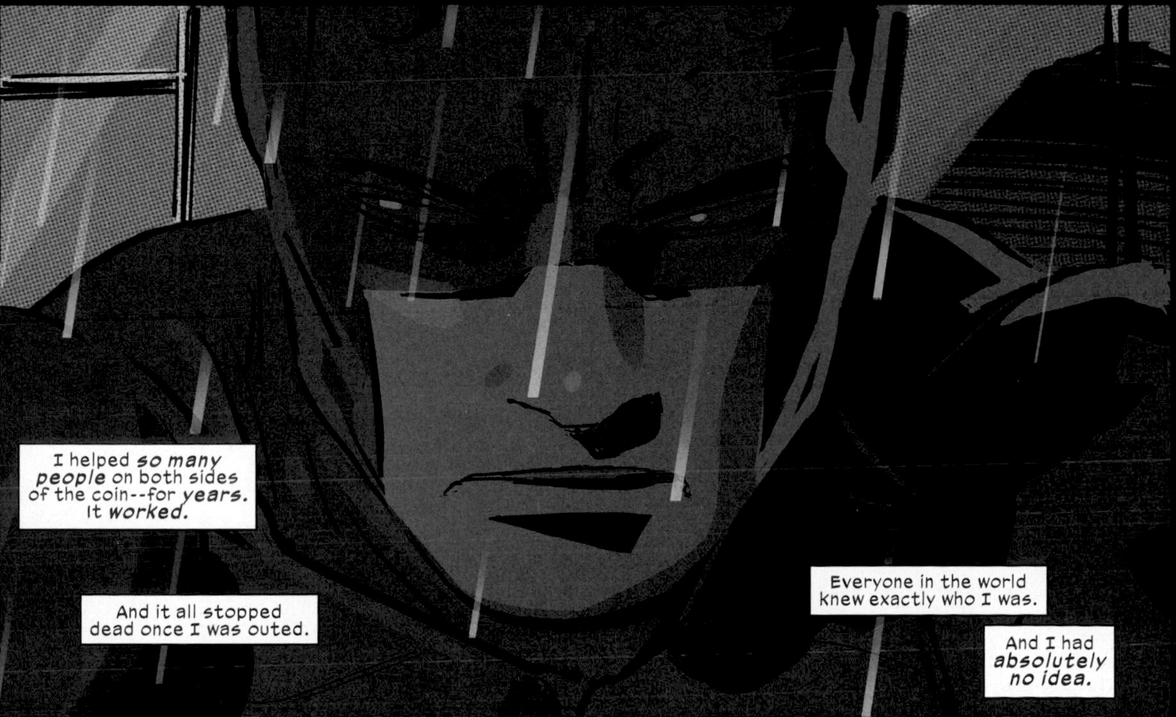
I helped *so many people* on both sides of the coin--for *years*. It *worked*.
And it all stopped dead once I was outed.
Everyone in the world knew exactly who I was.
And I had *absolutely no idea*.

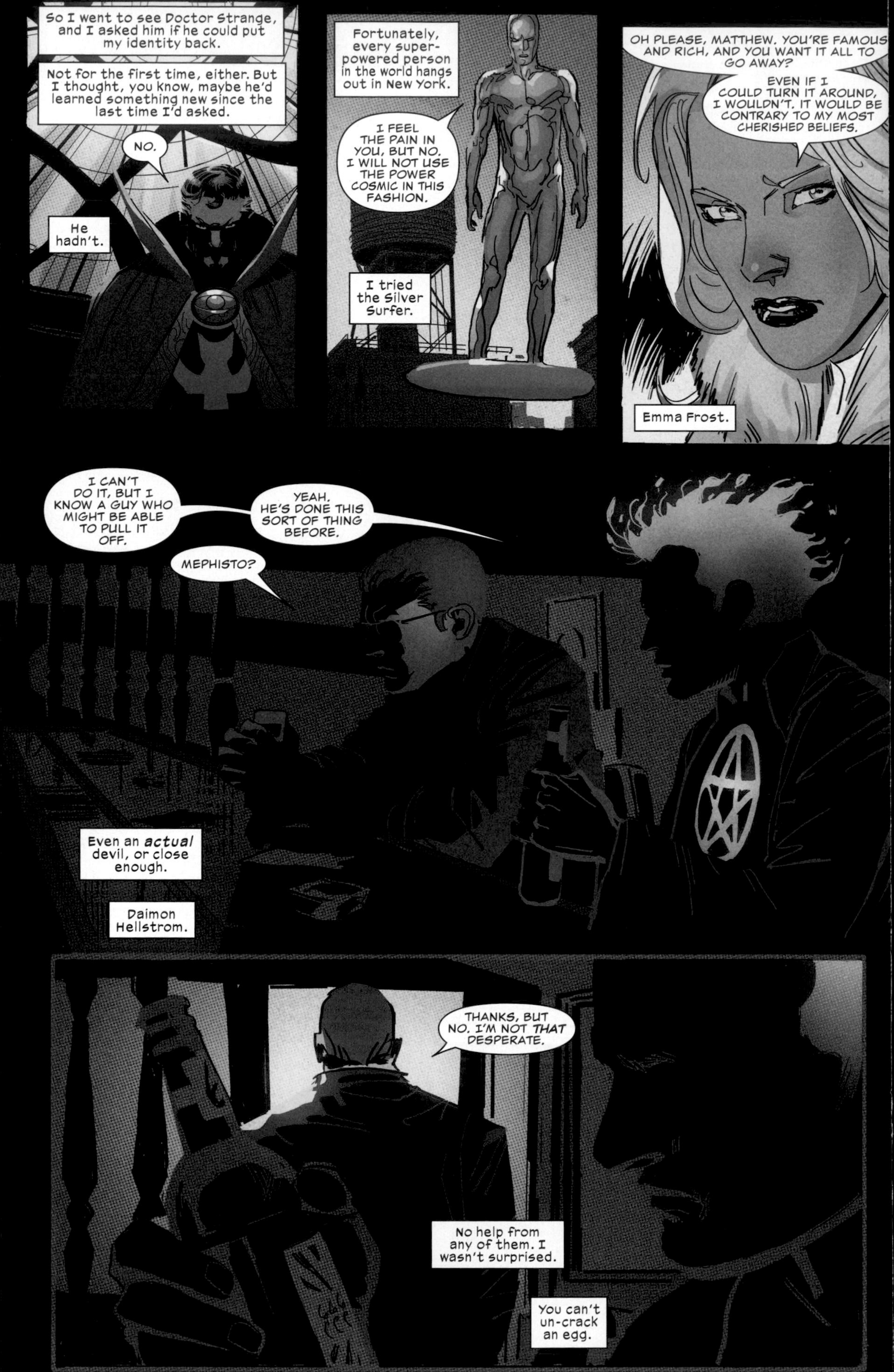
So I went to see Doctor Strange, and I asked him if he could put my identity back.
Not for the first time, either. But I thought, you know, maybe he'd learned something new since the last time I'd asked.
NO.
He hadn't.
Fortunately, every super-powered person in the world hangs out in New York.
I FEEL THE PAIN IN YOU, BUT NO. I WILL NOT USE THE POWER COSMIC IN THIS FASHION.
I tried the Silver Surfer.
OH PLEASE, MATTHEW. YOU'RE FAMOUS AND RICH, AND YOU WANT IT ALL TO GO AWAY?
EVEN IF I COULD TURN IT AROUND, I WOULDN'T. IT WOULD BE CONTRARY TO MY MOST CHERISHED BELIEFS.
Emma Frost.
I CAN'T DO IT, BUT I KNOW A GUY WHO MIGHT BE ABLE TO PULL IT OFF.
YEAH. HE'S DONE THIS SORT OF THING BEFORE.
MEPHISTO?
Even an *actual* devil, or close enough.
Daimon Hellstrom.
THANKS, BUT NO. I'M NOT *THAT* DESPERATE.
No help from any of them. I wasn't surprised.
You can't un-crack an egg.

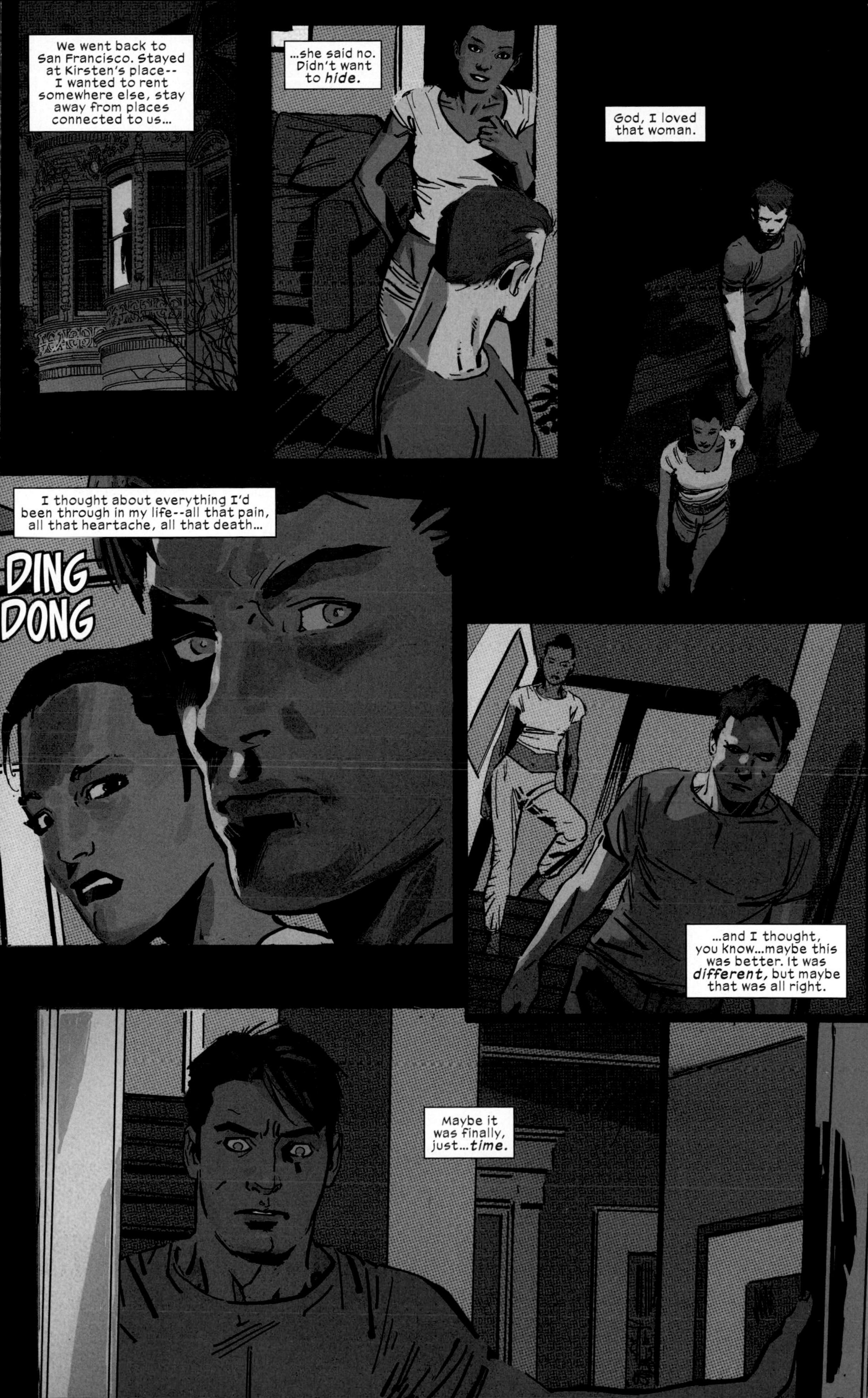

We went back to San Francisco. Stayed at Kirsten's place-- I wanted to rent somewhere else, stay away from places connected to us...
...she said no. Didn't want to *hide.*
God, I loved that woman.
I thought about everything I'd been through in my life--all that pain, all that heartache, all that death...
...and I thought, you know...maybe this was better. It was *different,* but maybe that was all right.
DING DONG
Maybe it was finally, just...*time.*

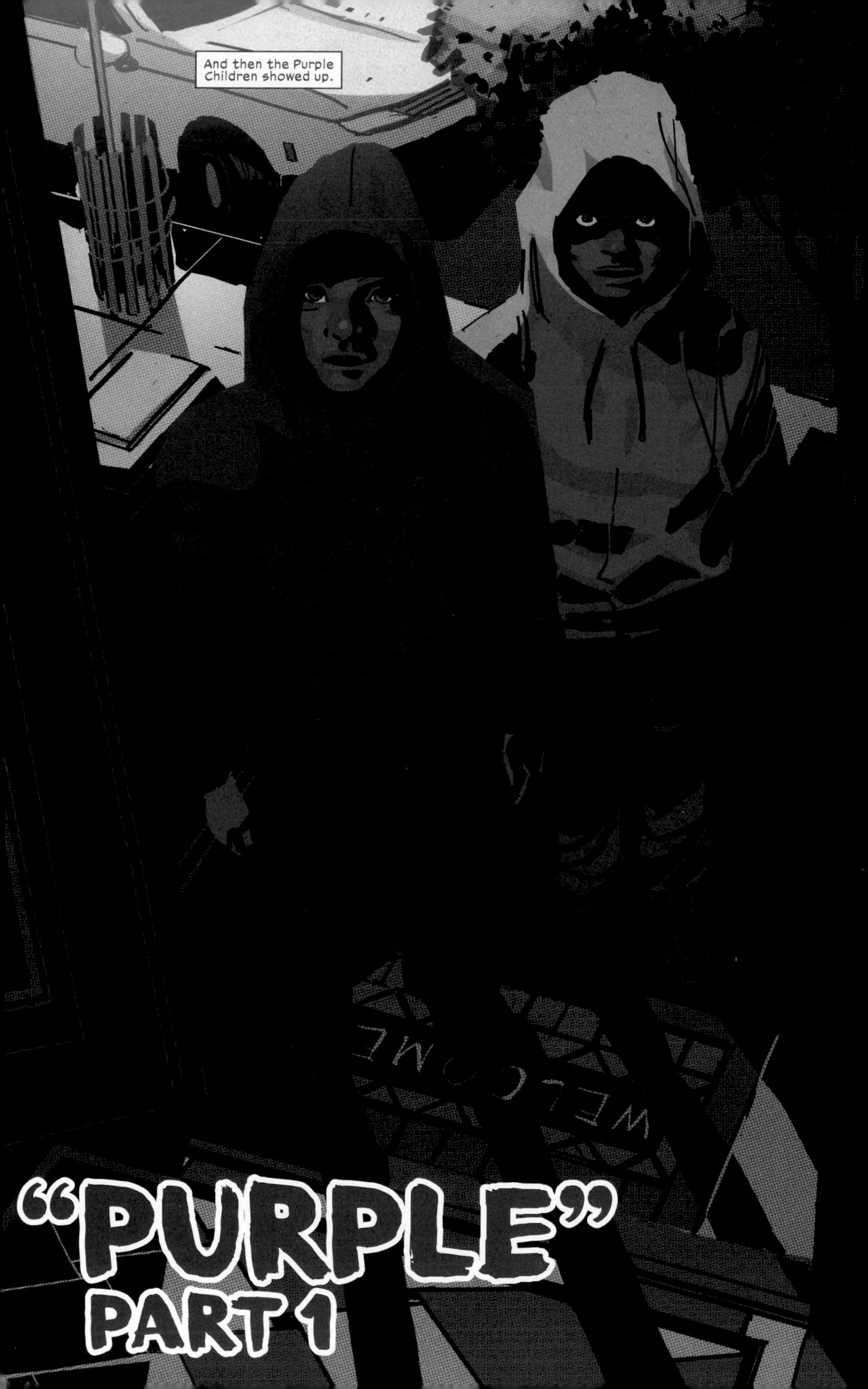
And then the Purple Children showed up.
WELCOME
"PURPLE"
PART 1

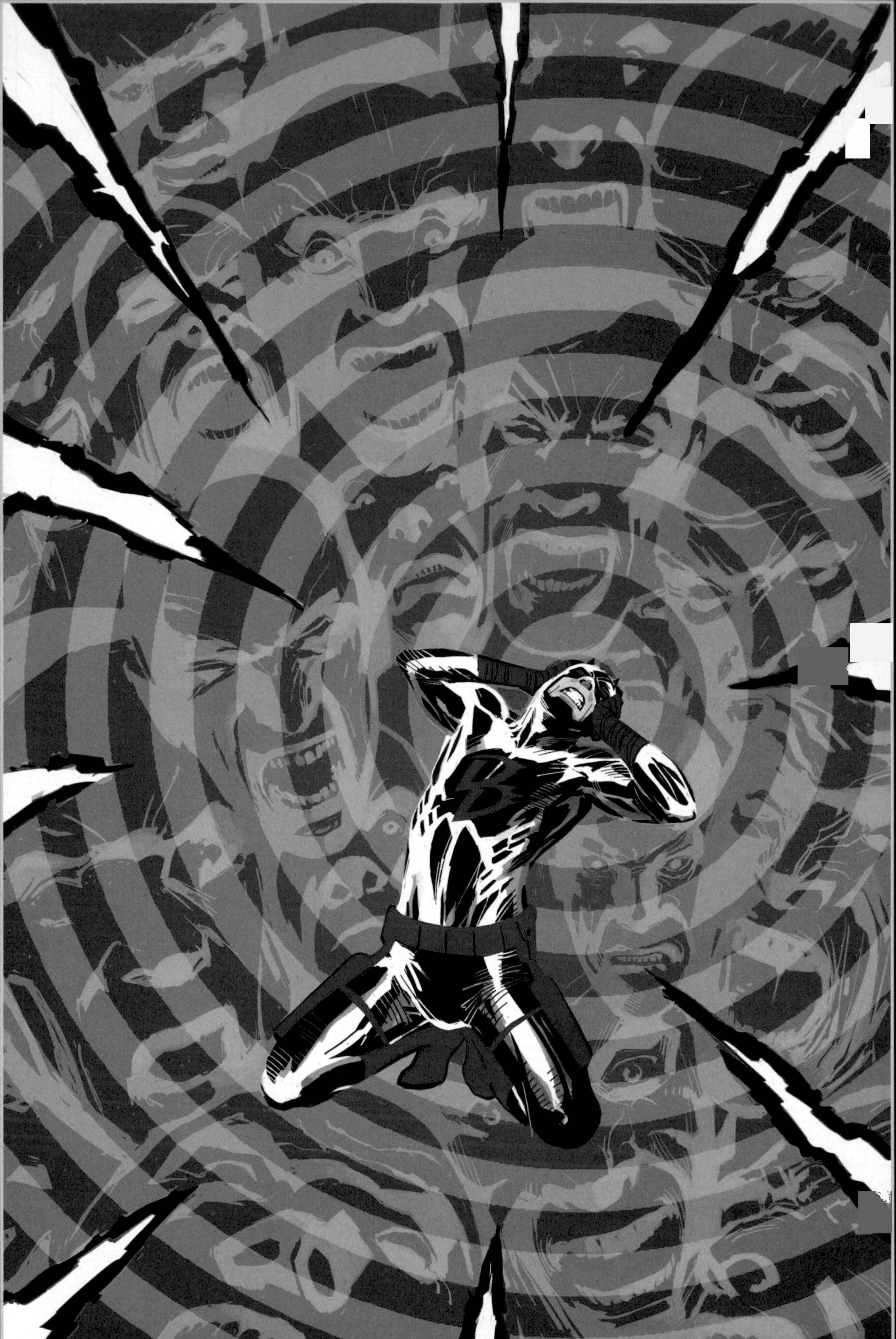

I WAS LOST.

I THINK THAT'S HOW EVERYTHING HAPPENED. MY COMPASS WAS OFF. I COULDN'T SEE MYSELF, AND IT MADE ME *WEAK*.

MATT, I'M SYMPATHETIC--BUT I DON'T THINK YOU'RE BEING FAIR TO YOURSELF.

UNCERTAINTY DOESN'T MAKE YOU WEAK. IT MAKES YOU *HUMAN*.

UH-HUH. I'M *DAREDEVIL*, FATHER JORDAN. I'M SUPPOSED TO BE *SUPERHUMAN*, REMEMBER? ALL DAY, EVERY DAY, EIGHT DAYS A WEEK.

MM, PERHAPS...LET'S JUST KEEP TALKING.

YOU SAID...*PURPLE CHILDREN* CAME TO SEE YOU?

NOT PURPLE CHILDREN. *THE PURPLE CHILDREN,* TWO OF THEM. TWO OUT OF FIVE.

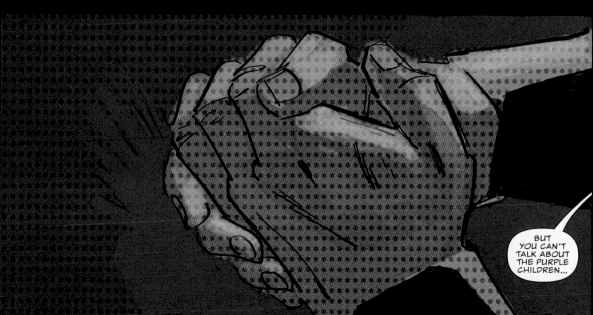

BUT YOU CAN'T TALK ABOUT THE PURPLE CHILDREN...

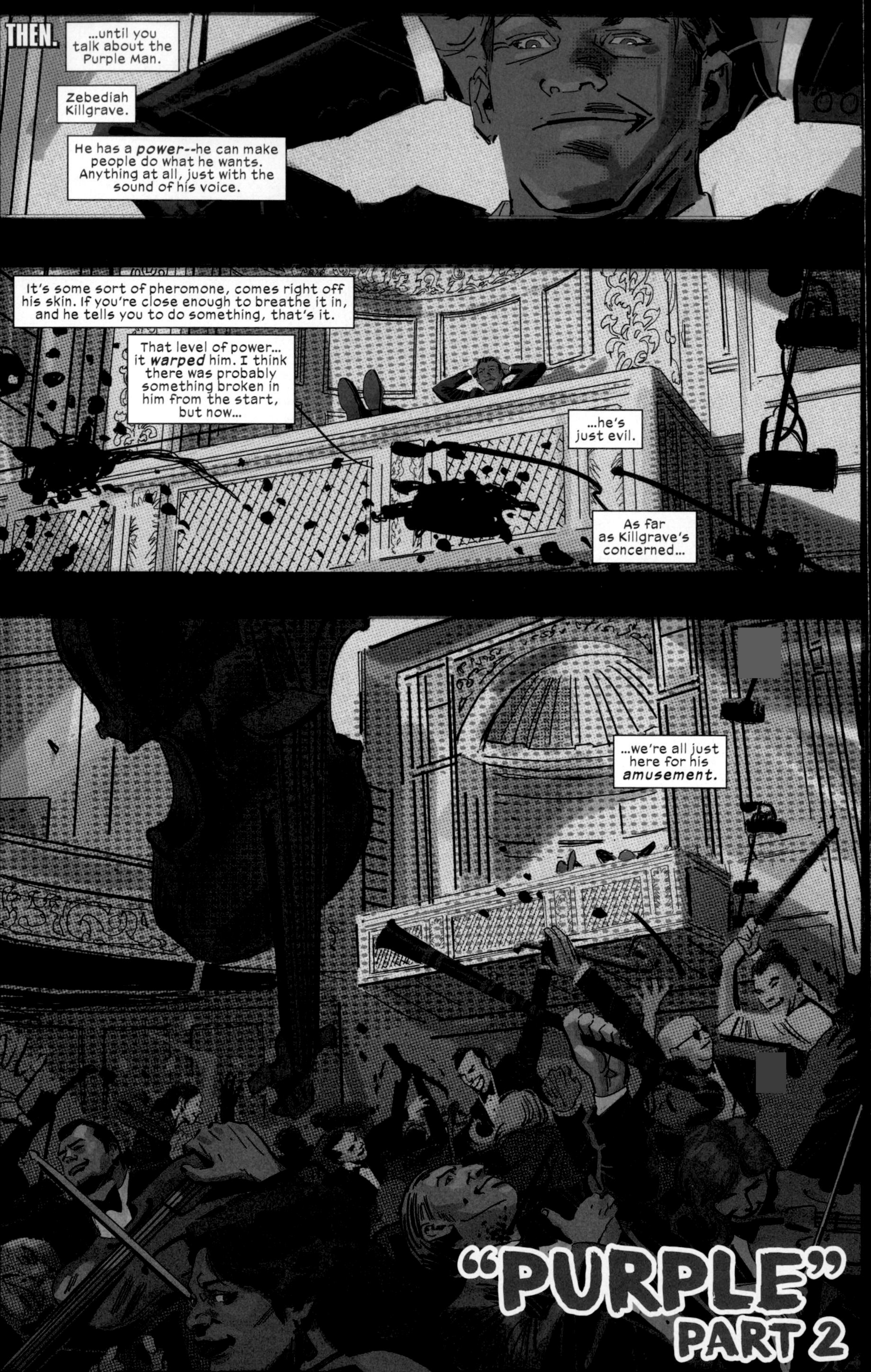
THEN.
...until you talk about the Purple Man.
Zebediah Killgrave.
He has a *power*--he can make people do what he wants. Anything at all, just with the sound of his voice.
It's some sort of pheromone, comes right off his skin. If you're close enough to breathe it in, and he tells you to do something, that's it.
That level of power... it *warped* him. I think there was probably something broken in him from the start, but now...
...he's just evil.
As far as Killgrave's concerned...
...we're all just here for his *amusement*.
"PURPLE"
PART 2

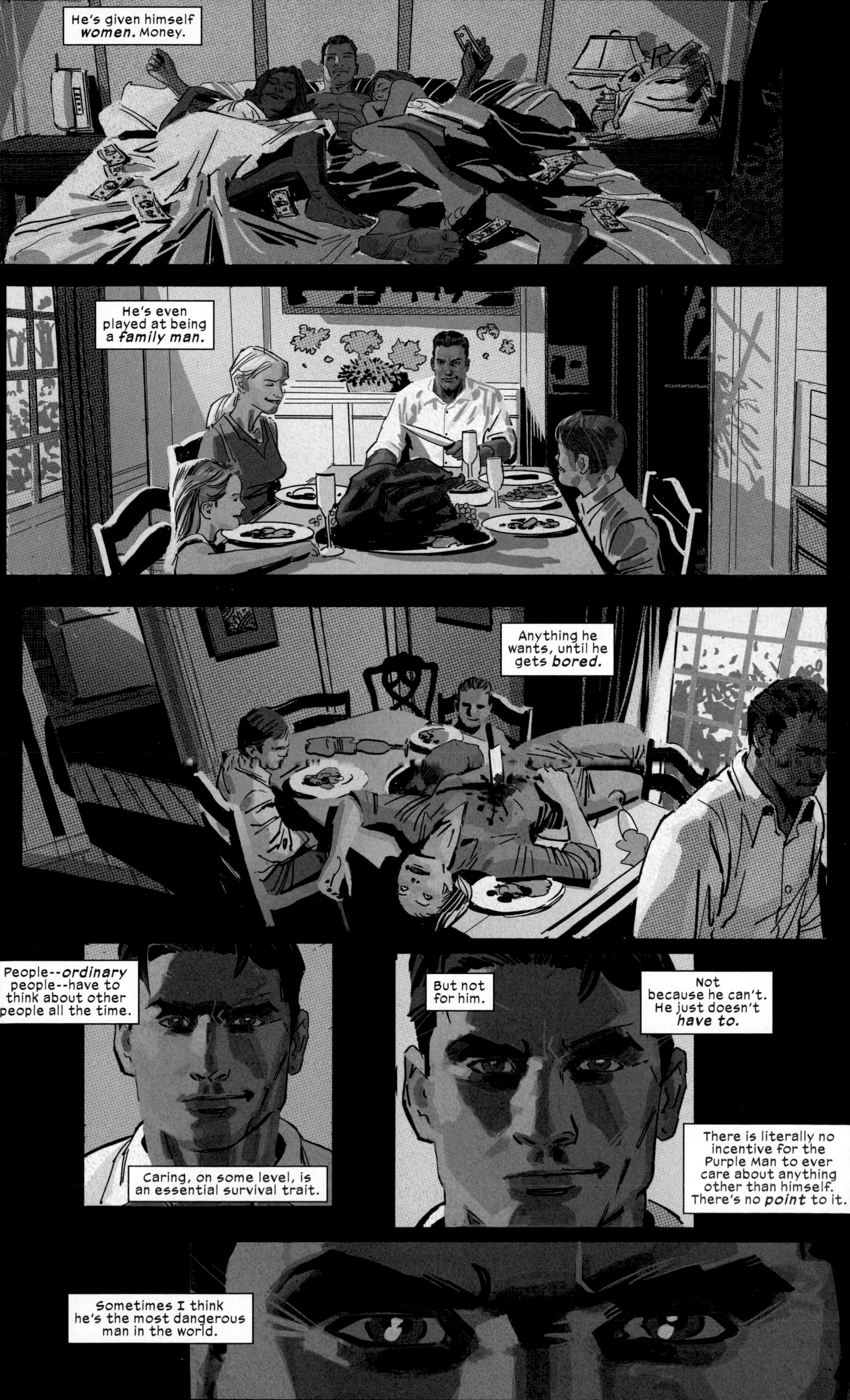
He's given himself *women.* Money.
He's even played at being a *family man.*
Anything he wants, until he gets *bored.*
People--*ordinary* people--have to think about other people all the time.
Caring, on some level, is an essential survival trait.
But not for him.
Not because he can't. He just doesn't *have to.*
There is literally no incentive for the Purple Man to ever care about anything other than himself. There's no *point* to it.
Sometimes I think he's the most dangerous man in the world.

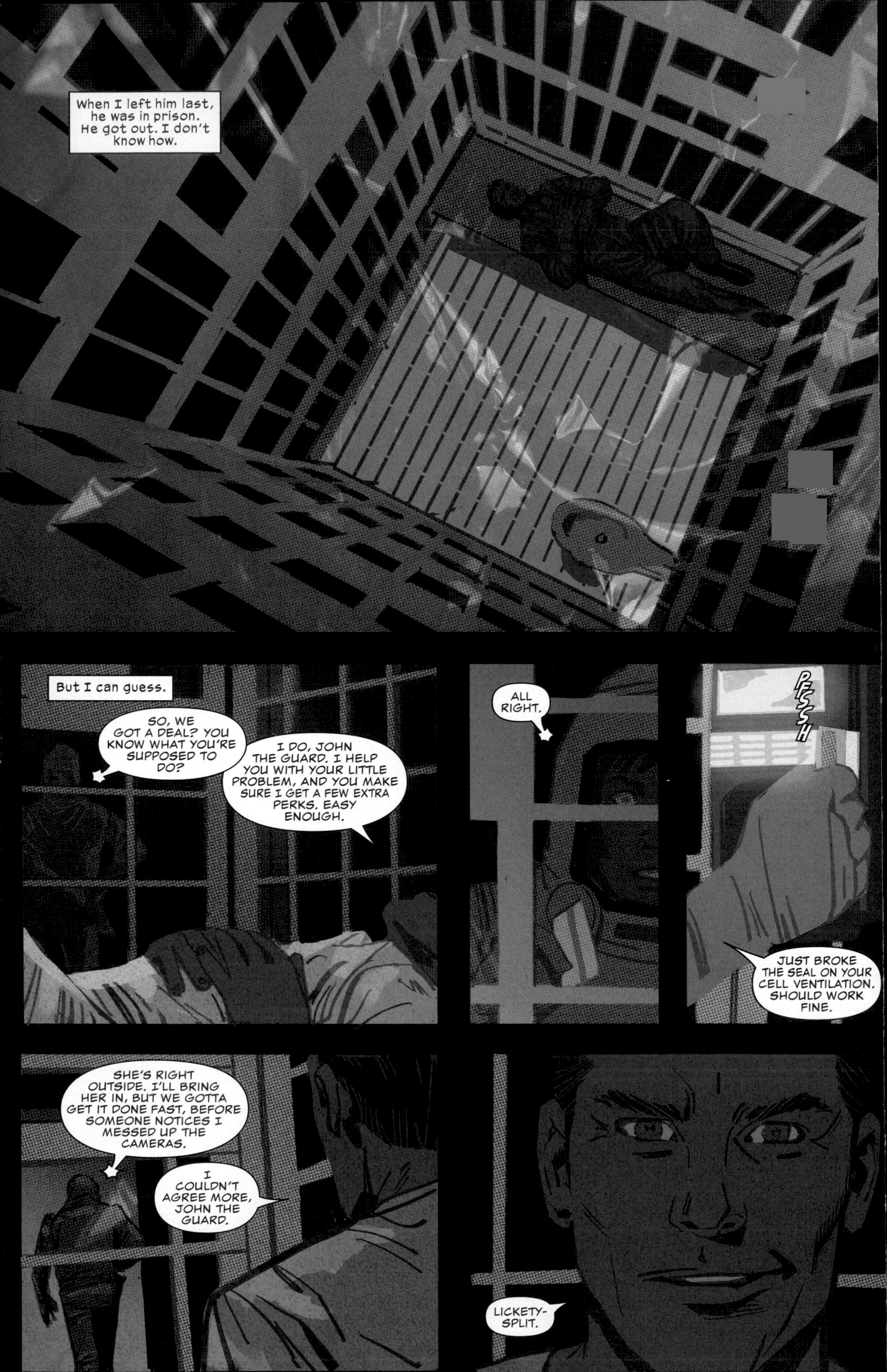
When I left him last, he was in prison. He got out. I don't know how.
But I can guess.
SO, WE GOT A DEAL? YOU KNOW WHAT YOU'RE SUPPOSED TO DO?
I DO, JOHN THE GUARD. I HELP YOU WITH YOUR LITTLE PROBLEM, AND YOU MAKE SURE I GET A FEW EXTRA PERKS. EASY ENOUGH.
ALL RIGHT.
PFSSH
JUST BROKE THE SEAL ON YOUR CELL VENTILATION. SHOULD WORK FINE.
SHE'S RIGHT OUTSIDE. I'LL BRING HER IN, BUT WE GOTTA GET IT DONE FAST, BEFORE SOMEONE NOTICES I MESSED UP THE CAMERAS.
I COULDN'T AGREE MORE, JOHN THE GUARD.
LICKETY-SPLIT.

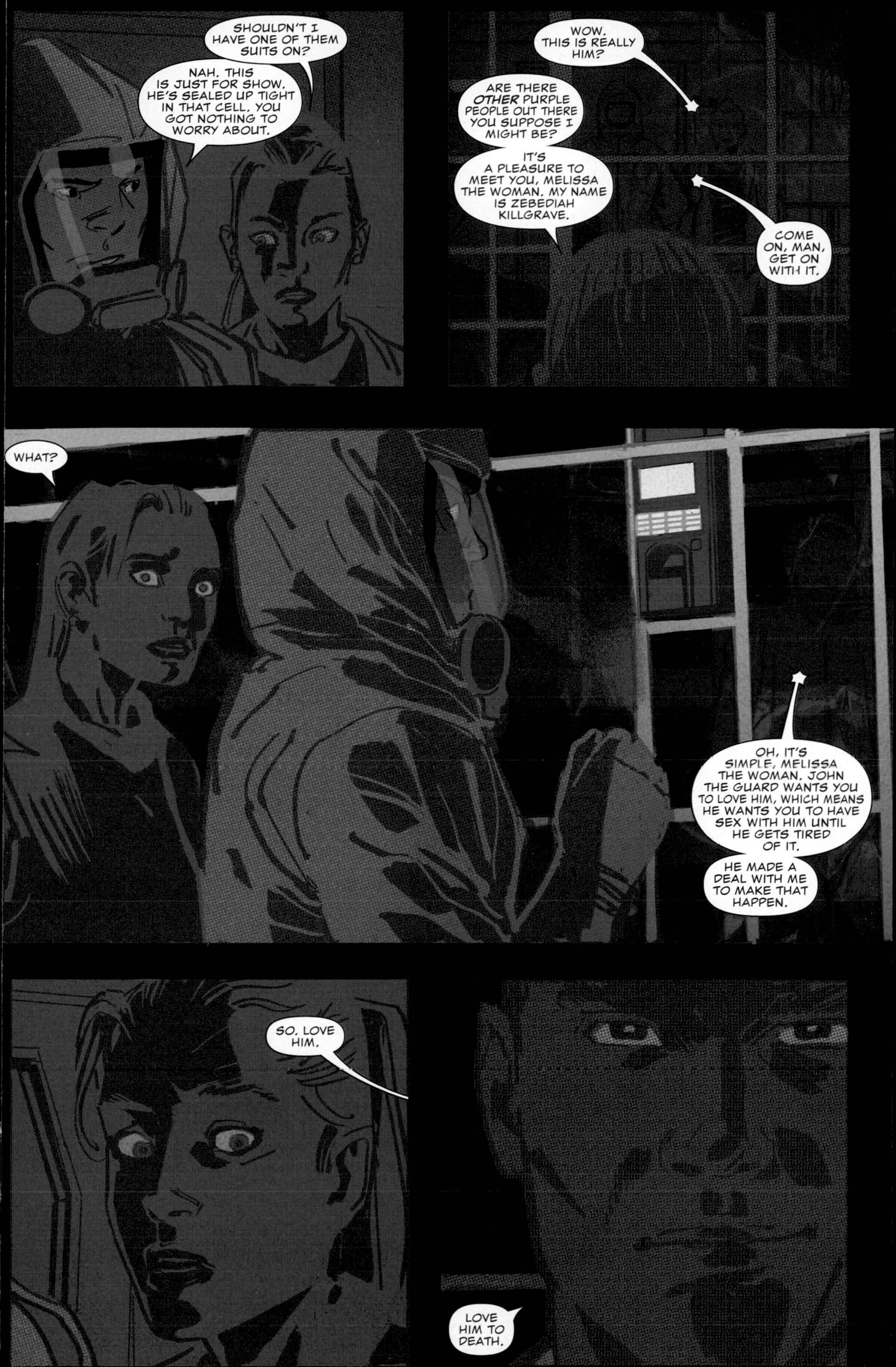
SHOULDN'T I HAVE ONE OF THEM SUITS ON?
NAH. THIS IS JUST FOR SHOW. HE'S SEALED UP TIGHT IN THAT CELL. YOU GOT NOTHING TO WORRY ABOUT.
WOW. THIS IS REALLY HIM?
ARE THERE OTHER PURPLE PEOPLE OUT THERE YOU SUPPOSE I MIGHT BE?
IT'S A PLEASURE TO MEET YOU, MELISSA THE WOMAN. MY NAME IS ZEBEDIAH KILLGRAVE.
COME ON, MAN, GET ON WITH IT.
WHAT?
OH, IT'S SIMPLE, MELISSA THE WOMAN. JOHN THE GUARD WANTS YOU TO LOVE HIM, WHICH MEANS HE WANTS YOU TO HAVE SEX WITH HIM UNTIL HE GETS TIRED OF IT.
HE MADE A DEAL WITH ME TO MAKE THAT HAPPEN.
SO, LOVE HIM.
LOVE HIM TO DEATH.

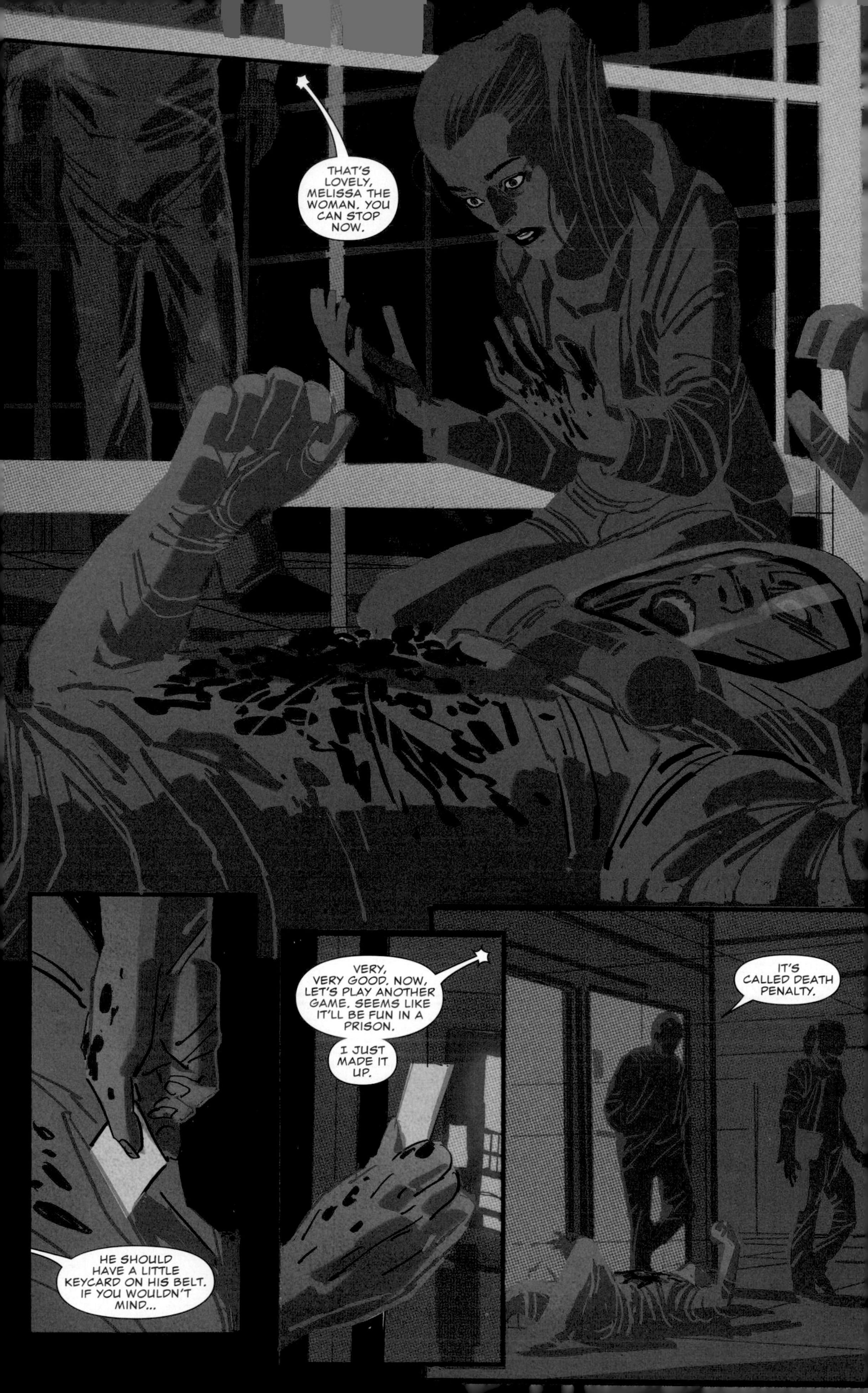
THAT'S LOVELY, MELISSA THE WOMAN. YOU CAN STOP NOW.
HE SHOULD HAVE A LITTLE KEYCARD ON HIS BELT. IF YOU WOULDN'T MIND...
VERY, VERY GOOD. NOW, LET'S PLAY ANOTHER GAME. SEEMS LIKE IT'LL BE FUN IN A PRISON.
I JUST MADE IT UP.
IT'S CALLED DEATH PENALTY.

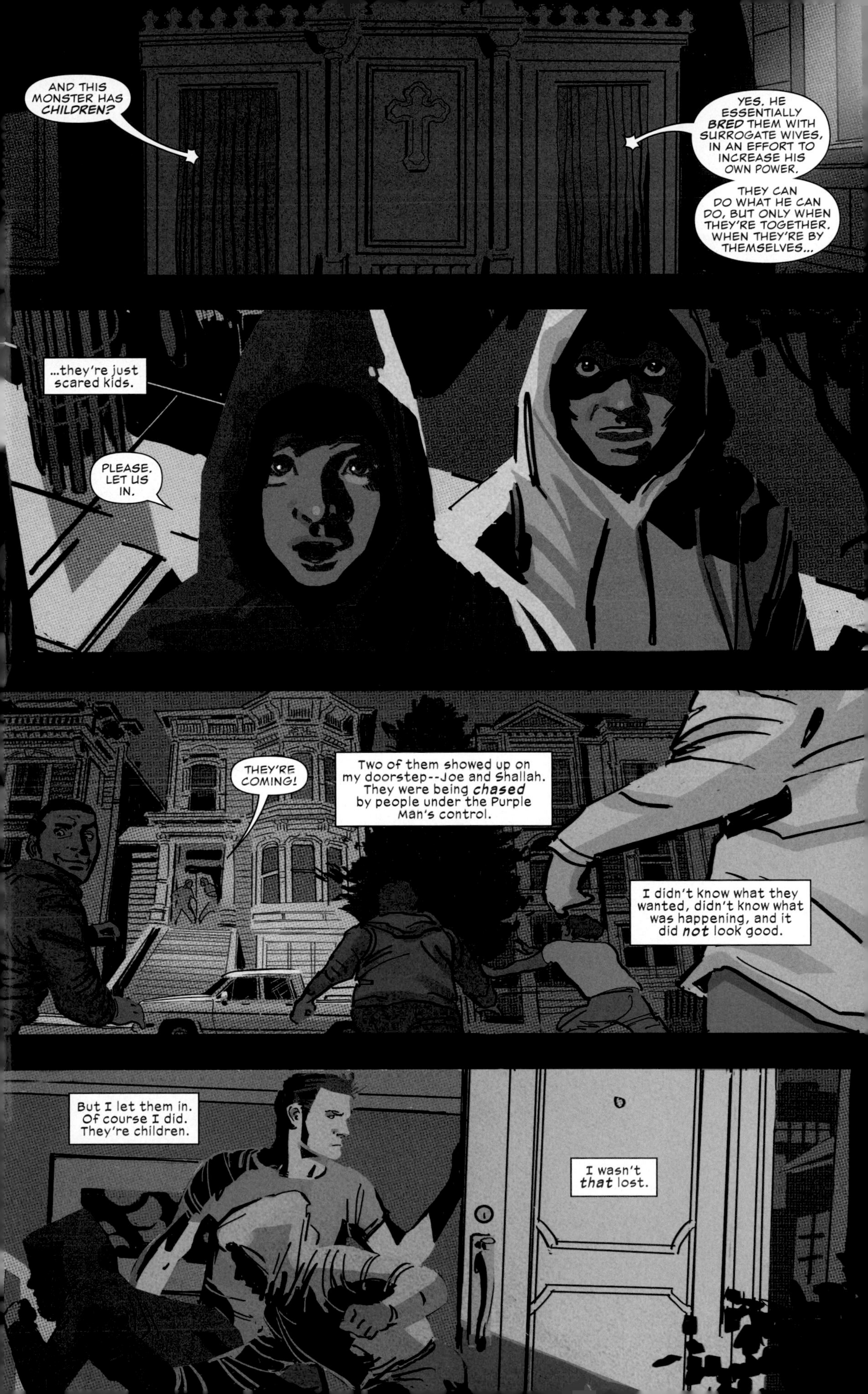
AND THIS MONSTER HAS CHILDREN?
YES. HE ESSENTIALLY BRED THEM WITH SURROGATE WIVES, IN AN EFFORT TO INCREASE HIS OWN POWER.
THEY CAN DO WHAT HE CAN DO, BUT ONLY WHEN THEY'RE TOGETHER. WHEN THEY'RE BY THEMSELVES...
...they're just scared kids.
PLEASE. LET US IN.
THEY'RE COMING!
Two of them showed up on my doorstep--Joe and Shallah. They were being chased by people under the Purple Man's control.
I didn't know what they wanted, didn't know what was happening, and it did not look good.
But I let them in. Of course I did. They're children.
I wasn't that lost.

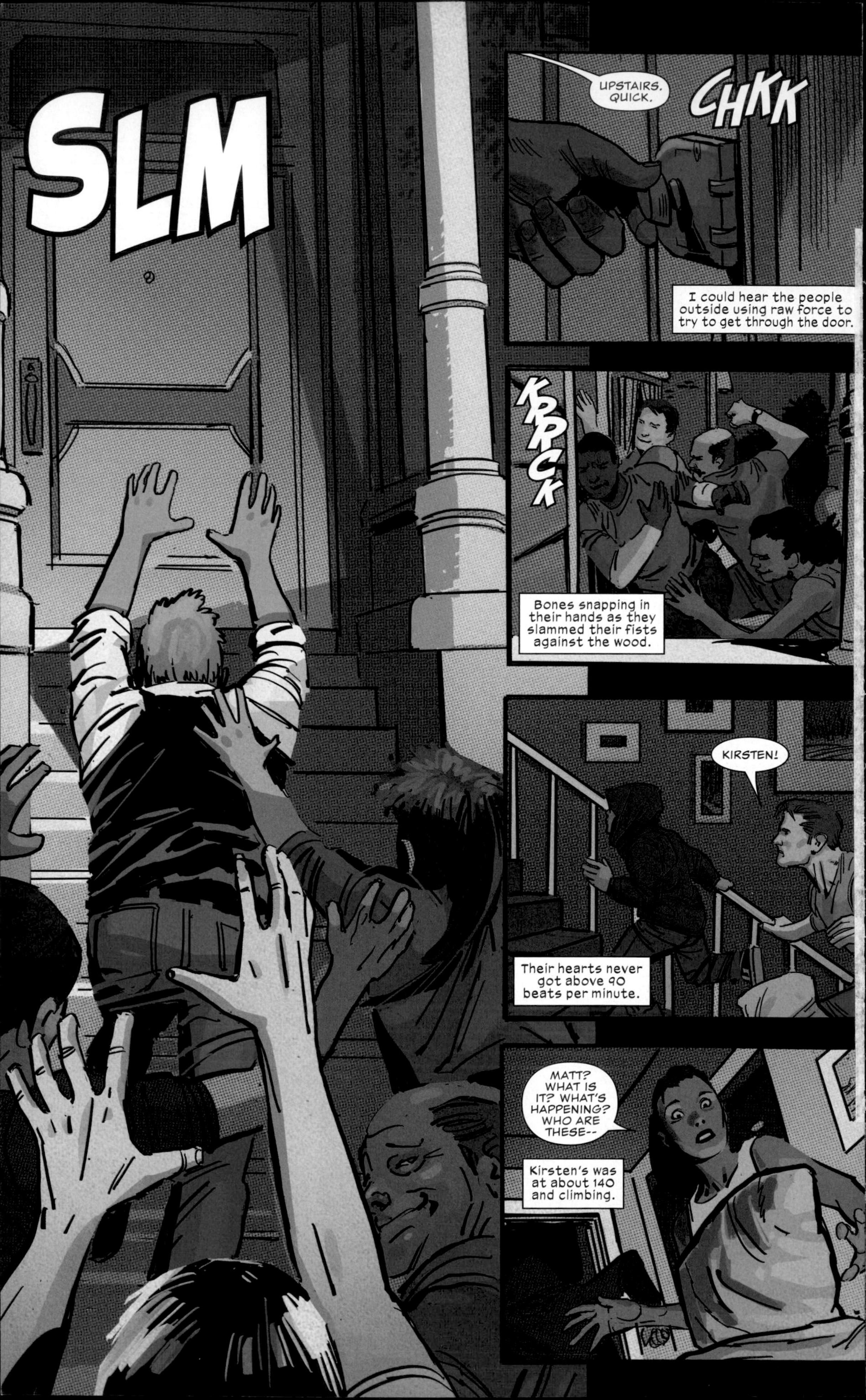
SLM
UPSTAIRS. QUICK.
CHKK
I could hear the people outside using raw force to try to get through the door.
KRRCK
Bones snapping in their hands as they slammed their fists against the wood.
KIRSTEN!
Their hearts never got above 90 beats per minute.
MATT? WHAT IS IT? WHAT'S HAPPENING? WHO ARE THESE--
Kirsten's was at about 140 and climbing.

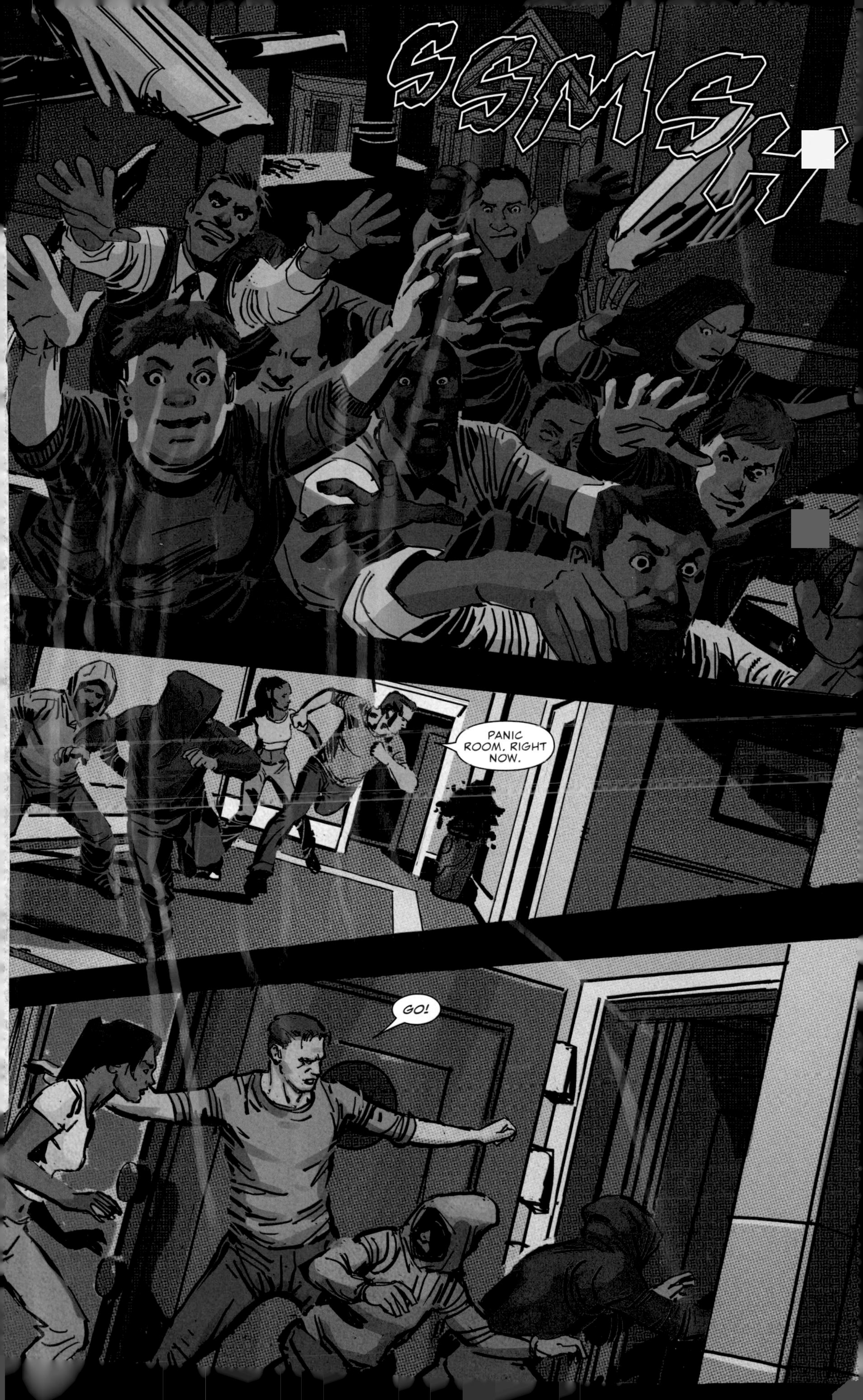
SSMSH
PANIC ROOM. RIGHT NOW.
GO!

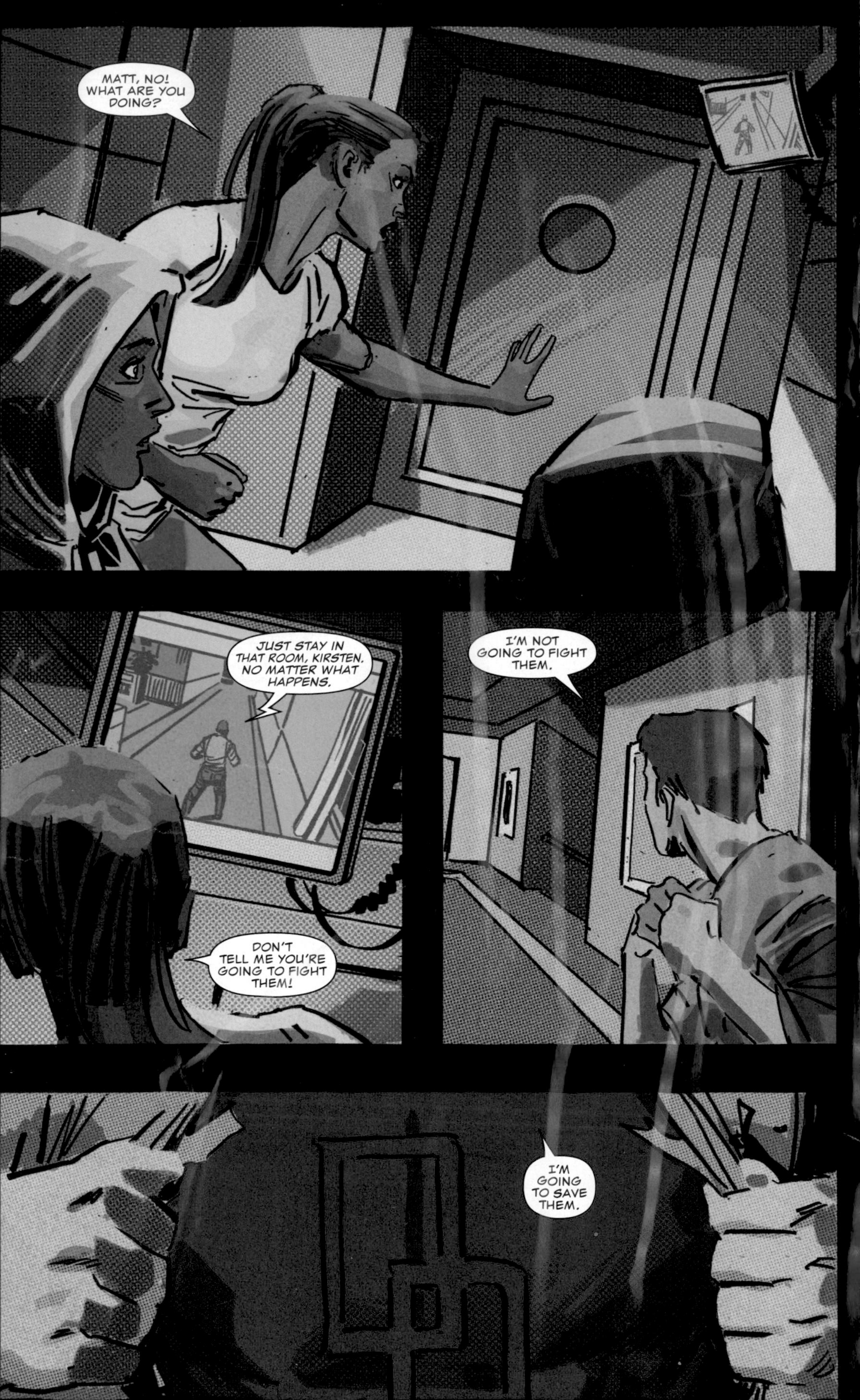
MATT, NO! WHAT ARE YOU DOING?
JUST STAY IN THAT ROOM, KIRSTEN. NO MATTER WHAT HAPPENS.
DON'T TELL ME YOU'RE GOING TO FIGHT THEM!
I'M NOT GOING TO FIGHT THEM.
I'M GOING TO SAVE THEM.

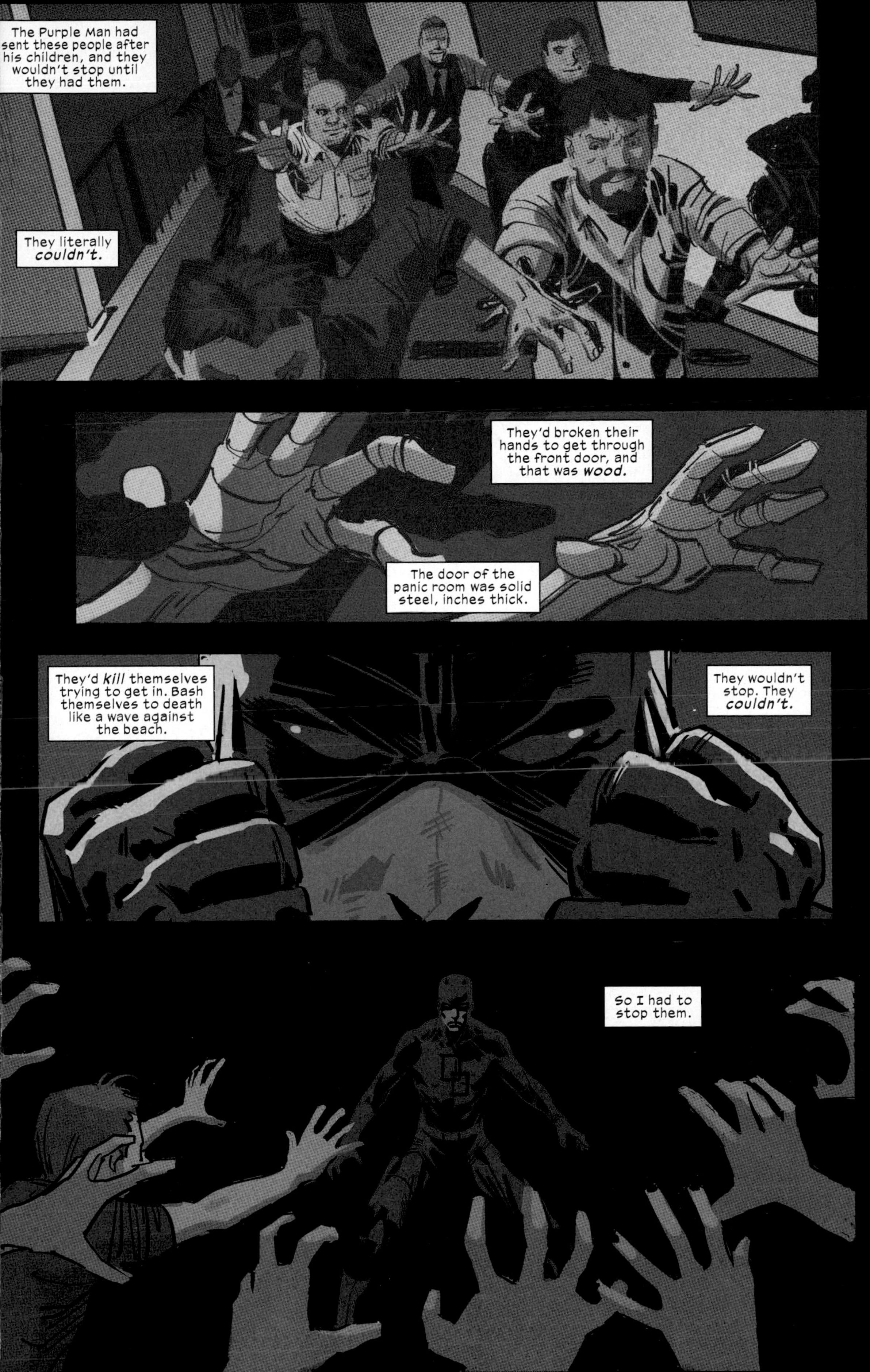
The Purple Man had sent these people after his children, and they wouldn't stop until they had them.
They literally *couldn't.*
They'd broken their hands to get through the front door, and that was *wood.*
The door of the panic room was solid steel, inches thick.
They'd *kill* themselves trying to get in. Bash themselves to death like a wave against the beach.
They wouldn't stop. They *couldn't.*
So I had to stop them.

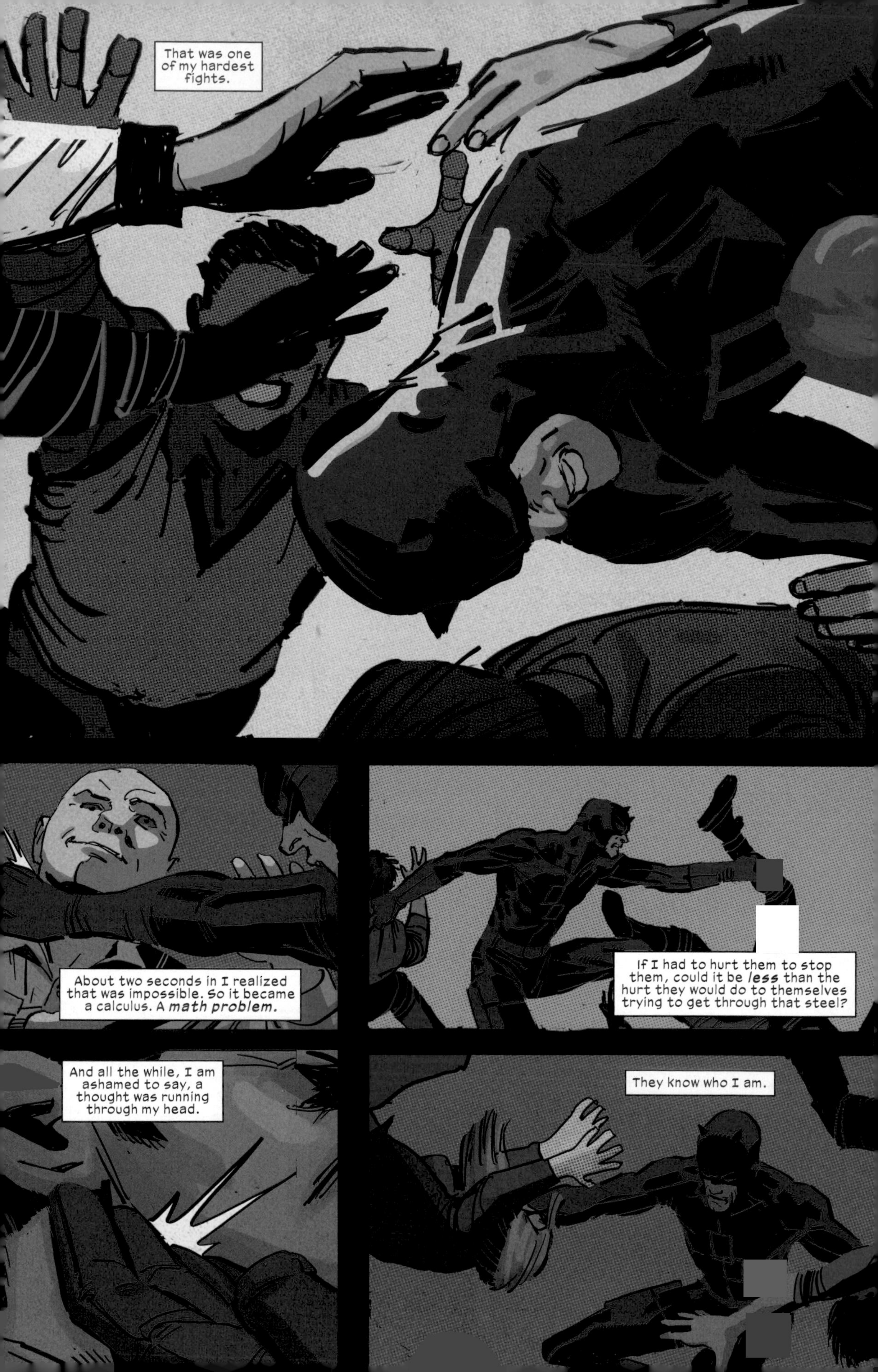
That was one of my hardest fights.
About two seconds in I realized that was impossible. So it became a calculus. A *math problem.*
If I had to hurt them to stop them, could it be *less* than the hurt they would do to themselves trying to get through that steel?
And all the while, I am ashamed to say, a thought was running through my head.
They know who I am.

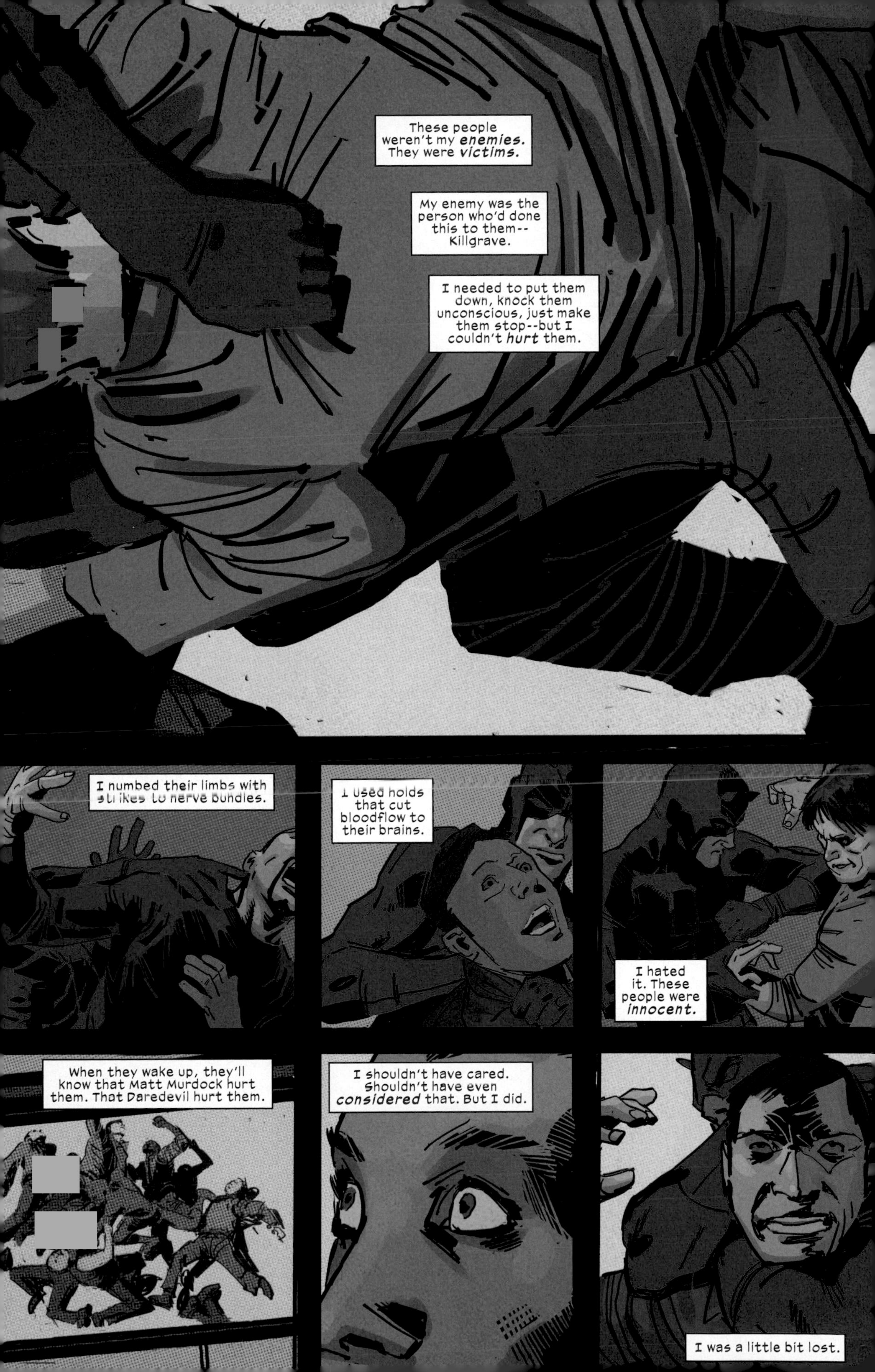
These people weren't my enemies. They were victims.
My enemy was the person who'd done this to them--Killgrave.
I needed to put them down, knock them unconscious, just make them stop--but I couldn't hurt them.
I numbed their limbs with strikes to nerve bundles.
I used holds that cut bloodflow to their brains.
I hated it. These people were innocent.
When they wake up, they'll know that Matt Murdock hurt them. That Daredevil hurt them.
I shouldn't have cared. Shouldn't have even considered that. But I did.
I was a little bit lost.

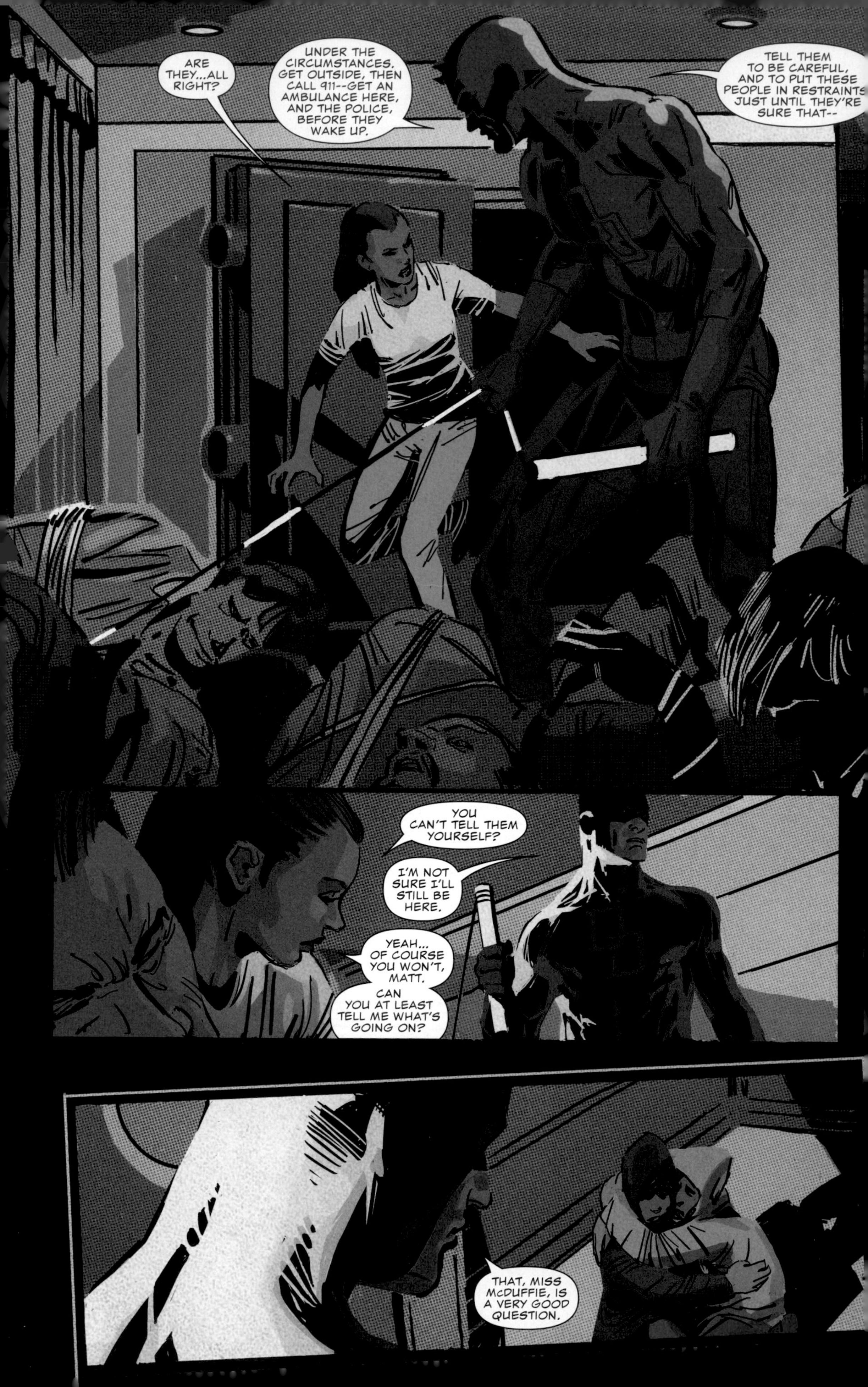
ARE THEY...ALL RIGHT?
UNDER THE CIRCUMSTANCES. GET OUTSIDE, THEN CALL 911--GET AN AMBULANCE HERE, AND THE POLICE, BEFORE THEY WAKE UP.
TELL THEM TO BE CAREFUL, AND TO PUT THESE PEOPLE IN RESTRAINTS JUST UNTIL THEY'RE SURE THAT--
YOU CAN'T TELL THEM YOURSELF?
I'M NOT SURE I'LL STILL BE HERE.
YEAH... OF COURSE YOU WON'T, MATT.
CAN YOU AT LEAST TELL ME WHAT'S GOING ON?
THAT, MISS McDUFFIE, IS A VERY GOOD QUESTION.

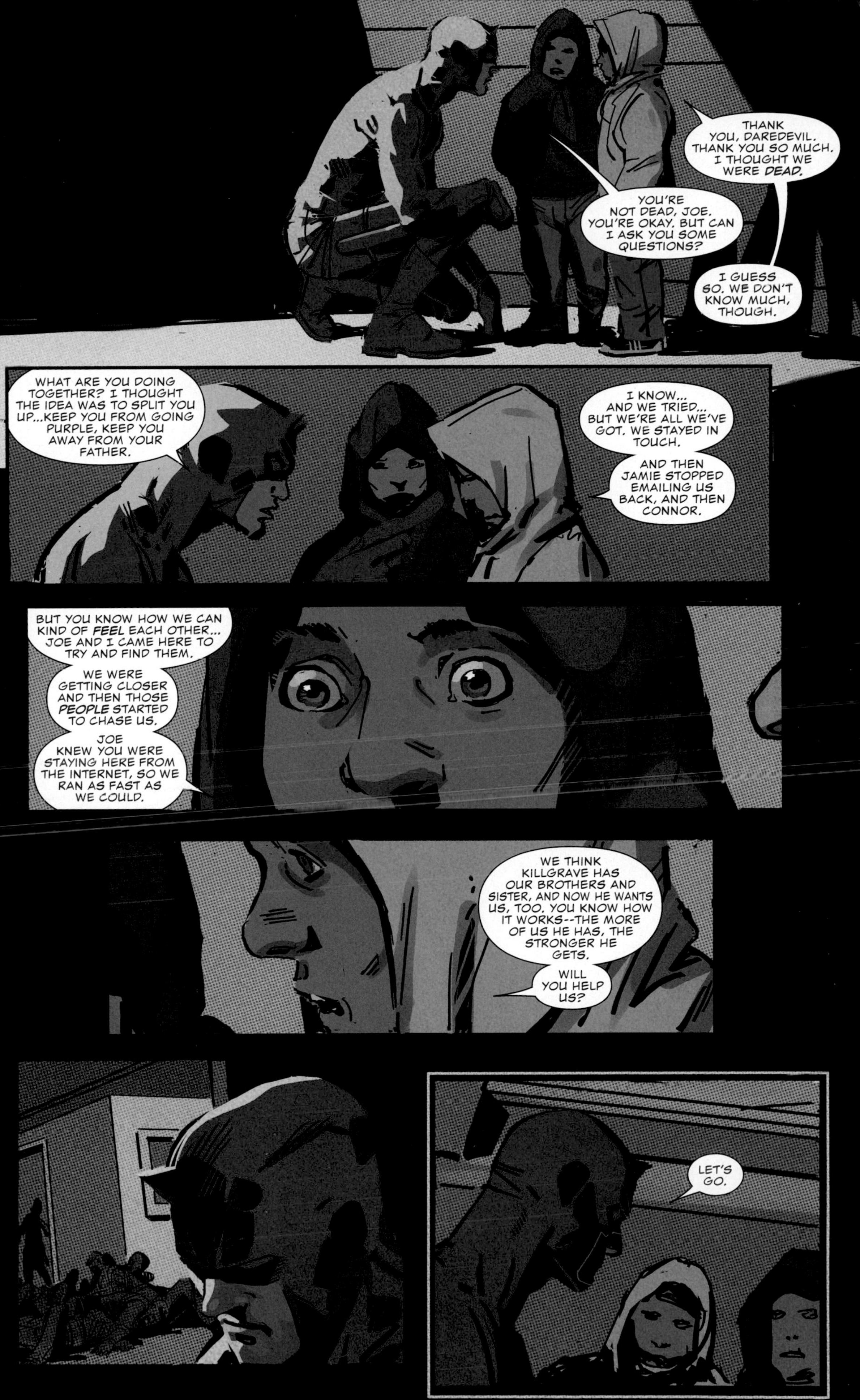
THANK YOU, DAREDEVIL. THANK YOU SO MUCH. I THOUGHT WE WERE *DEAD.*
YOU'RE NOT DEAD, JOE. YOU'RE OKAY. BUT CAN I ASK YOU SOME QUESTIONS?
I GUESS SO. WE DON'T KNOW MUCH, THOUGH.
WHAT ARE YOU DOING TOGETHER? I THOUGHT THE IDEA WAS TO SPLIT YOU UP...KEEP YOU FROM GOING PURPLE, KEEP YOU AWAY FROM YOUR FATHER.
I KNOW... AND WE TRIED... BUT WE'RE ALL WE'VE GOT. WE STAYED IN TOUCH.
AND THEN JAMIE STOPPED EMAILING US BACK, AND THEN CONNOR.
BUT YOU KNOW HOW WE CAN KIND OF *FEEL* EACH OTHER... JOE AND I CAME HERE TO TRY AND FIND THEM.
WE WERE GETTING CLOSER AND THEN THOSE *PEOPLE* STARTED TO CHASE US.
JOE KNEW YOU WERE STAYING HERE FROM THE INTERNET, SO WE RAN AS FAST AS WE COULD.
WE THINK KILLGRAVE HAS OUR BROTHERS AND SISTER, AND NOW HE WANTS US, TOO. YOU KNOW HOW IT WORKS--THE MORE OF US HE HAS, THE STRONGER HE GETS.
WILL YOU HELP US?
LET'S GO.

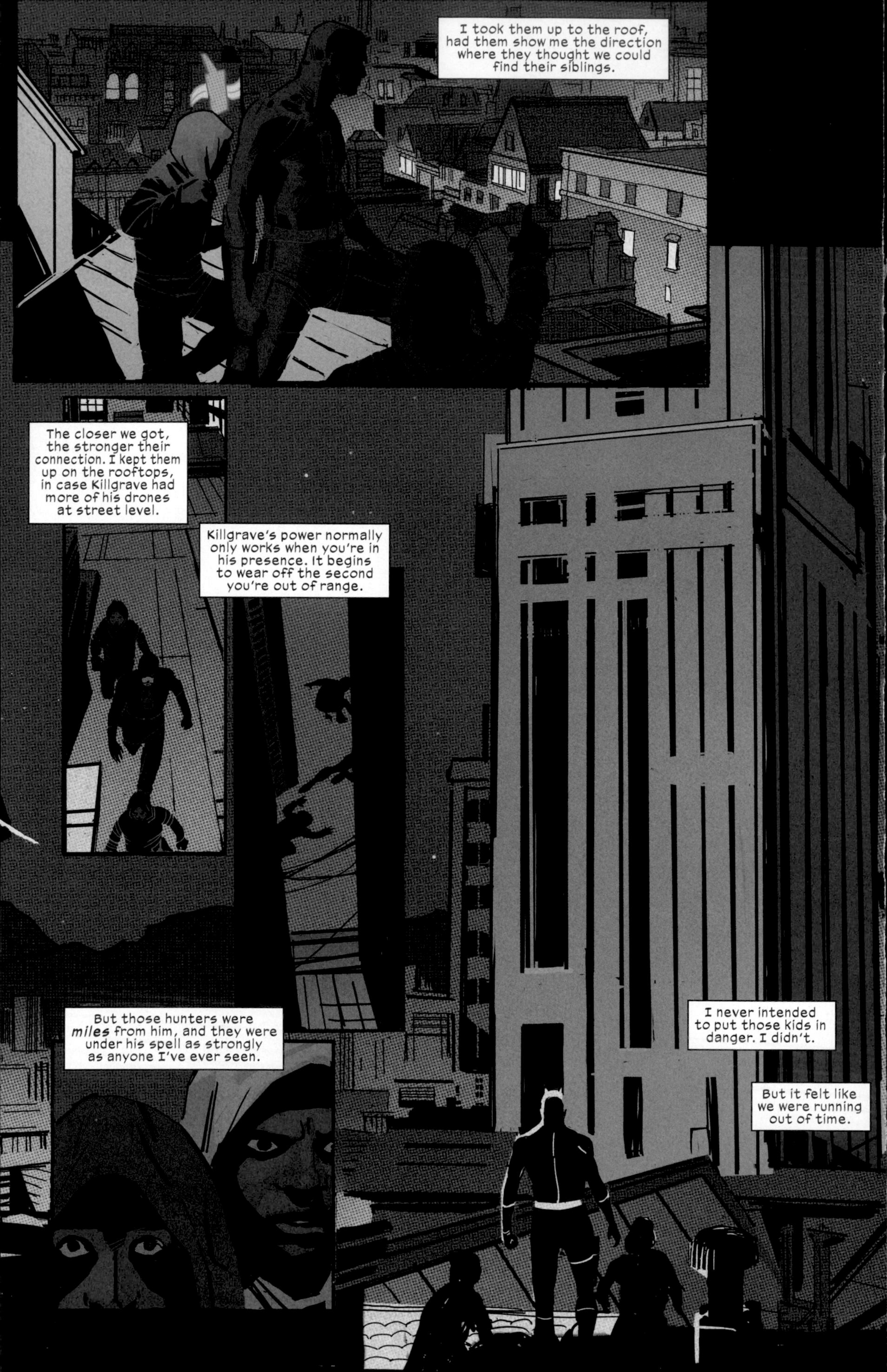
I took them up to the roof, had them show me the direction where they thought we could find their siblings.
The closer we got, the stronger their connection. I kept them up on the rooftops, in case Killgrave had more of his drones at street level.
Killgrave's power normally only works when you're in his presence. It begins to wear off the second you're out of range.
But those hunters were *miles* from him, and they were under his spell as strongly as anyone I've ever seen.
I never intended to put those kids in danger. I didn't.
But it felt like we were running out of time.

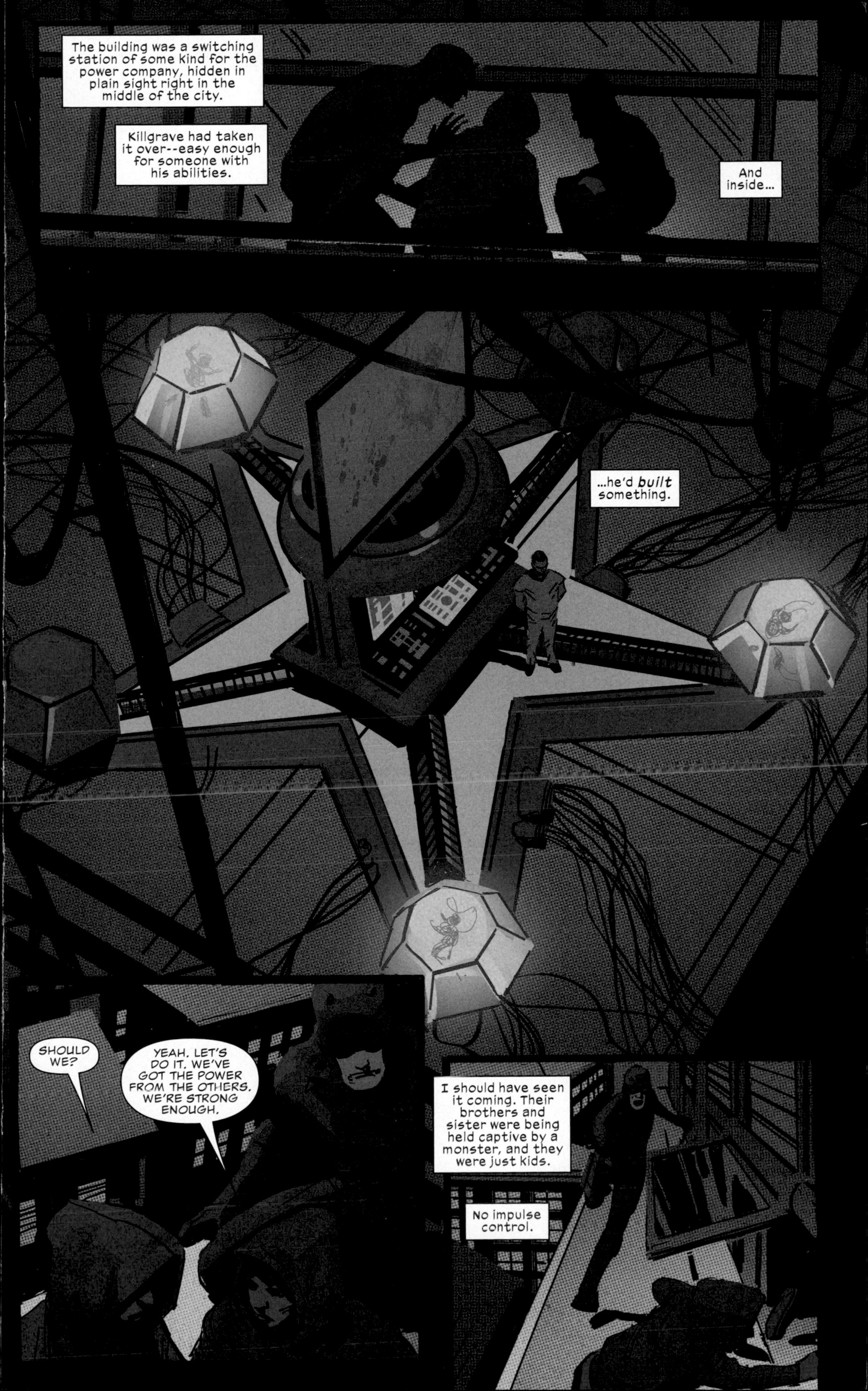
The building was a switching station of some kind for the power company, hidden in plain sight right in the middle of the city.
Killgrave had taken it over--easy enough for someone with his abilities.
And inside...
...he'd *built* something.
SHOULD WE?
YEAH, LET'S DO IT. WE'VE GOT THE POWER FROM THE OTHERS. WE'RE STRONG ENOUGH.
I should have seen it coming. Their brothers and sister were being held captive by a monster, and they were just kids.
No impulse control.

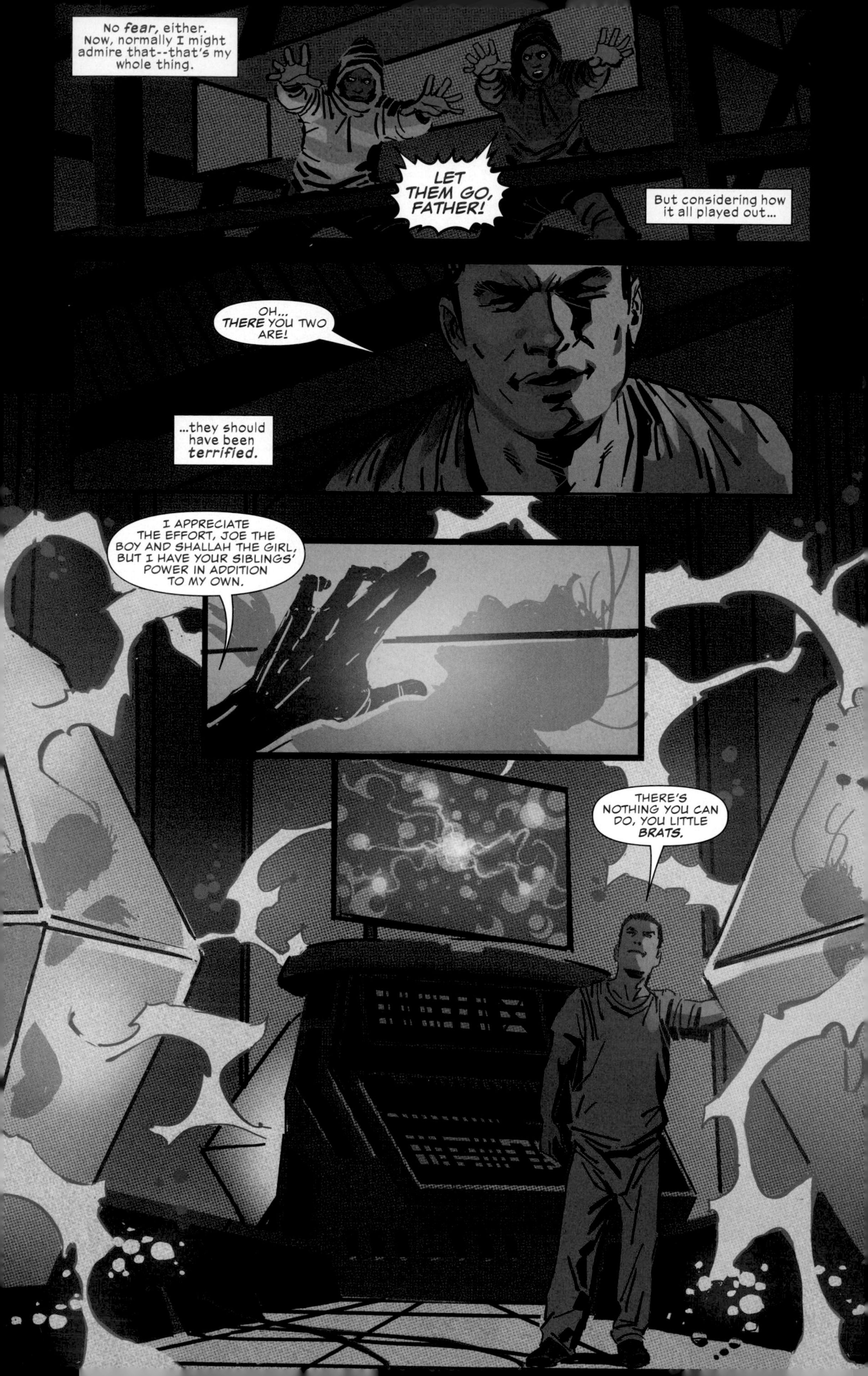
No fear, either. Now, normally I might admire that--that's my whole thing.
LET THEM GO, FATHER!
But considering how it all played out...
OH... THERE YOU TWO ARE!
...they should have been terrified.
I APPRECIATE THE EFFORT, JOE THE BOY AND SHALLAH THE GIRL, BUT I HAVE YOUR SIBLINGS' POWER IN ADDITION TO MY OWN.
THERE'S NOTHING YOU CAN DO, YOU LITTLE BRATS.

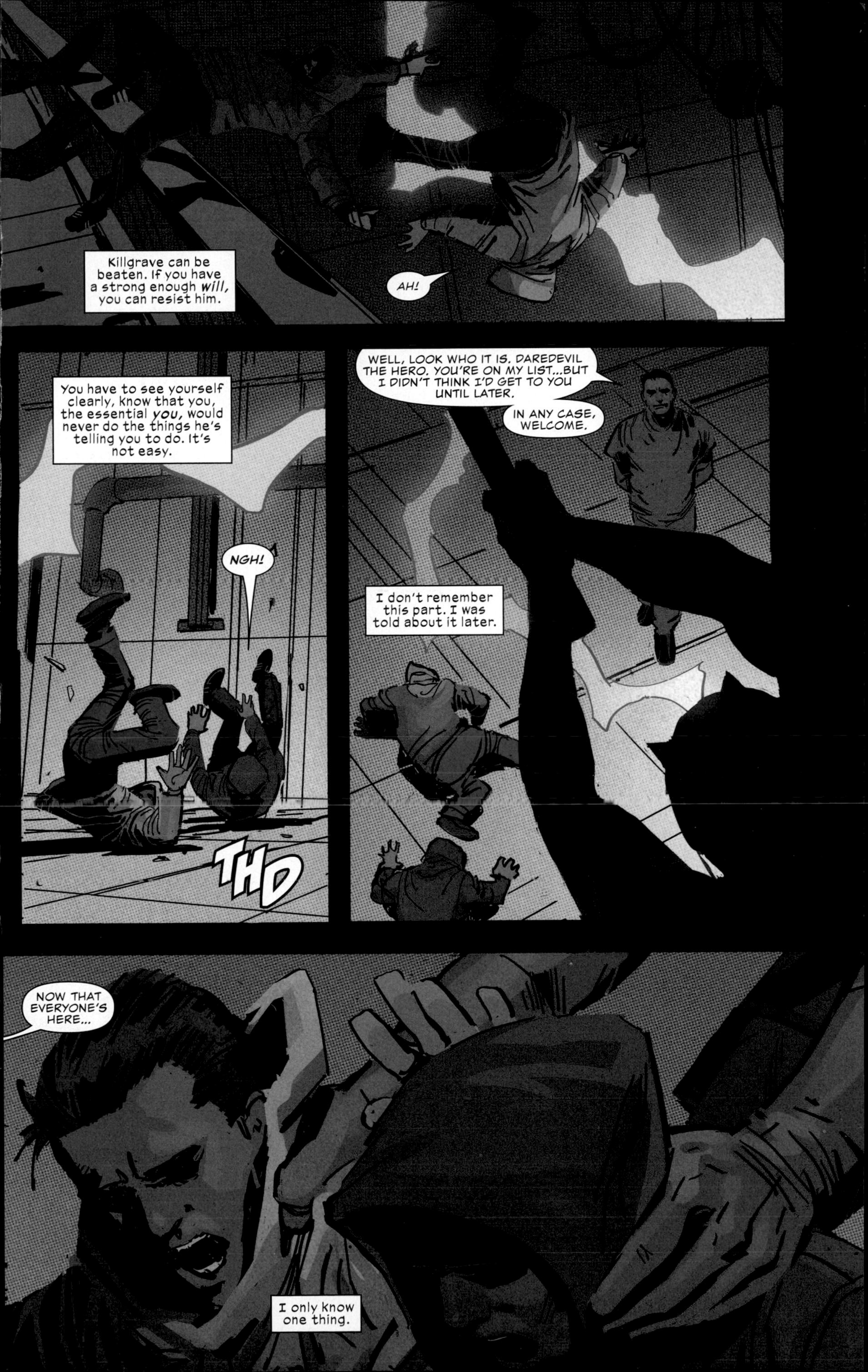
Killgrave can be beaten. If you have a strong enough *will*, you can resist him.
AH!
You have to see yourself clearly, know that you, the essential *you*, would never do the things he's telling you to do. It's not easy.
NGH!
THD
WELL, LOOK WHO IT IS. DAREDEVIL THE HERO. YOU'RE ON MY LIST...BUT I DIDN'T THINK I'D GET TO YOU UNTIL LATER.
IN ANY CASE, WELCOME.
I don't remember this part. I was told about it later.
NOW THAT EVERYONE'S HERE...
I only know one thing.

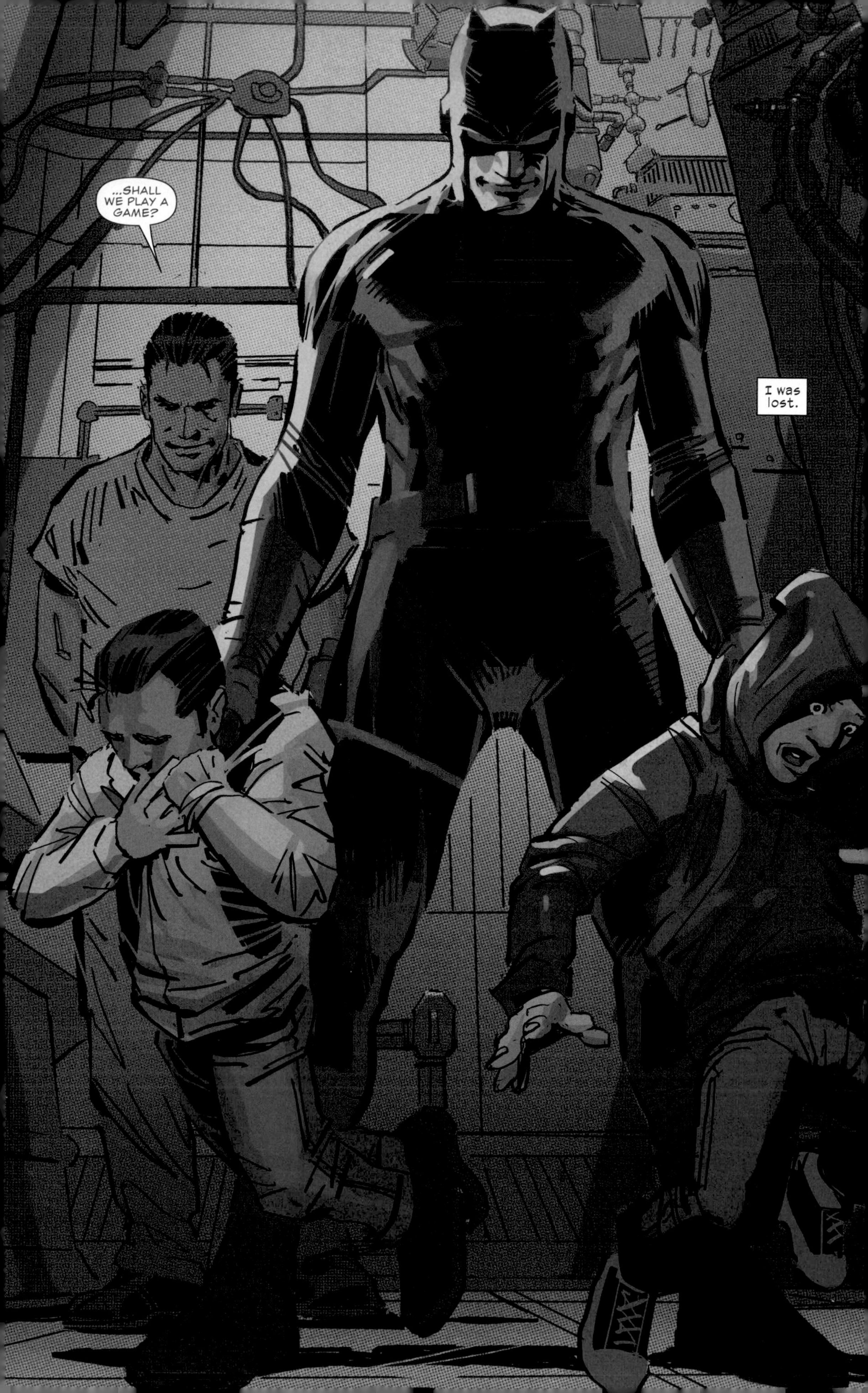
...SHALL WE PLAY A GAME?
I was lost.

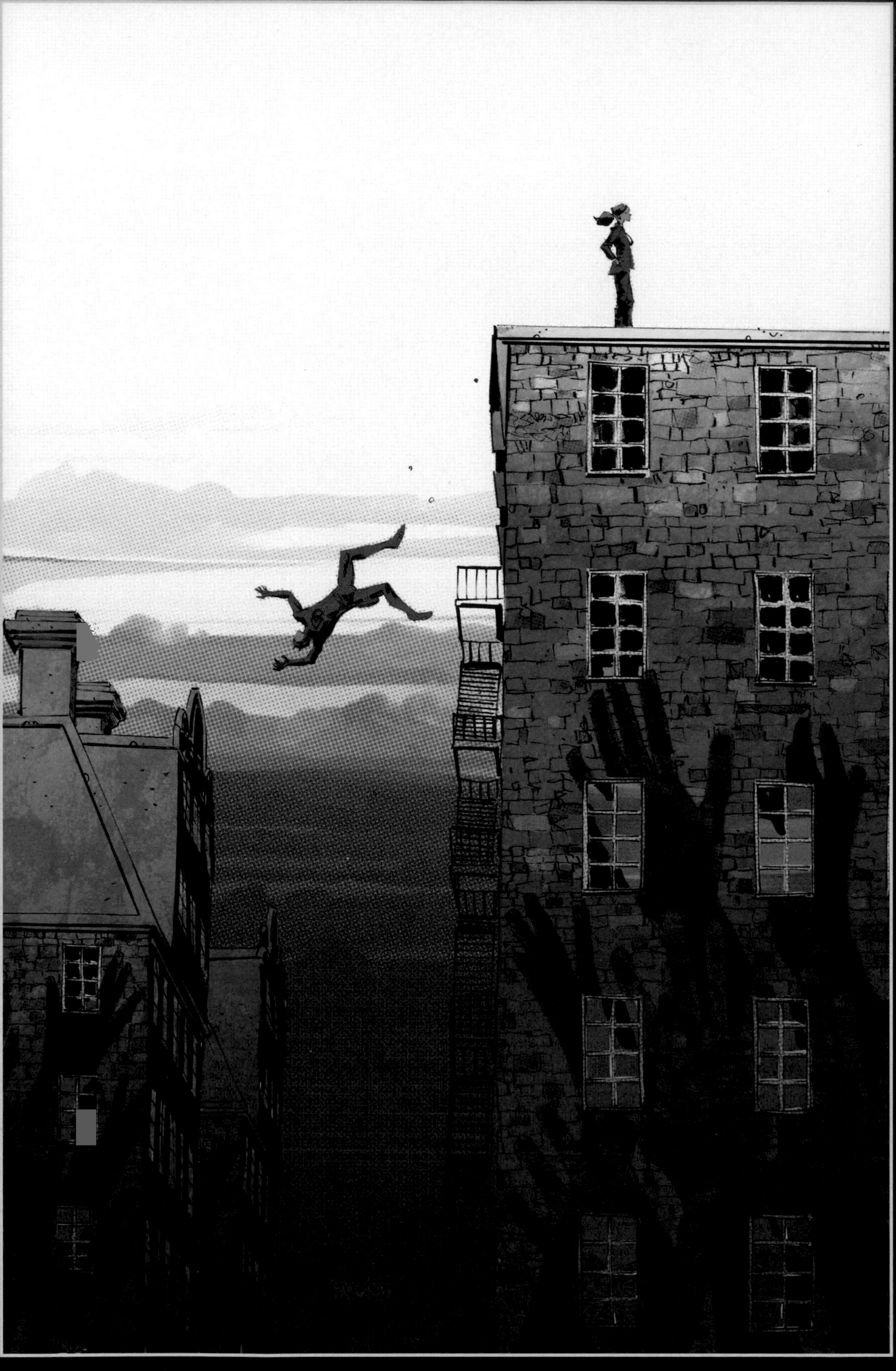

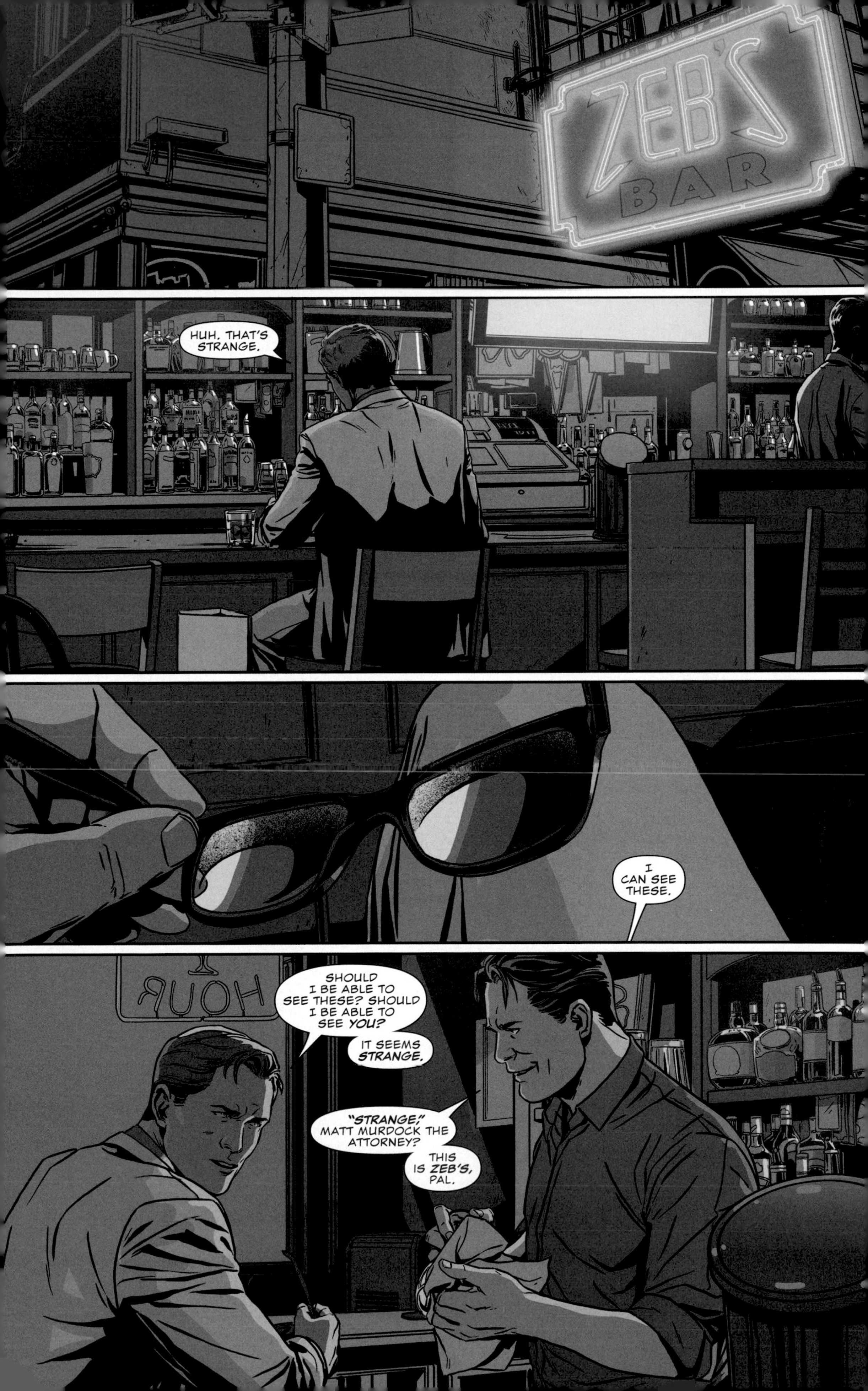
ZEB'S
BAR
HUH. THAT'S STRANGE.
I CAN SEE THESE.
HOUR
SHOULD I BE ABLE TO SEE THESE? SHOULD I BE ABLE TO SEE *YOU?*
IT SEEMS *STRANGE.*
"STRANGE," MATT MURDOCK THE ATTORNEY?
THIS IS *ZEB'S,* PAL.

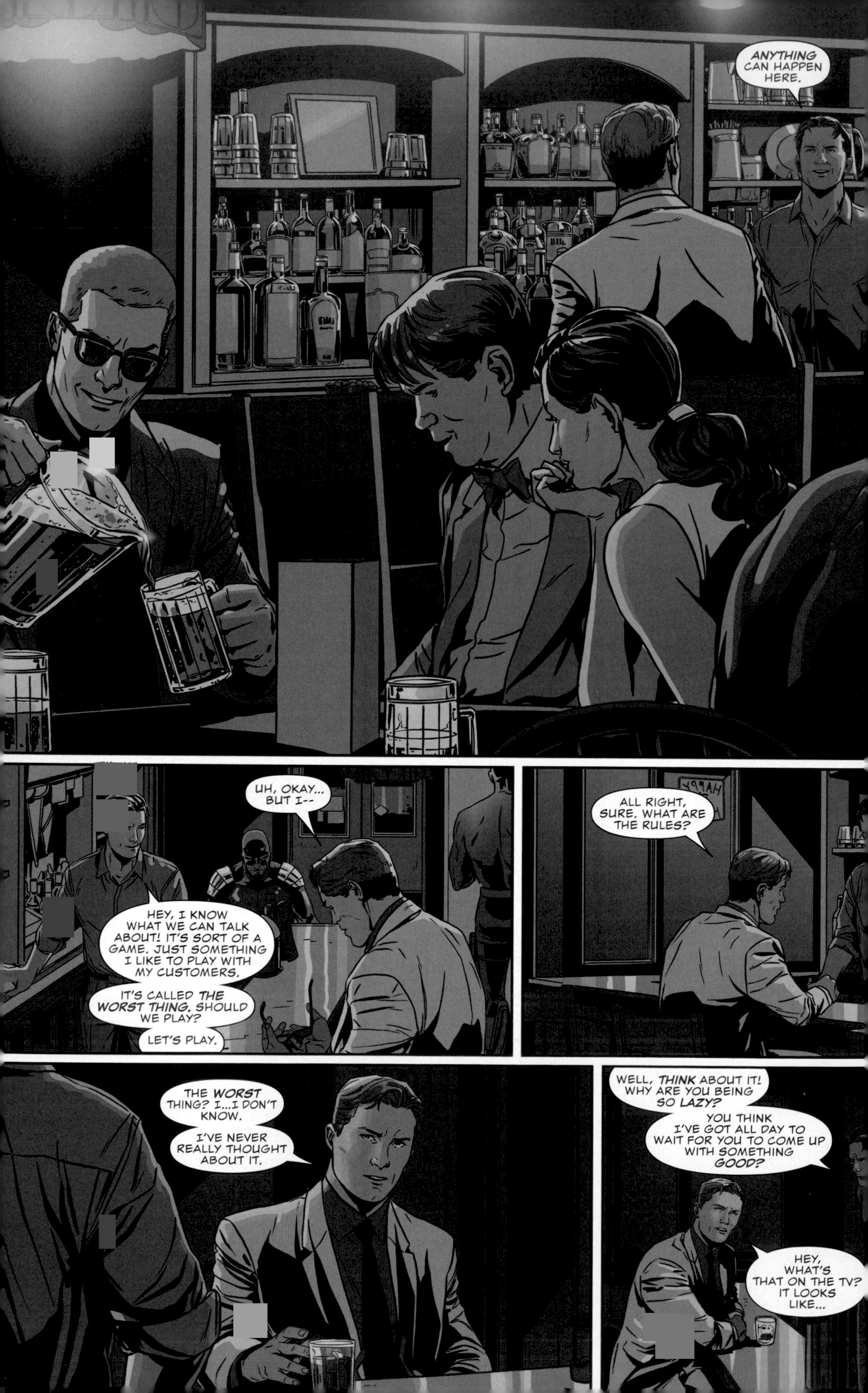
ANYTHING CAN HAPPEN HERE.
UH, OKAY... BUT I--
HEY, I KNOW WHAT WE CAN TALK ABOUT! IT'S SORT OF A GAME. JUST SOMETHING I LIKE TO PLAY WITH MY CUSTOMERS.
IT'S CALLED THE WORST THING. SHOULD WE PLAY?
LET'S PLAY.
ALL RIGHT, SURE. WHAT ARE THE RULES?
THE WORST THING? I...I DON'T KNOW.
I'VE NEVER REALLY THOUGHT ABOUT IT.
WELL, THINK ABOUT IT! WHY ARE YOU BEING SO LAZY?
YOU THINK I'VE GOT ALL DAY TO WAIT FOR YOU TO COME UP WITH SOMETHING GOOD?
HEY, WHAT'S THAT ON THE TV? IT LOOKS LIKE...

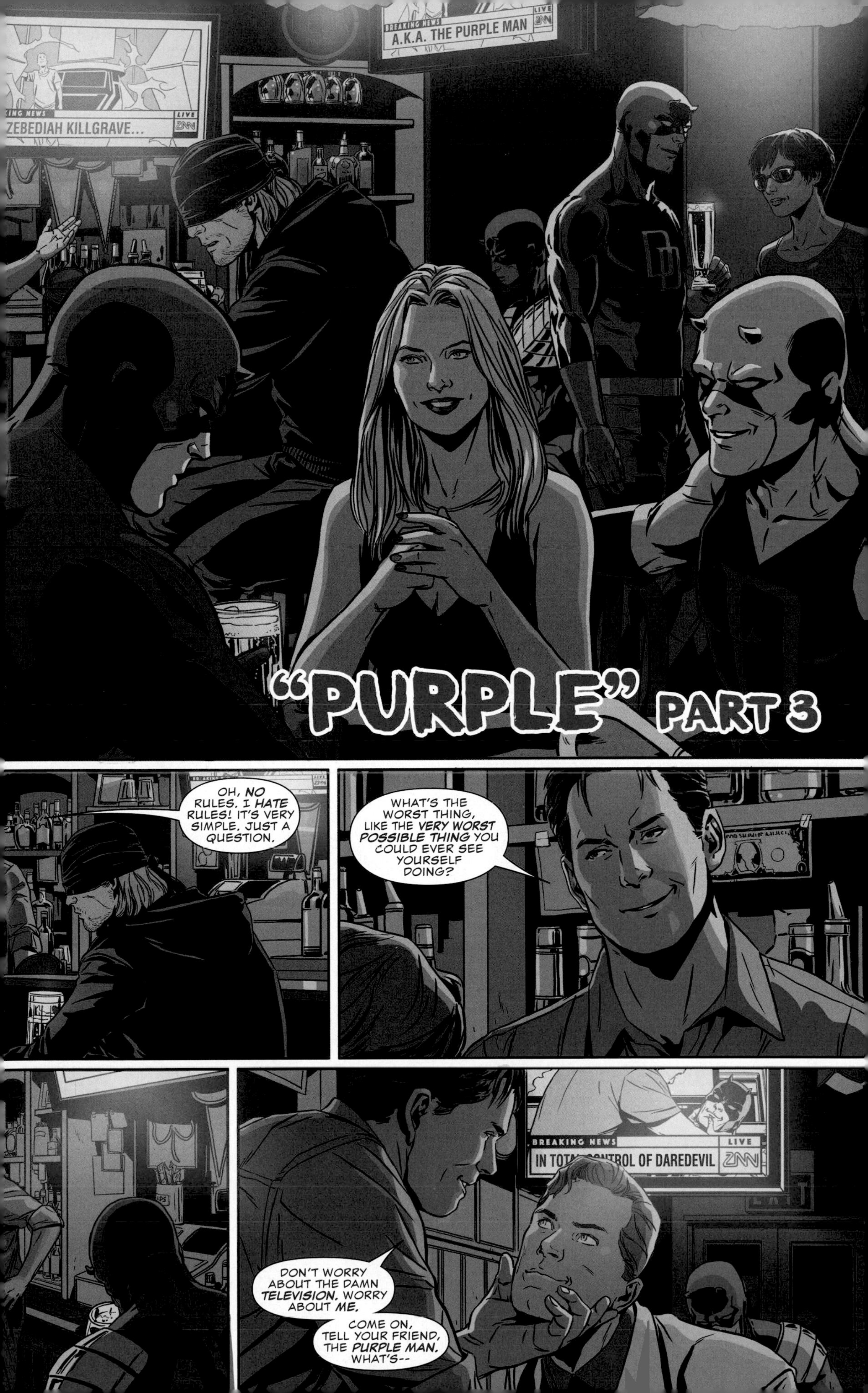
BREAKING NEWS
A.K.A. THE PURPLE MAN
LIVE
ZEBEDIAH KILLGRAVE...
LIVE
"PURPLE" PART 3
OH, NO RULES. I HATE RULES! IT'S VERY SIMPLE. JUST A QUESTION.
WHAT'S THE WORST THING, LIKE THE VERY WORST POSSIBLE THING YOU COULD EVER SEE YOURSELF DOING?
BREAKING NEWS
LIVE
IN TOTAL CONTROL OF DAREDEVIL
DON'T WORRY ABOUT THE DAMN TELEVISION. WORRY ABOUT ME.
COME ON, TELL YOUR FRIEND, THE PURPLE MAN. WHAT'S--

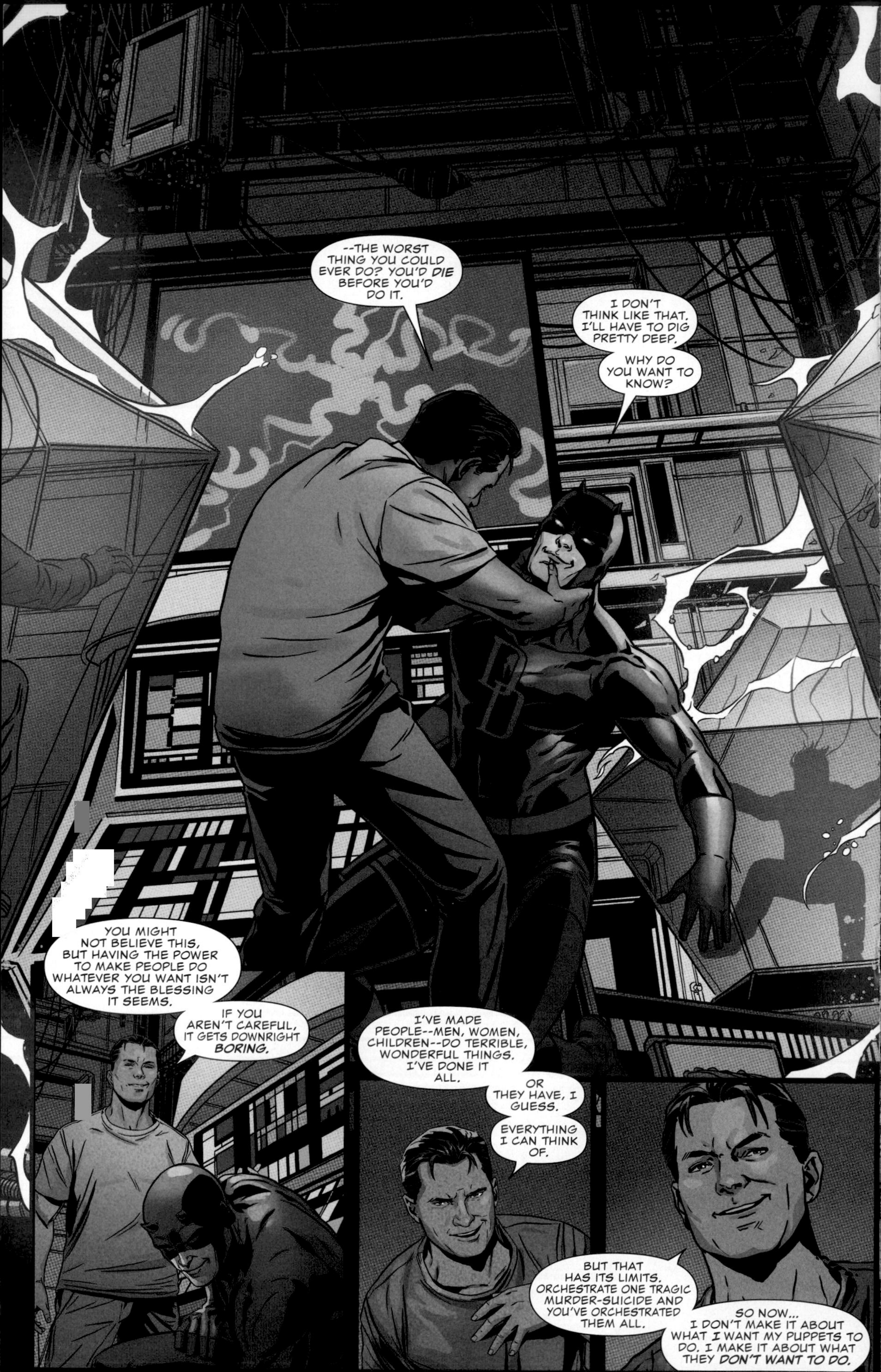
--THE WORST THING YOU COULD EVER DO? YOU'D DIE BEFORE YOU'D DO IT.
I DON'T THINK LIKE THAT. I'LL HAVE TO DIG PRETTY DEEP.
WHY DO YOU WANT TO KNOW?
YOU MIGHT NOT BELIEVE THIS, BUT HAVING THE POWER TO MAKE PEOPLE DO WHATEVER YOU WANT ISN'T ALWAYS THE BLESSING IT SEEMS.
IF YOU AREN'T CAREFUL, IT GETS DOWNRIGHT BORING.
I'VE MADE PEOPLE--MEN, WOMEN, CHILDREN--DO TERRIBLE, WONDERFUL THINGS. I'VE DONE IT ALL.
OR THEY HAVE, I GUESS.
EVERYTHING I CAN THINK OF.
BUT THAT HAS ITS LIMITS. ORCHESTRATE ONE TRAGIC MURDER-SUICIDE AND YOU'VE ORCHESTRATED THEM ALL.
SO NOW... I DON'T MAKE IT ABOUT WHAT I WANT MY PUPPETS TO DO. I MAKE IT ABOUT WHAT THEY DON'T WANT TO DO.

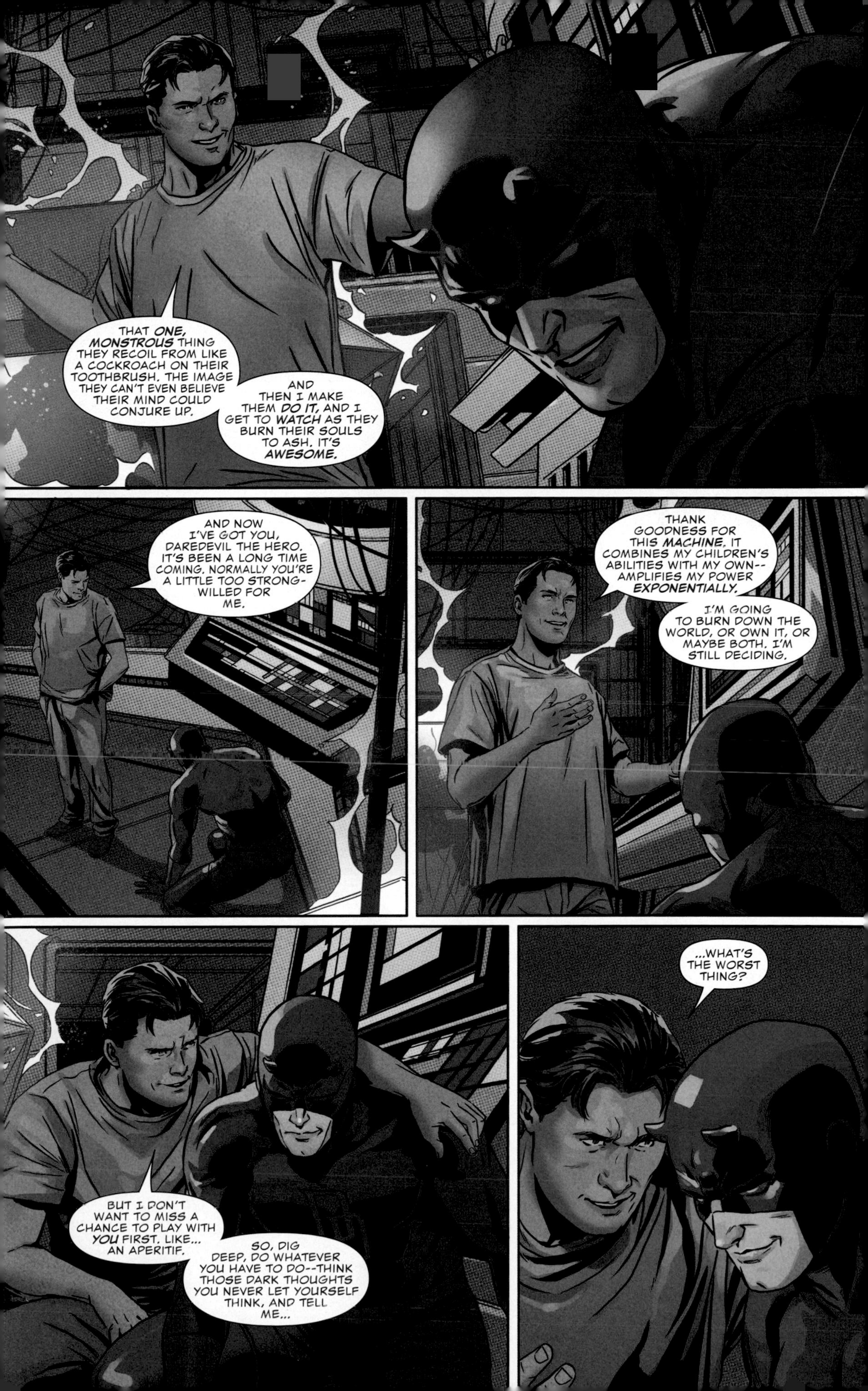

THAT ONE, MONSTROUS THING THEY RECOIL FROM LIKE A COCKROACH ON THEIR TOOTHBRUSH. THE IMAGE THEY CAN'T EVEN BELIEVE THEIR MIND COULD CONJURE UP.
AND THEN I MAKE THEM DO IT, AND I GET TO WATCH AS THEY BURN THEIR SOULS TO ASH. IT'S AWESOME.
AND NOW I'VE GOT YOU, DAREDEVIL THE HERO. IT'S BEEN A LONG TIME COMING. NORMALLY YOU'RE A LITTLE TOO STRONG-WILLED FOR ME.
THANK GOODNESS FOR THIS MACHINE. IT COMBINES MY CHILDREN'S ABILITIES WITH MY OWN--AMPLIFIES MY POWER EXPONENTIALLY.
I'M GOING TO BURN DOWN THE WORLD, OR OWN IT, OR MAYBE BOTH. I'M STILL DECIDING.
BUT I DON'T WANT TO MISS A CHANCE TO PLAY WITH YOU FIRST. LIKE... AN APERITIF.
SO, DIG DEEP, DO WHATEVER YOU HAVE TO DO--THINK THOSE DARK THOUGHTS YOU NEVER LET YOURSELF THINK, AND TELL ME...
...WHAT'S THE WORST THING?

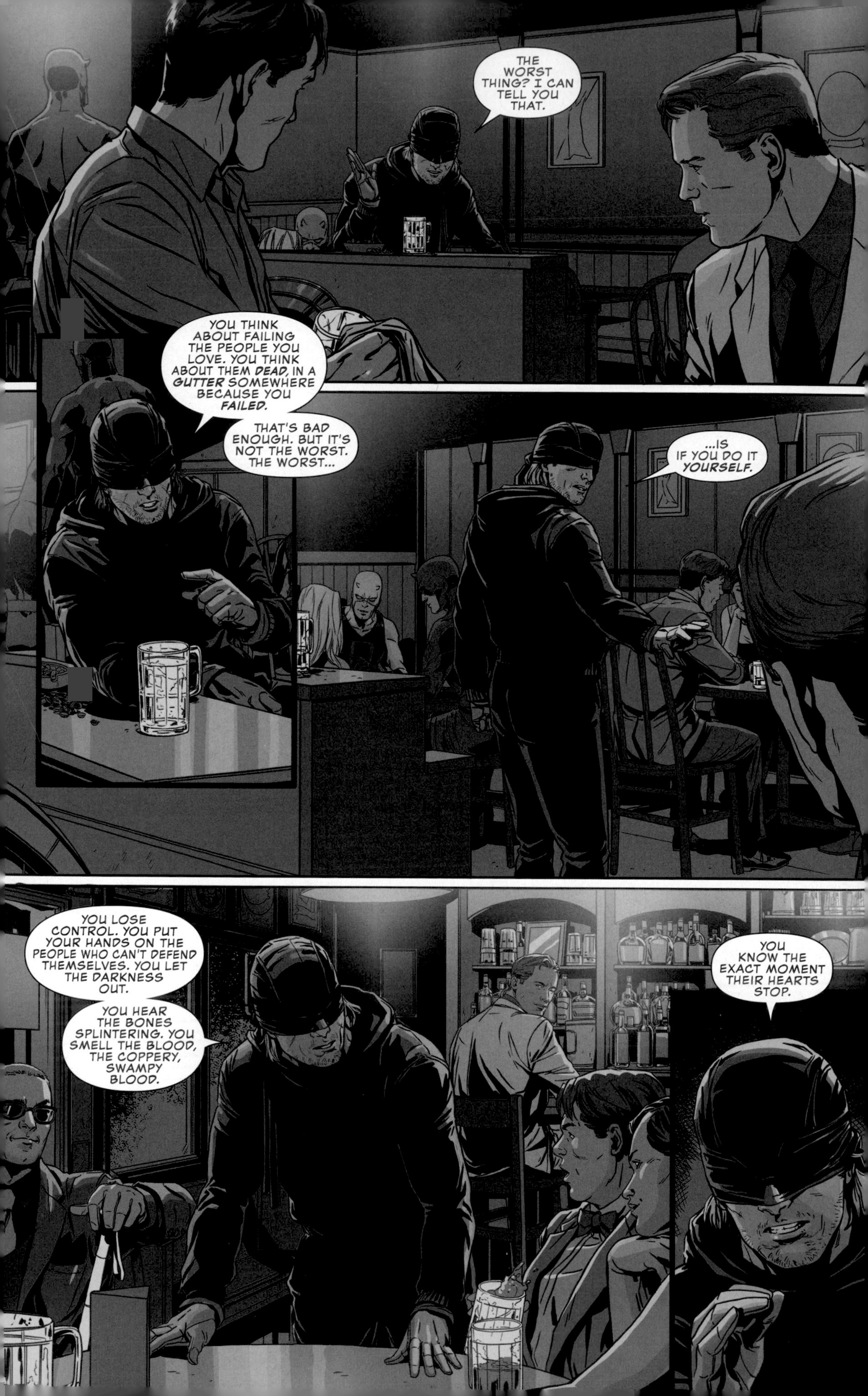
THE WORST THING? I CAN TELL YOU THAT.
YOU THINK ABOUT FAILING THE PEOPLE YOU LOVE. YOU THINK ABOUT THEM DEAD, IN A GUTTER SOMEWHERE BECAUSE YOU FAILED.
THAT'S BAD ENOUGH. BUT IT'S NOT THE WORST. THE WORST...
...IS IF YOU DO IT YOURSELF.
YOU LOSE CONTROL. YOU PUT YOUR HANDS ON THE PEOPLE WHO CAN'T DEFEND THEMSELVES. YOU LET THE DARKNESS OUT.
YOU HEAR THE BONES SPLINTERING. YOU SMELL THE BLOOD, THE COPPERY, SWAMPY BLOOD.
YOU KNOW THE EXACT MOMENT THEIR HEARTS STOP.

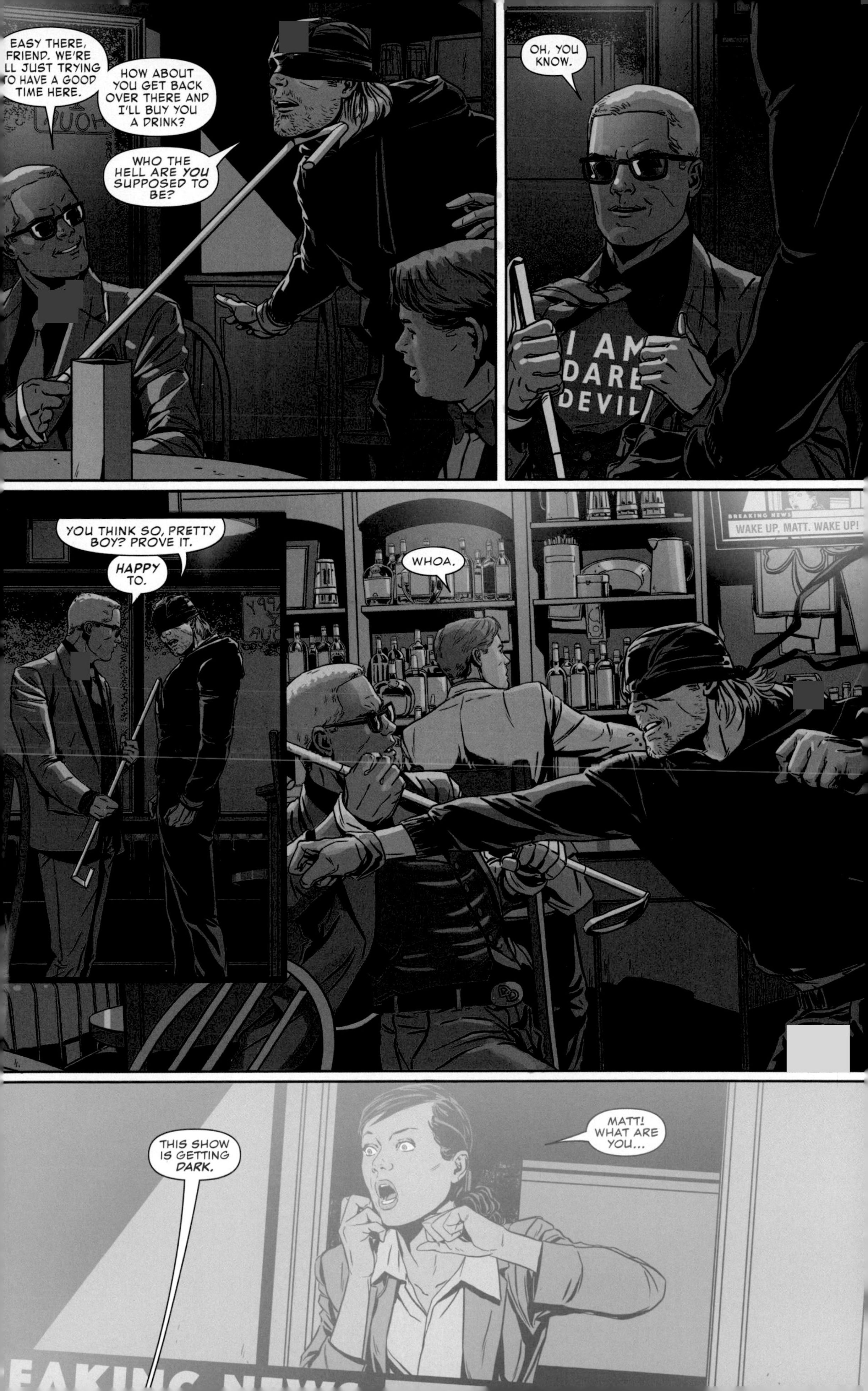
EASY THERE, FRIEND. WE'RE LL JUST TRYING O HAVE A GOOD TIME HERE.
HOW ABOUT YOU GET BACK OVER THERE AND I'LL BUY YOU A DRINK?
WHO THE HELL ARE *YOU* SUPPOSED TO BE?
OH, YOU KNOW.
I AM DARE DEVIL
YOU THINK SO, PRETTY BOY? PROVE IT.
HAPPY TO.
WHOA.
BREAKING NEWS
WAKE UP, MATT. WAKE UP!
THIS SHOW IS GETTING *DARK.*
MATT! WHAT ARE YOU...

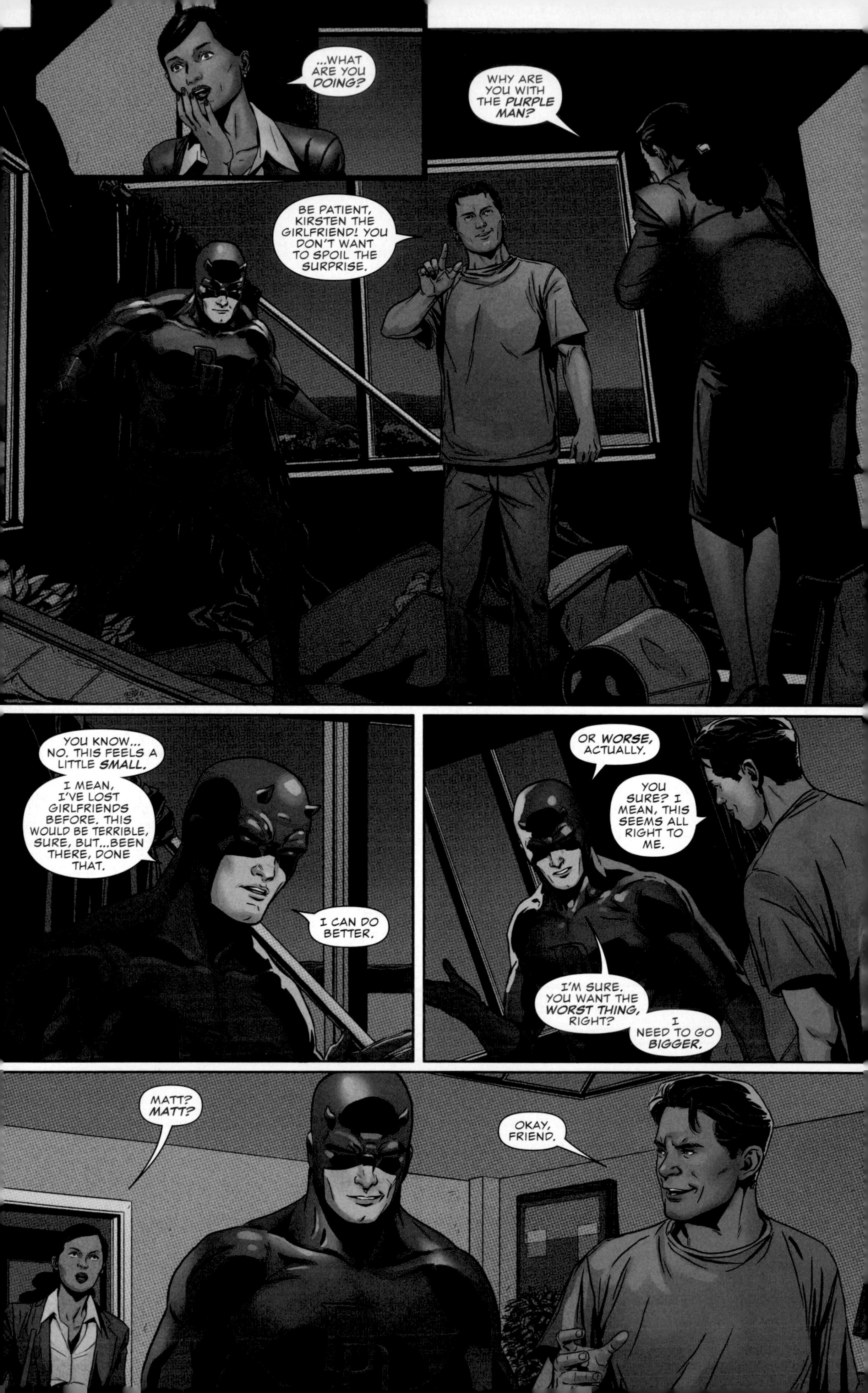
...WHAT ARE YOU DOING?
WHY ARE YOU WITH THE PURPLE MAN?
BE PATIENT, KIRSTEN THE GIRLFRIEND! YOU DON'T WANT TO SPOIL THE SURPRISE.
YOU KNOW... NO. THIS FEELS A LITTLE SMALL.
I MEAN, I'VE LOST GIRLFRIENDS BEFORE. THIS WOULD BE TERRIBLE, SURE, BUT...BEEN THERE, DONE THAT.
I CAN DO BETTER.
OR WORSE, ACTUALLY.
YOU SURE? I MEAN, THIS SEEMS ALL RIGHT TO ME.
I'M SURE. YOU WANT THE WORST THING, RIGHT?
I NEED TO GO BIGGER.
MATT? MATT?
OKAY, FRIEND.

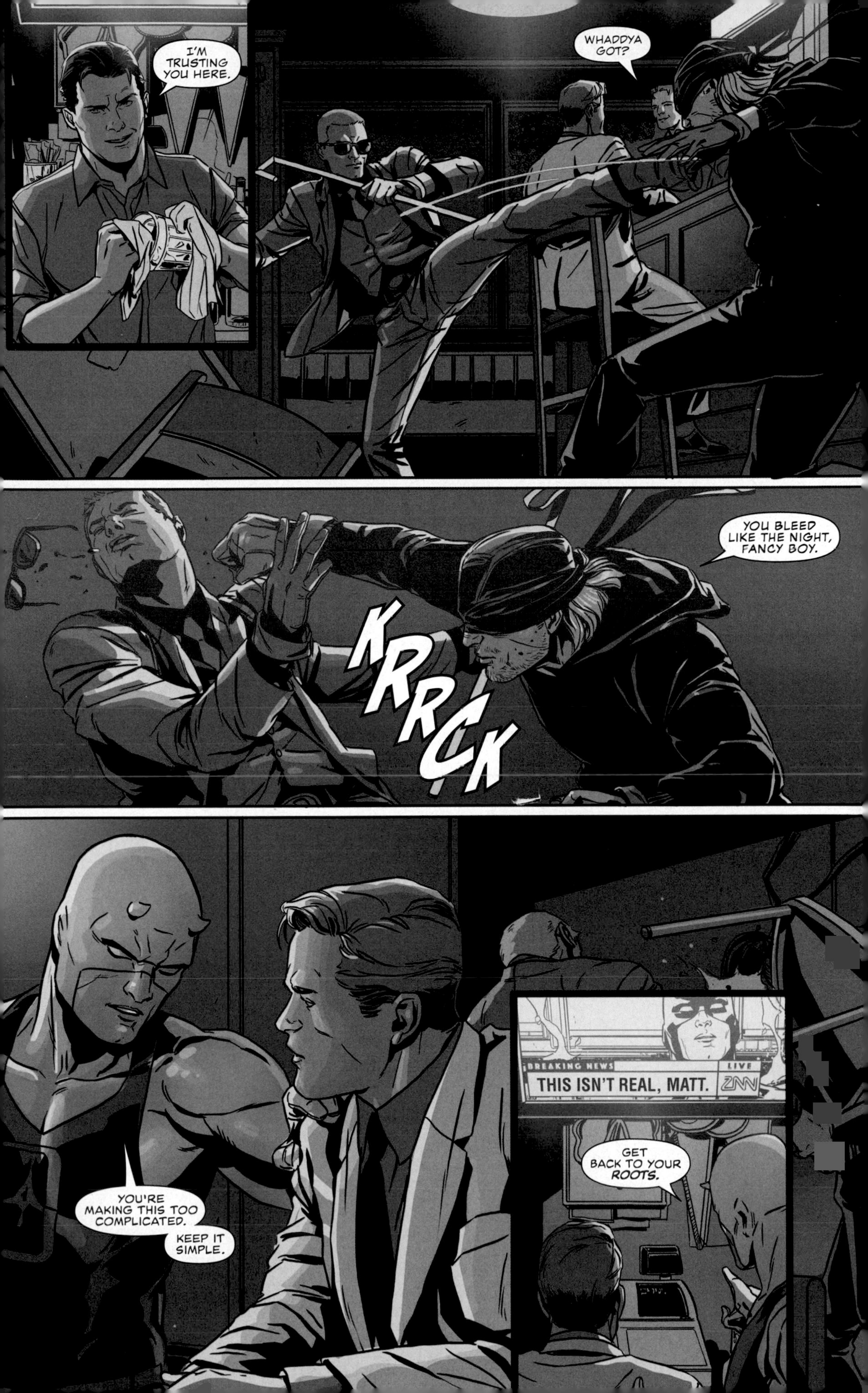
I'M TRUSTING YOU HERE.
WHADDYA GOT?
YOU BLEED LIKE THE NIGHT, FANCY BOY.
KRRCK
YOU'RE MAKING THIS TOO COMPLICATED.
KEEP IT SIMPLE.
BREAKING NEWS
LIVE
THIS ISN'T REAL, MATT.
GET BACK TO YOUR ROOTS.

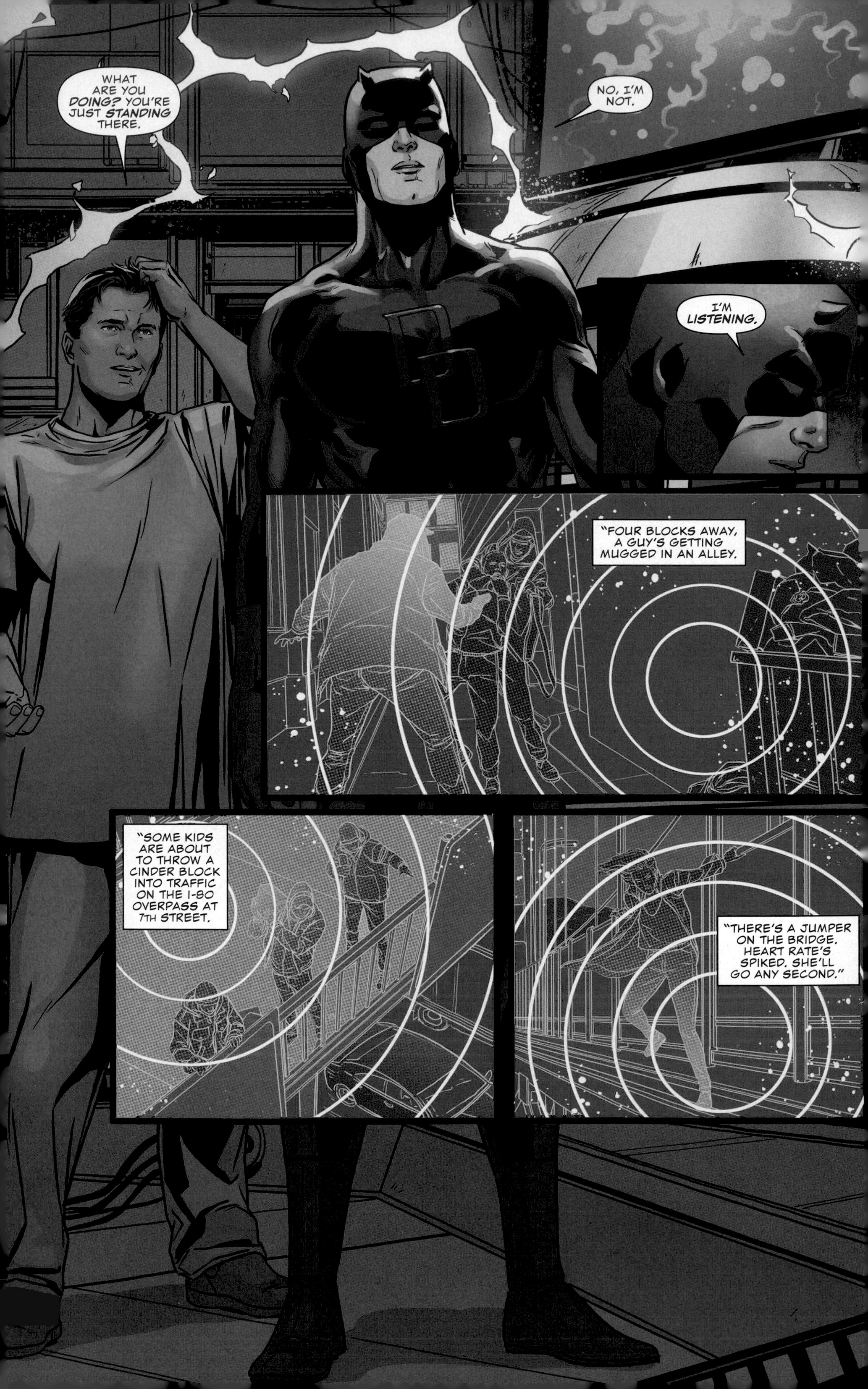
WHAT ARE YOU DOING? YOU'RE JUST STANDING THERE.
NO, I'M NOT.
I'M LISTENING.
"FOUR BLOCKS AWAY, A GUY'S GETTING MUGGED IN AN ALLEY.
"SOME KIDS ARE ABOUT TO THROW A CINDER BLOCK INTO TRAFFIC ON THE I-80 OVERPASS AT 7TH STREET.
"THERE'S A JUMPER ON THE BRIDGE. HEART RATE'S SPIKED. SHE'LL GO ANY SECOND."

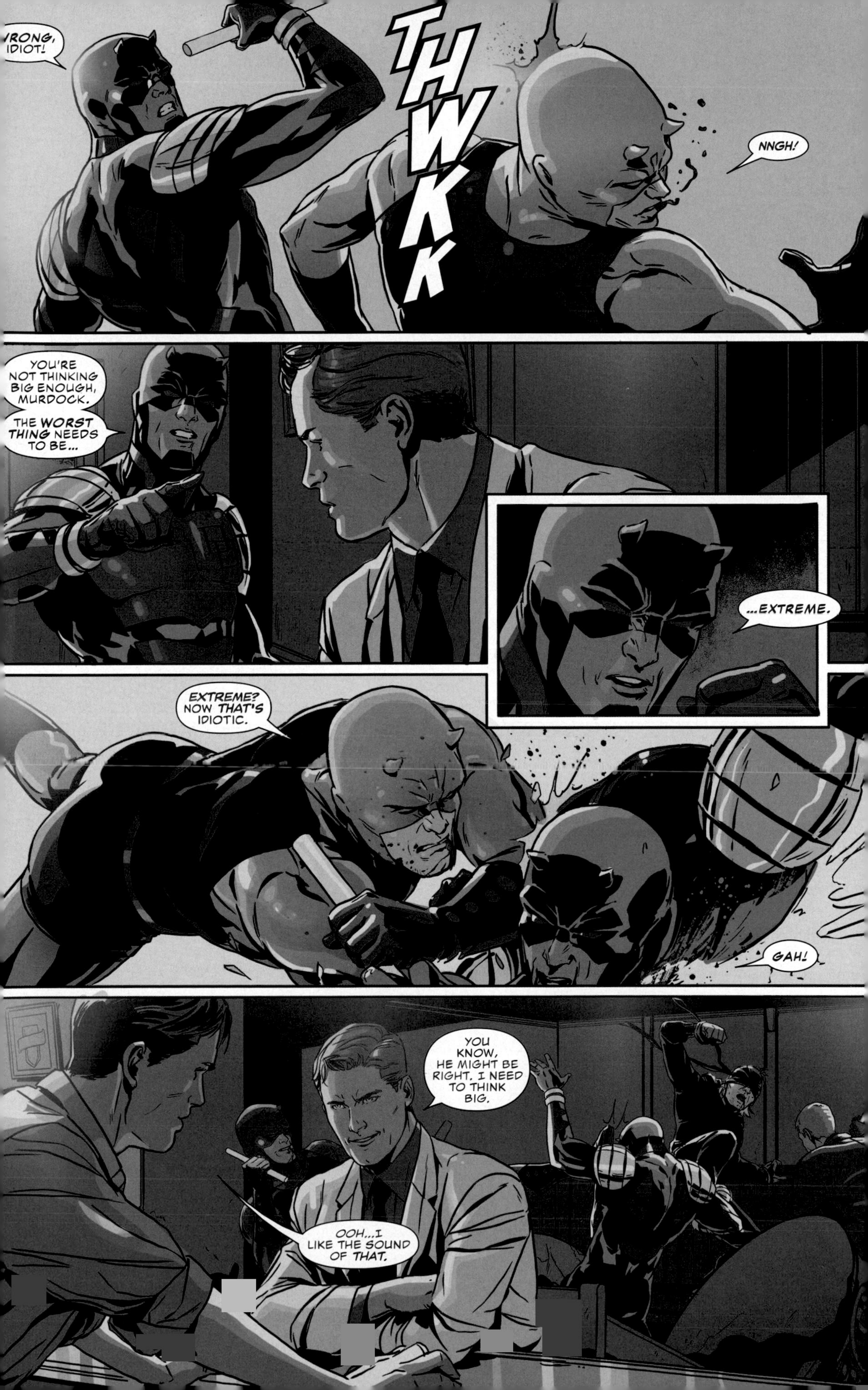
RONG, IDIOT!
THWKK
NNGH!
YOU'RE NOT THINKING BIG ENOUGH, MURDOCK.
THE WORST THING NEEDS TO BE...
...EXTREME.
EXTREME? NOW THAT'S IDIOTIC.
GAH!
YOU KNOW, HE MIGHT BE RIGHT. I NEED TO THINK BIG.
OOH...I LIKE THE SOUND OF THAT.

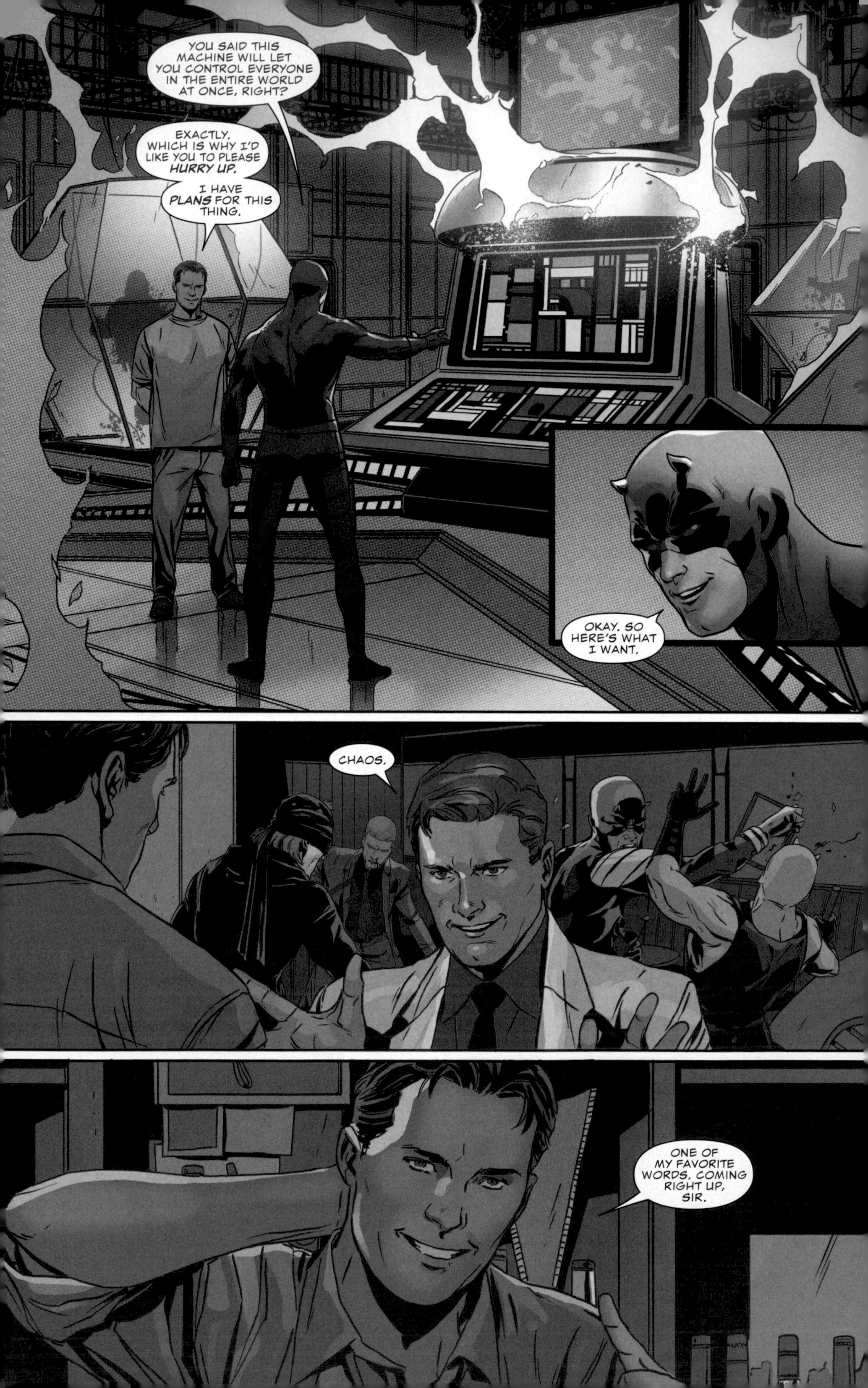
YOU SAID THIS MACHINE WILL LET YOU CONTROL EVERYONE IN THE ENTIRE WORLD AT ONCE, RIGHT?
EXACTLY. WHICH IS WHY I'D LIKE YOU TO PLEASE HURRY UP.
I HAVE PLANS FOR THIS THING.
OKAY. SO HERE'S WHAT I WANT.
CHAOS.
ONE OF MY FAVORITE WORDS. COMING RIGHT UP, SIR.

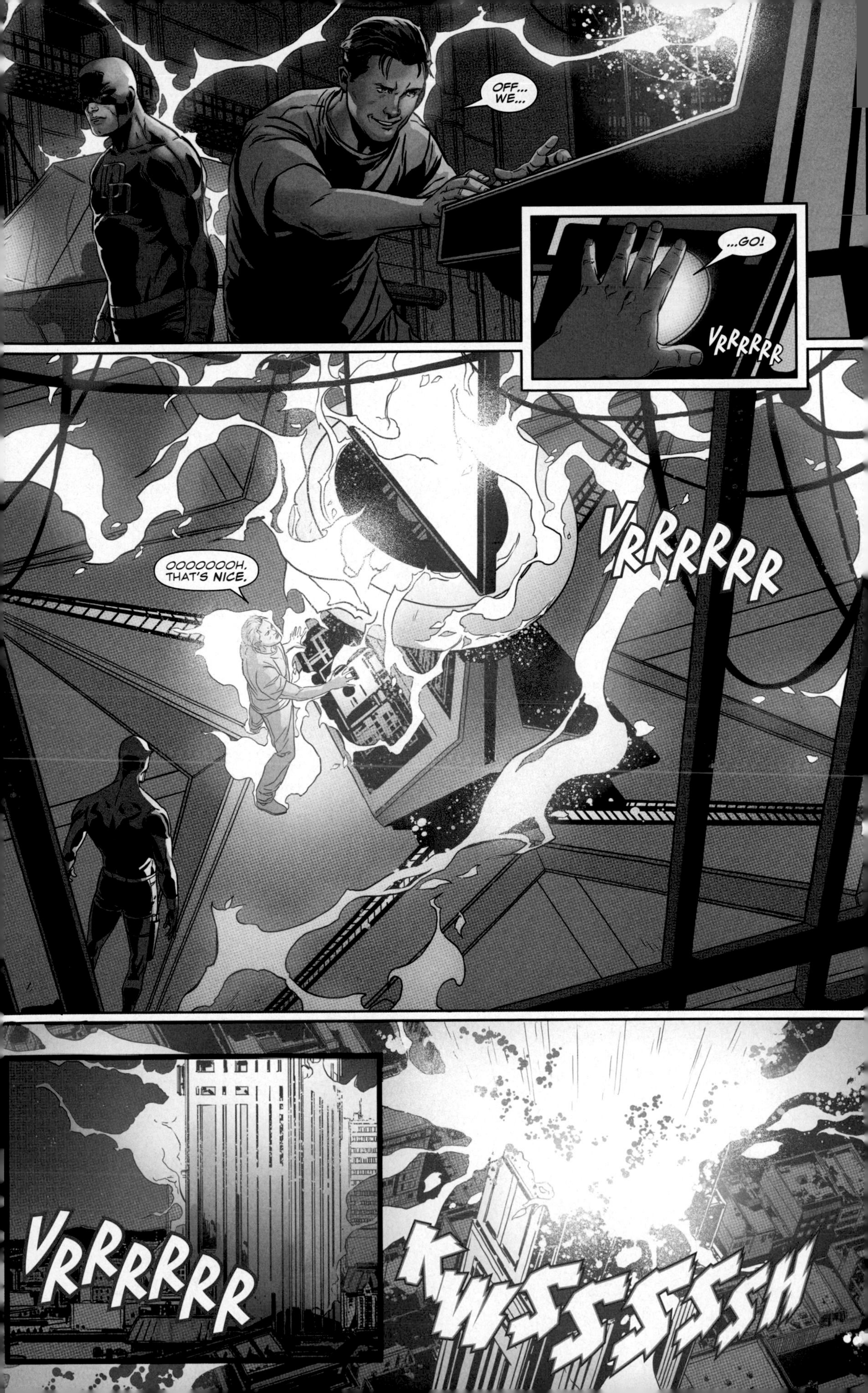
OFF... WE...
...GO!
VRRRRRR
VRRRRRRR
OOOOOOOH. THAT'S NICE.
VRRRRRR
KWSSSSSH

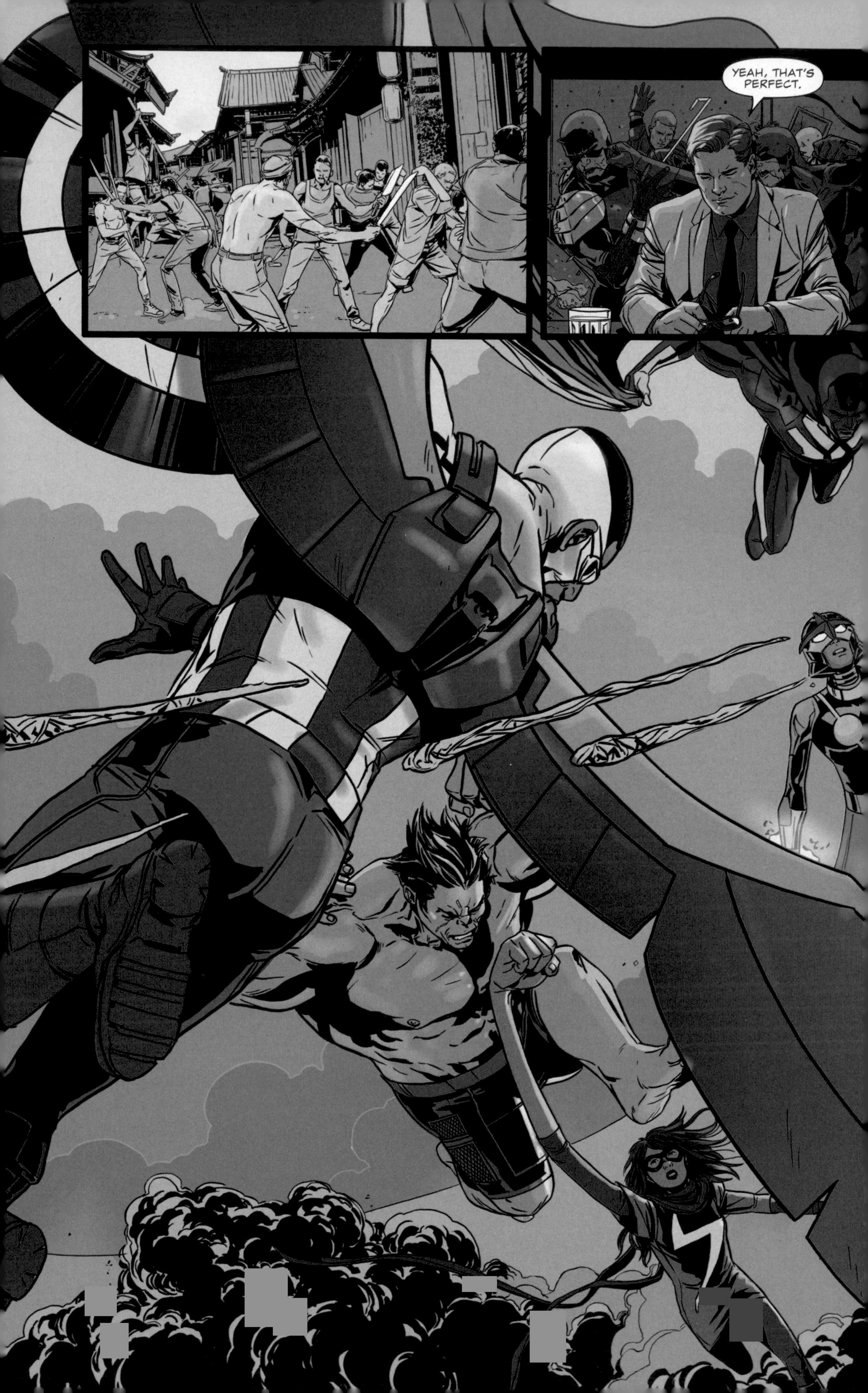
YEAH, THAT'S PERFECT.

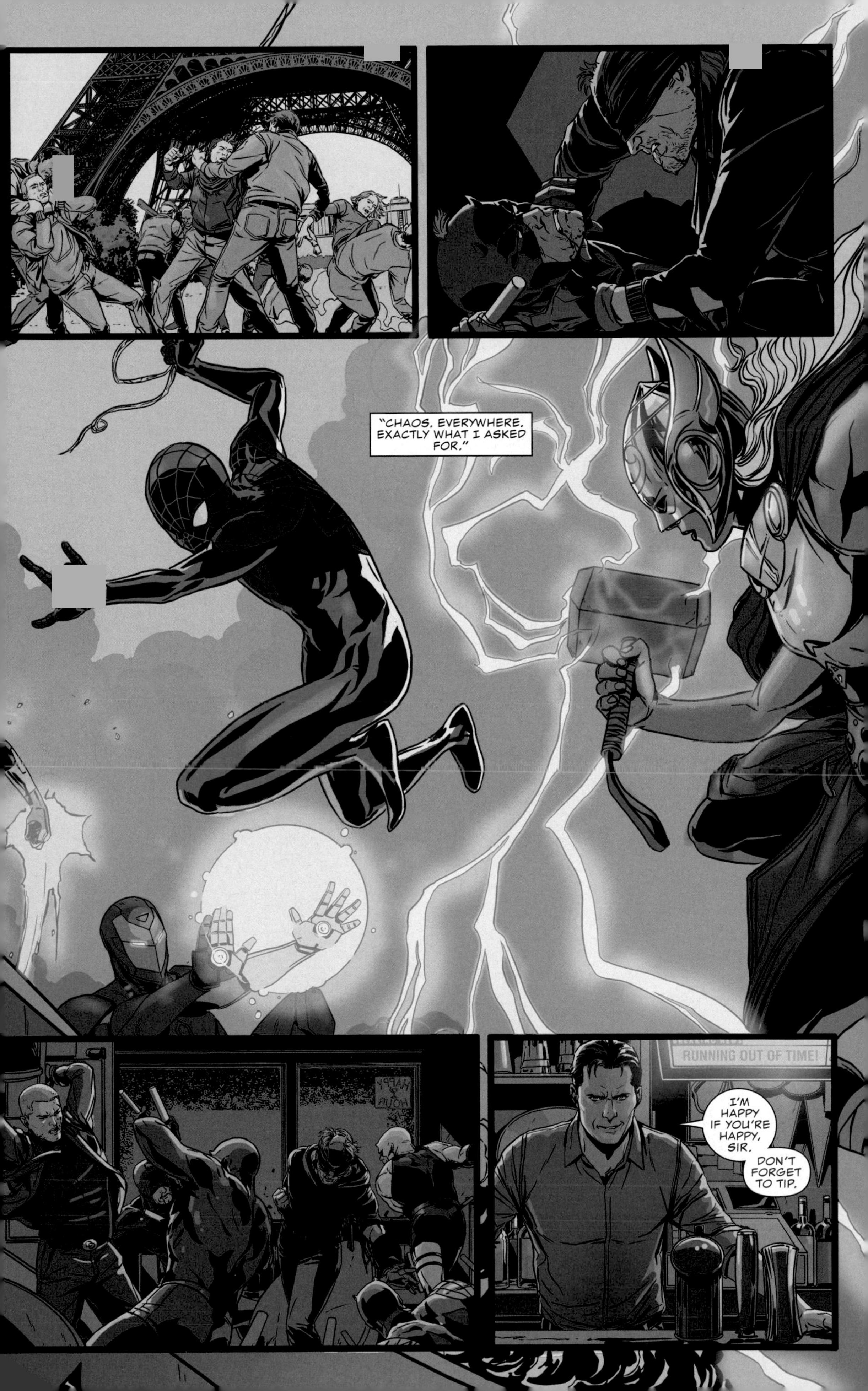
"CHAOS. EVERYWHERE. EXACTLY WHAT I ASKED FOR."
RUNNING OUT OF TIME!
I'M HAPPY IF YOU'RE HAPPY, SIR.
DON'T FORGET TO TIP.

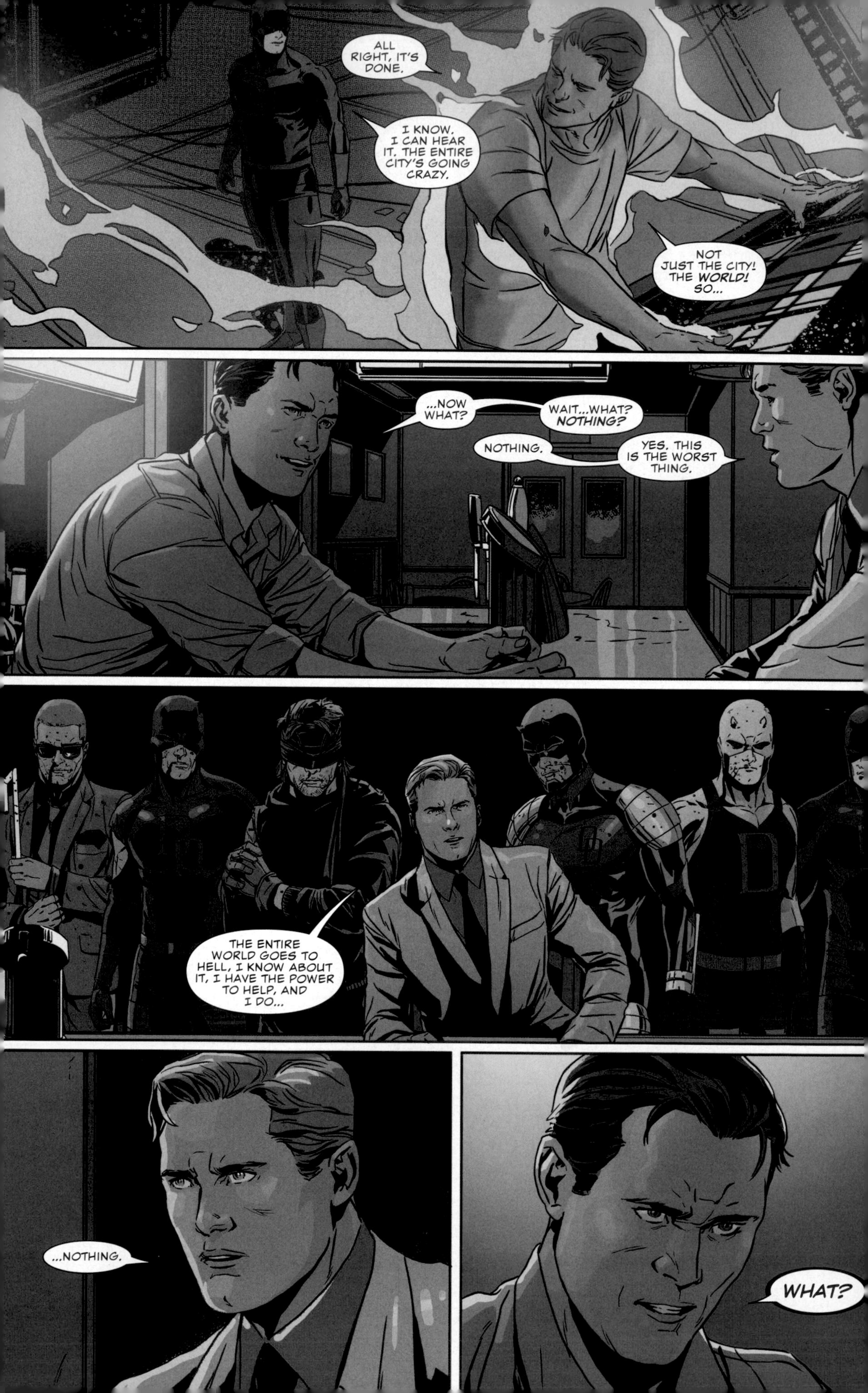
ALL RIGHT, IT'S DONE.
I KNOW. I CAN HEAR IT. THE ENTIRE CITY'S GOING CRAZY.
NOT JUST THE CITY! THE WORLD! SO...
...NOW WHAT?
WAIT...WHAT? NOTHING?
NOTHING.
YES. THIS IS THE WORST THING.
THE ENTIRE WORLD GOES TO HELL, I KNOW ABOUT IT, I HAVE THE POWER TO HELP, AND I DO...
...NOTHING.
WHAT?

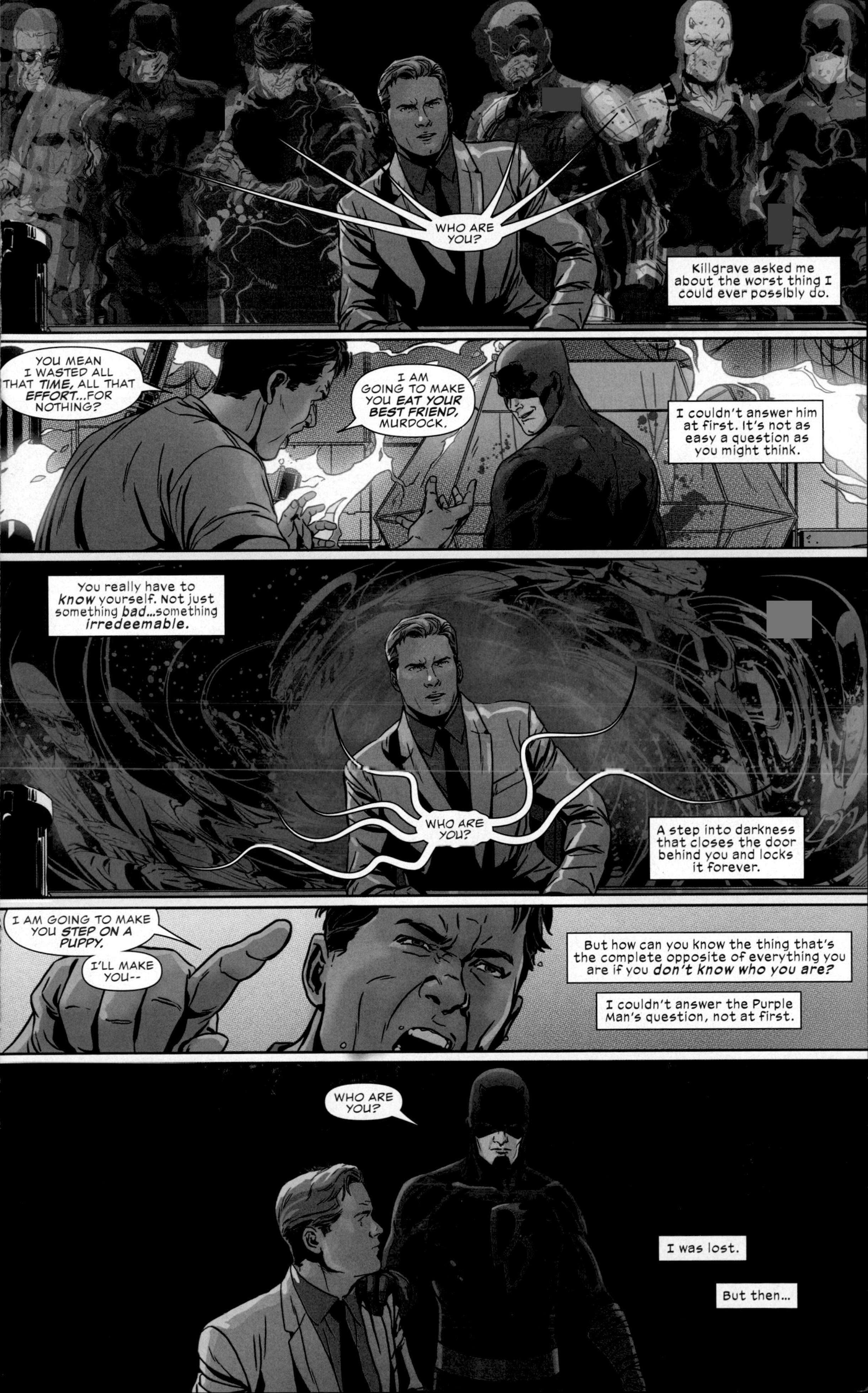
WHO ARE YOU?
Killgrave asked me about the worst thing I could ever possibly do.
YOU MEAN I WASTED ALL THAT TIME, ALL THAT EFFORT...FOR NOTHING?
I AM GOING TO MAKE YOU EAT YOUR BEST FRIEND, MURDOCK.
I couldn't answer him at first. It's not as easy a question as you might think.
You really have to know yourself. Not just something bad...something irredeemable.
WHO ARE YOU?
A step into darkness that closes the door behind you and locks it forever.
I AM GOING TO MAKE YOU STEP ON A PUPPY.
I'LL MAKE YOU--
But how can you know the thing that's the complete opposite of everything you are if you don't know who you are?
I couldn't answer the Purple Man's question, not at first.
WHO ARE YOU?
I was lost.
But then...

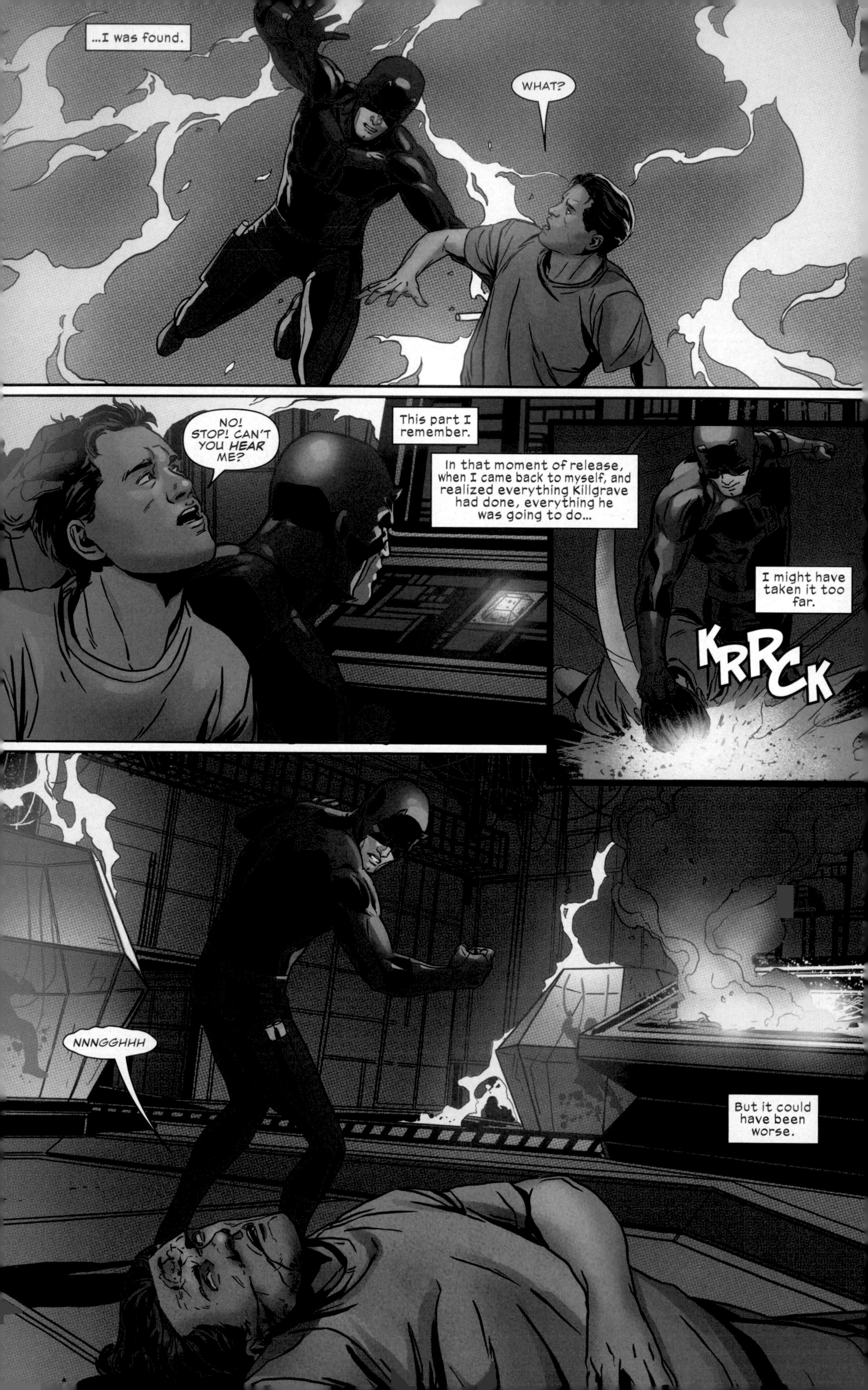

...I was found.
WHAT?
NO! STOP! CAN'T YOU HEAR ME?
This part I remember.
In that moment of release, when I came back to myself, and realized everything Killgrave had done, everything he was going to do...
I might have taken it too far.
KRRCK
NNNGGHHH
But it could have been worse.

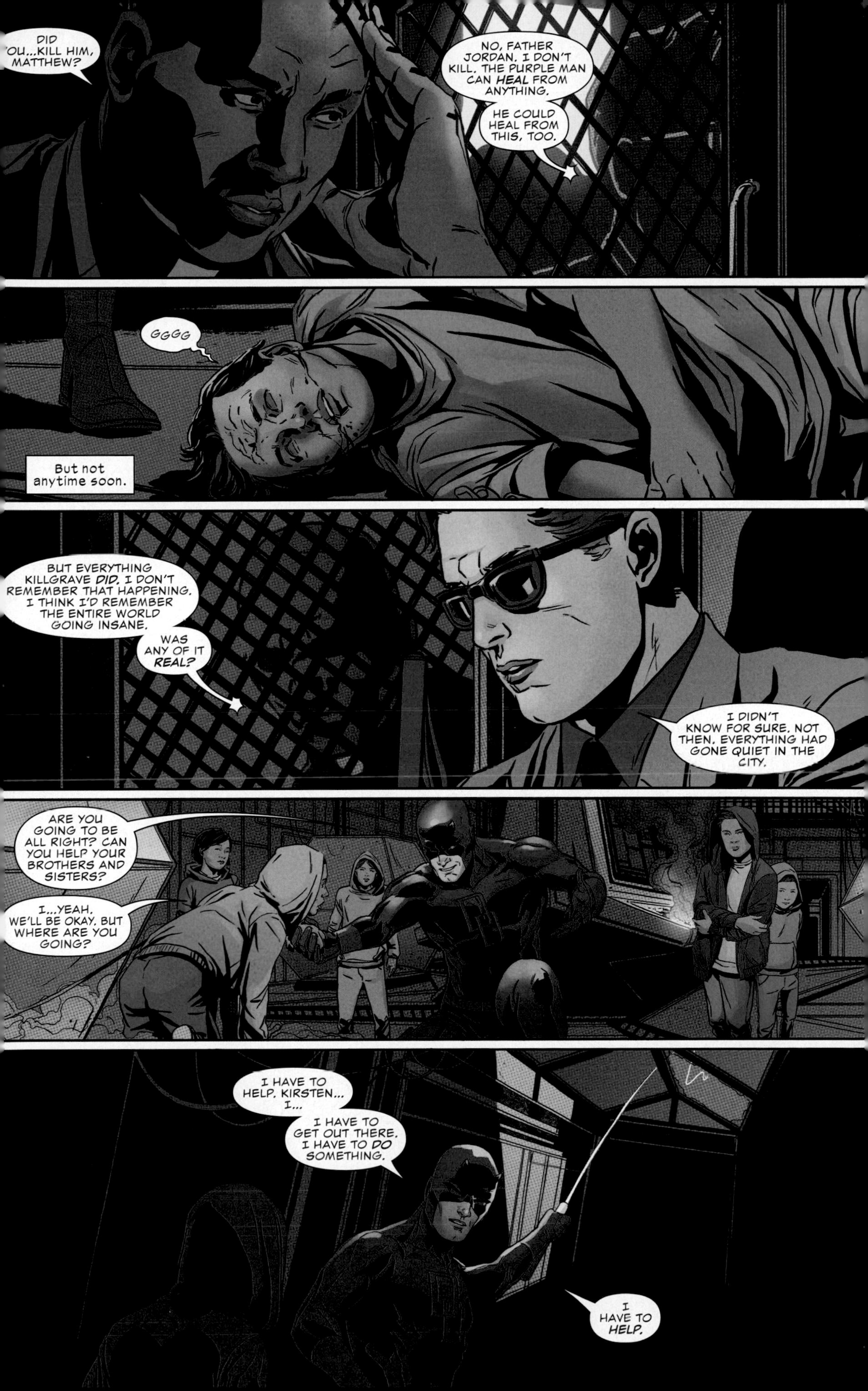
DID YOU...KILL HIM, MATTHEW?
NO, FATHER JORDAN. I DON'T KILL. THE PURPLE MAN CAN HEAL FROM ANYTHING.
HE COULD HEAL FROM THIS, TOO.
GGGG
But not anytime soon.
BUT EVERYTHING KILLGRAVE DID, I DON'T REMEMBER THAT HAPPENING. I THINK I'D REMEMBER THE ENTIRE WORLD GOING INSANE.
WAS ANY OF IT REAL?
I DIDN'T KNOW FOR SURE. NOT THEN. EVERYTHING HAD GONE QUIET IN THE CITY.
ARE YOU GOING TO BE ALL RIGHT? CAN YOU HELP YOUR BROTHERS AND SISTERS?
I...YEAH. WE'LL BE OKAY. BUT WHERE ARE YOU GOING?
I HAVE TO HELP, KIRSTEN... I...
I HAVE TO GET OUT THERE. I HAVE TO DO SOMETHING.
I HAVE TO HELP.

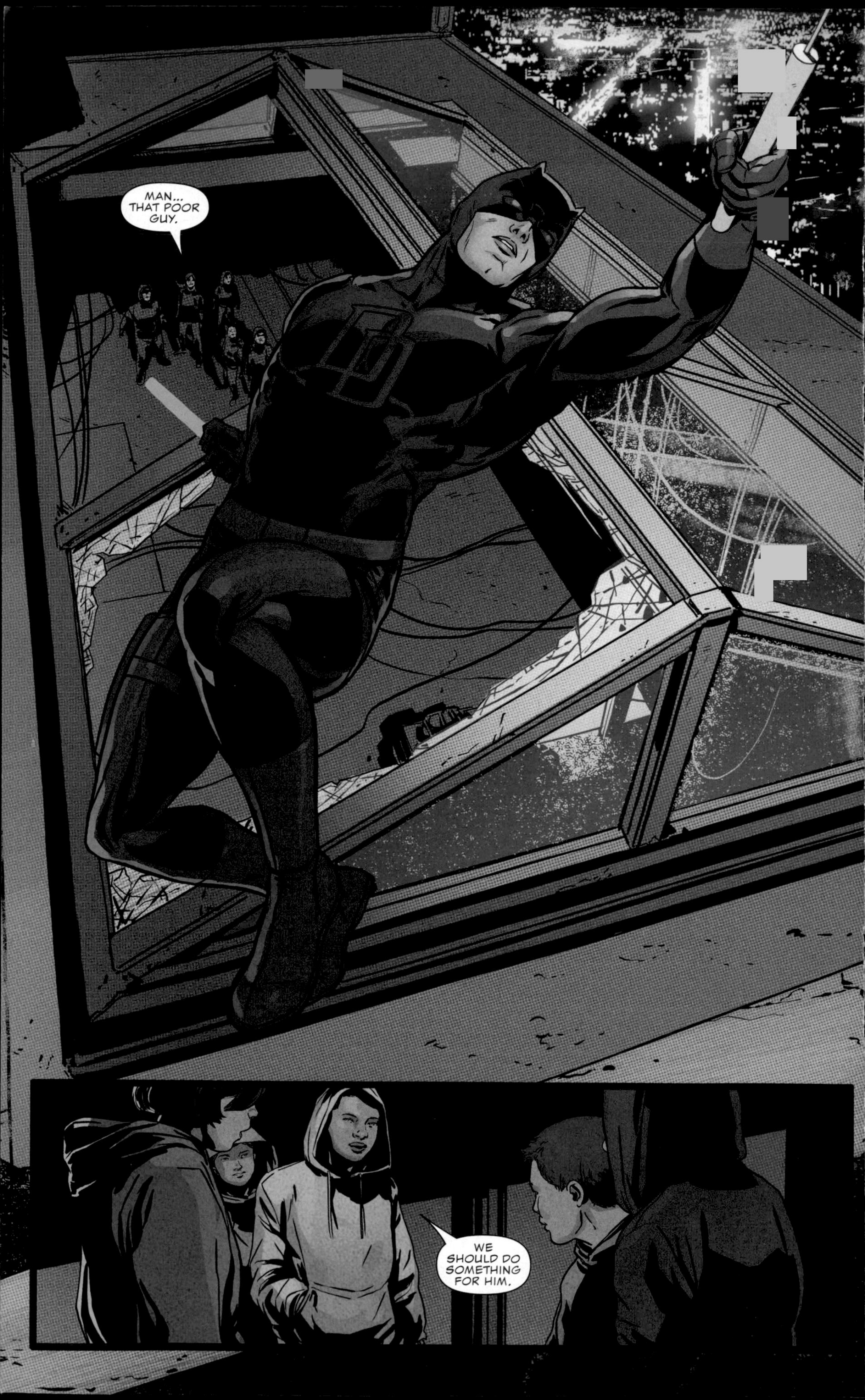
MAN... THAT POOR GUY.
WE SHOULD DO SOMETHING FOR HIM.

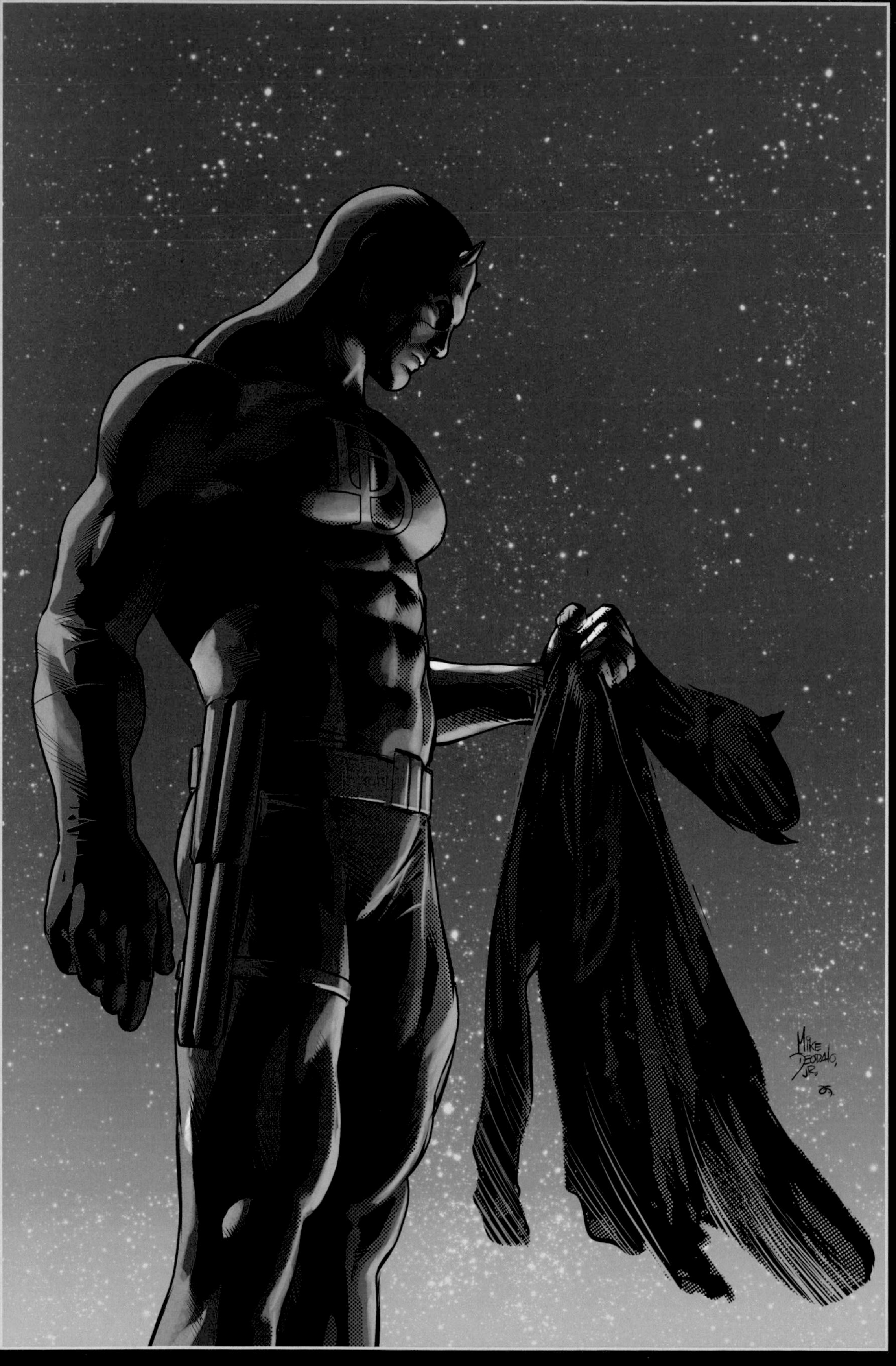

20

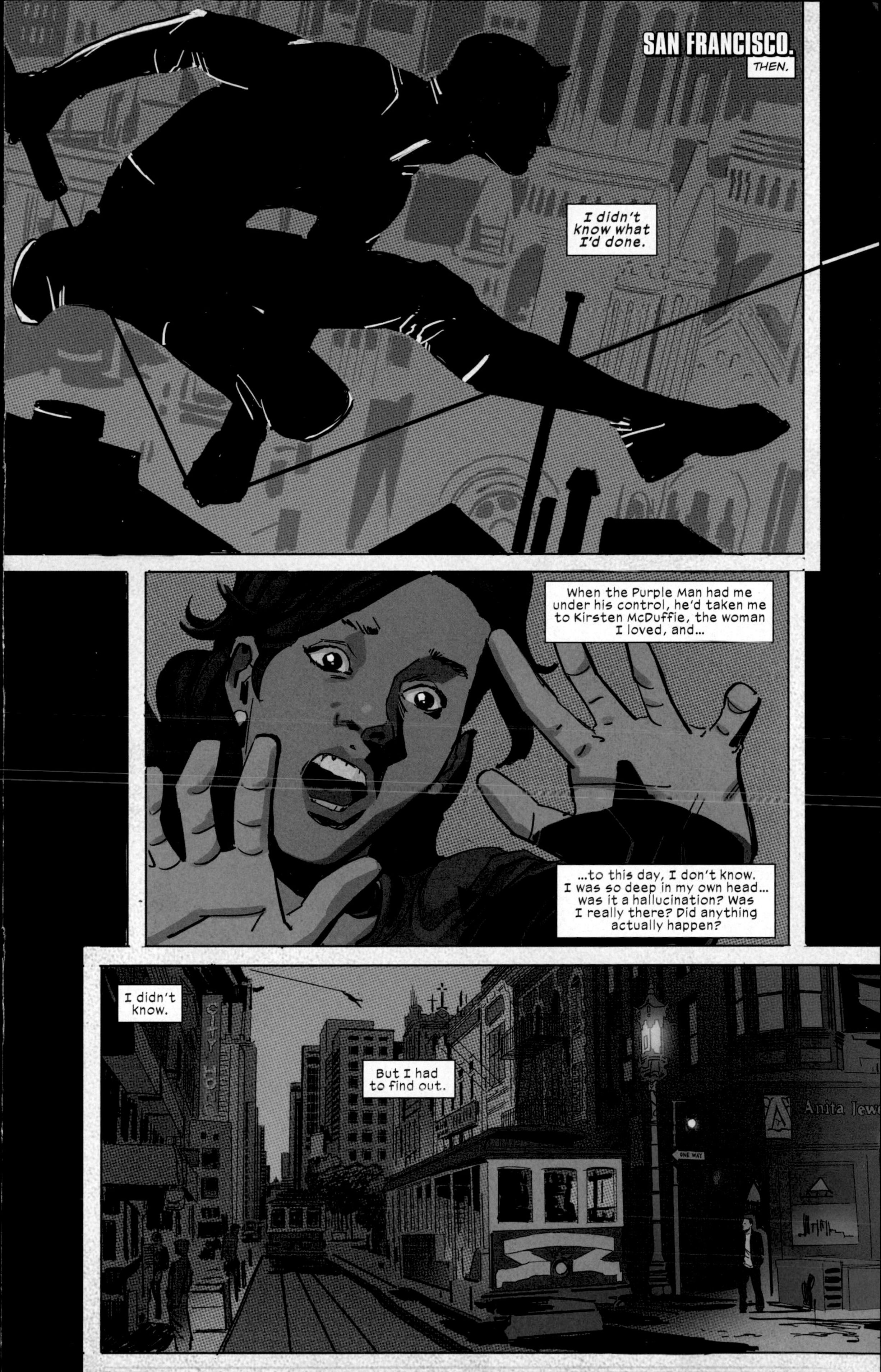
SAN FRANCISCO.
THEN.
I didn't know what I'd done.
When the Purple Man had me under his control, he'd taken me to Kirsten McDuffie, the woman I loved, and...
...to this day, I don't know. I was so deep in my own head... was it a hallucination? Was I really there? Did anything actually happen?
I didn't know.
But I had to find out.
ONE WAY

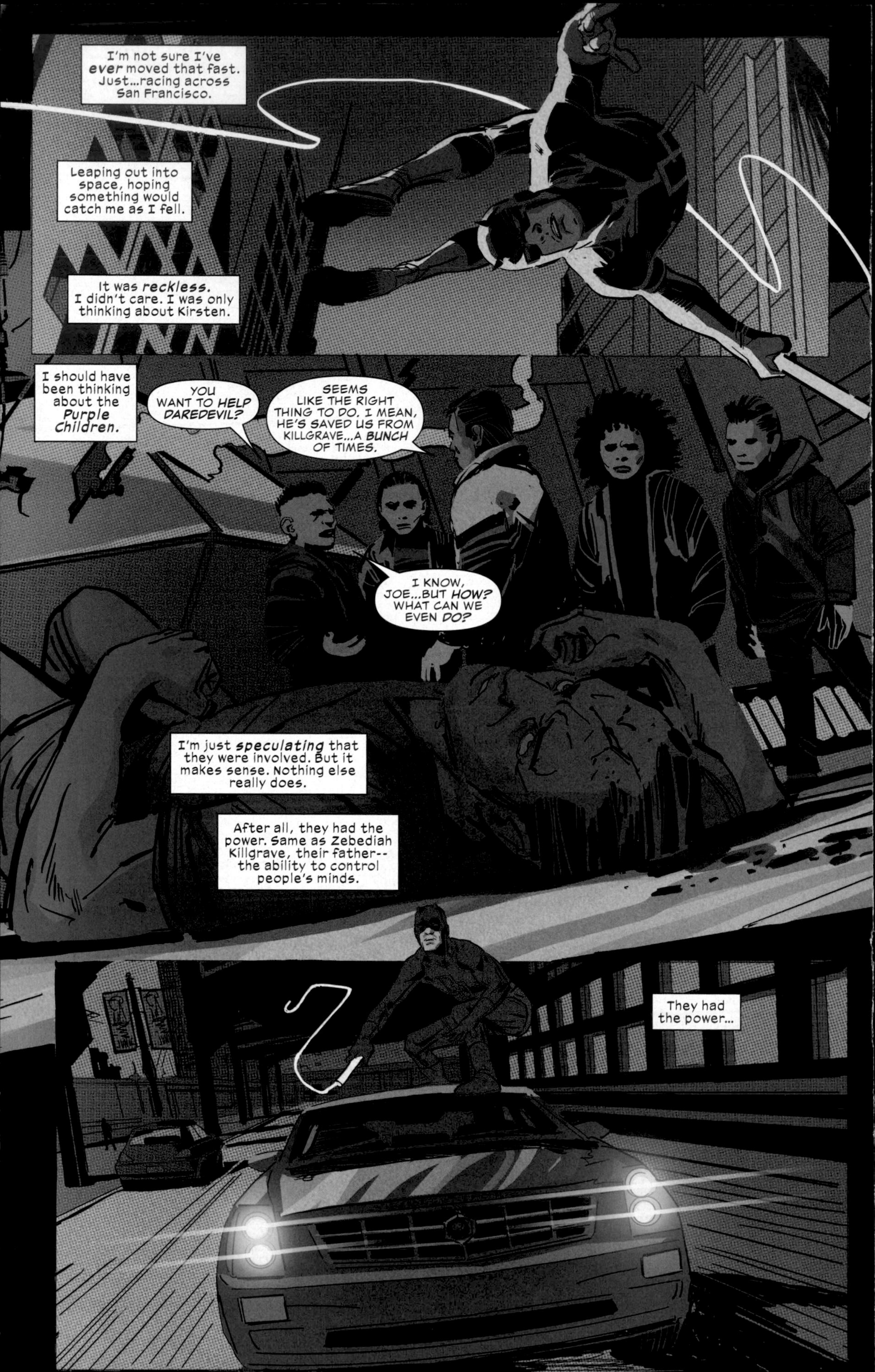
I'm not sure I've ever moved that fast. Just...racing across San Francisco.
Leaping out into space, hoping something would catch me as I fell.
It was reckless. I didn't care. I was only thinking about Kirsten.
I should have been thinking about the Purple Children.
YOU WANT TO HELP DAREDEVIL?
SEEMS LIKE THE RIGHT THING TO DO. I MEAN, HE'S SAVED US FROM KILLGRAVE...A BUNCH OF TIMES.
I KNOW, JOE...BUT HOW? WHAT CAN WE EVEN DO?
I'm just speculating that they were involved. But it makes sense. Nothing else really does.
After all, they had the power. Same as Zebediah Killgrave, their father-- the ability to control people's minds.
They had the power...

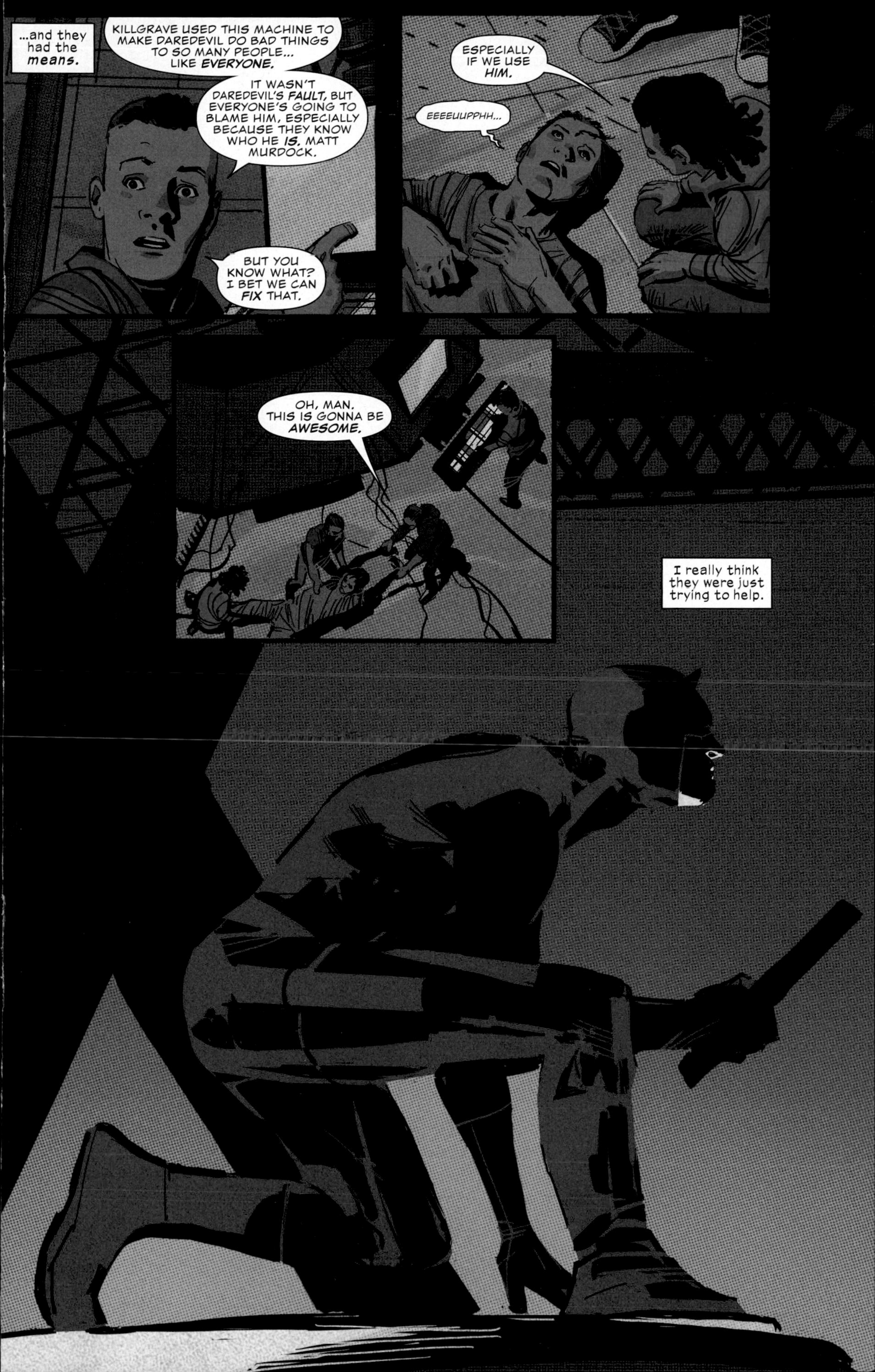
...and they had the *means.*
KILLGRAVE USED THIS MACHINE TO MAKE DAREDEVIL DO BAD THINGS TO SO MANY PEOPLE... LIKE *EVERYONE.*
IT WASN'T DAREDEVIL'S *FAULT,* BUT EVERYONE'S GOING TO BLAME HIM, ESPECIALLY BECAUSE THEY KNOW WHO HE *IS.* MATT MURDOCK.
BUT YOU KNOW WHAT? I BET WE CAN *FIX* THAT.
ESPECIALLY IF WE USE *HIM.*
EEEEUUPPHH...
OH, MAN. THIS IS GONNA BE *AWESOME.*
I really think they were just trying to help.

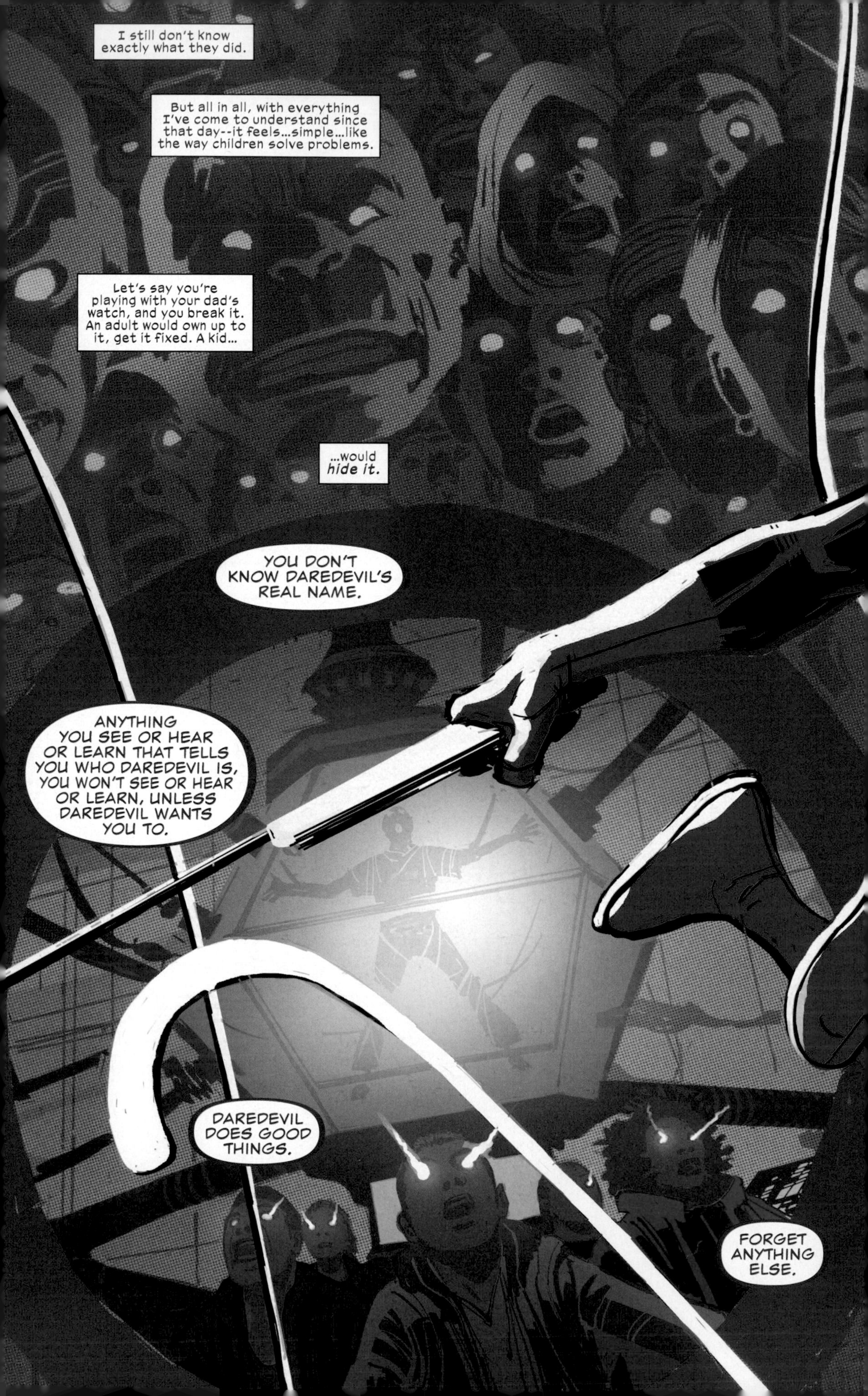

I still don't know exactly what they did.
But all in all, with everything I've come to understand since that day--it feels...simple...like the way children solve problems.
Let's say you're playing with your dad's watch, and you break it. An adult would own up to it, get it fixed. A kid...
...would *hide it.*
YOU DON'T KNOW DAREDEVIL'S REAL NAME.
ANYTHING YOU SEE OR HEAR OR LEARN THAT TELLS YOU WHO DAREDEVIL IS, YOU WON'T SEE OR HEAR OR LEARN, UNLESS DAREDEVIL WANTS YOU TO.
DAREDEVIL DOES GOOD THINGS.
FORGET ANYTHING ELSE.

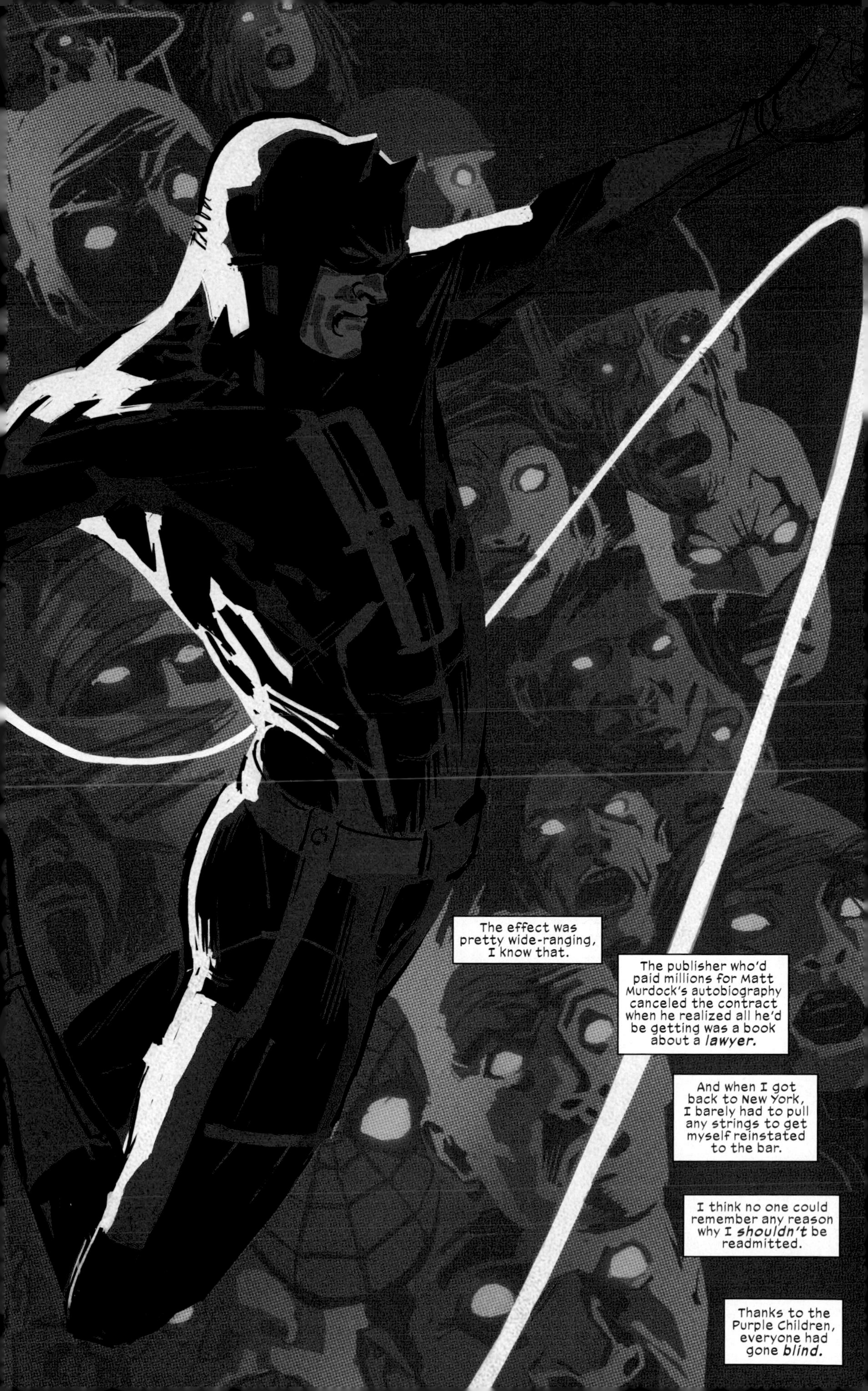

The effect was pretty wide-ranging, I know that.
The publisher who'd paid millions for Matt Murdock's autobiography canceled the contract when he realized all he'd be getting was a book about a *lawyer.*
And when I got back to New York, I barely had to pull any strings to get myself reinstated to the bar.
I think no one could remember any reason why I *shouldn't* be readmitted.
Thanks to the Purple Children, everyone had gone *blind.*

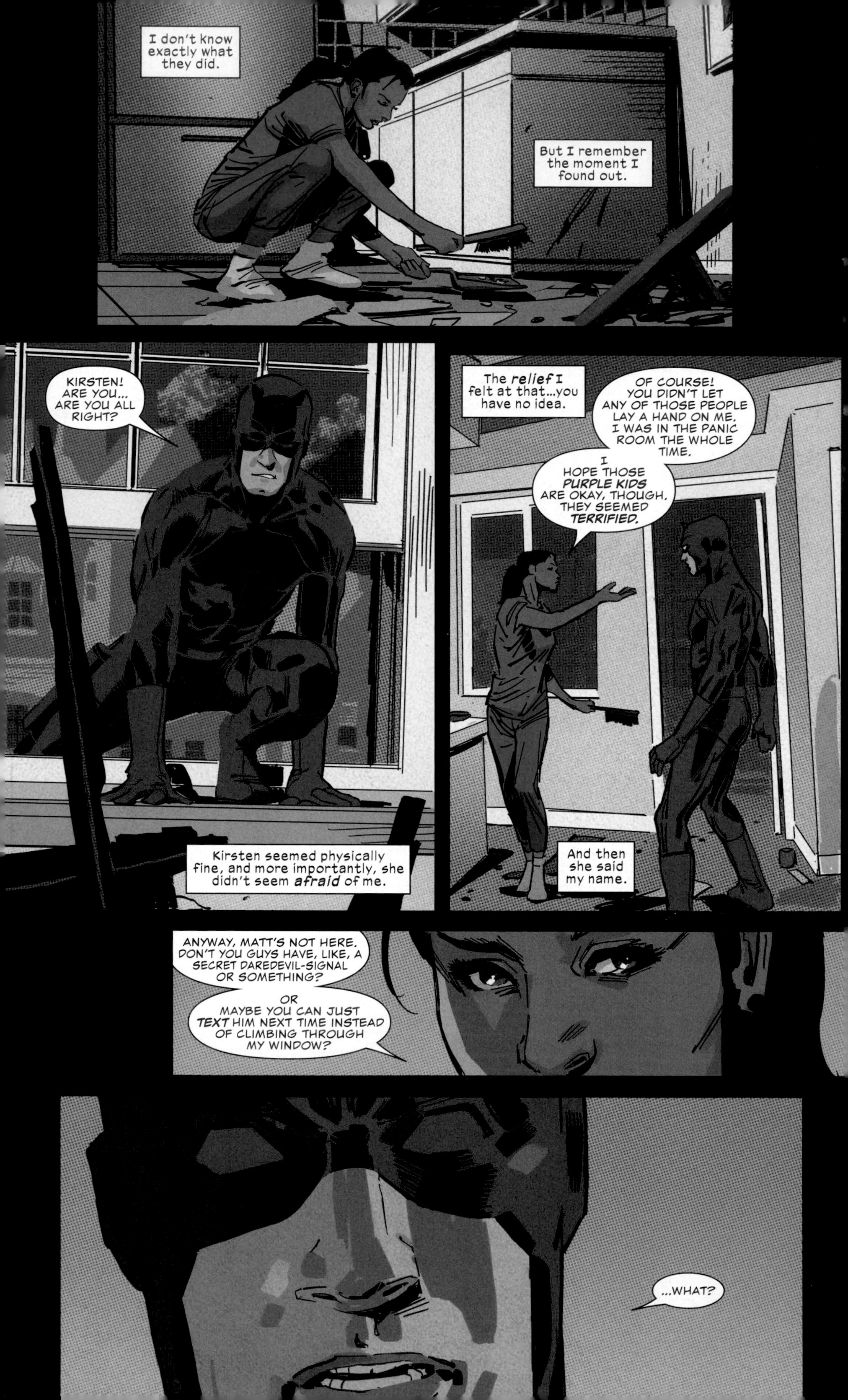
I don't know exactly what they did.
But I remember the moment I found out.
KIRSTEN! ARE YOU... ARE YOU ALL RIGHT?
Kirsten seemed physically fine, and more importantly, she didn't seem *afraid* of me.
The *relief* I felt at that...you have no idea.
OF COURSE! YOU DIDN'T LET ANY OF THOSE PEOPLE LAY A HAND ON ME. I WAS IN THE PANIC ROOM THE WHOLE TIME.
I HOPE THOSE *PURPLE KIDS* ARE OKAY, THOUGH. THEY SEEMED *TERRIFIED.*
And then she said my name.
ANYWAY, MATT'S NOT HERE. DON'T YOU GUYS HAVE, LIKE, A SECRET DAREDEVIL-SIGNAL OR SOMETHING?
OR MAYBE YOU CAN JUST *TEXT* HIM NEXT TIME INSTEAD OF CLIMBING THROUGH MY WINDOW?
...WHAT?

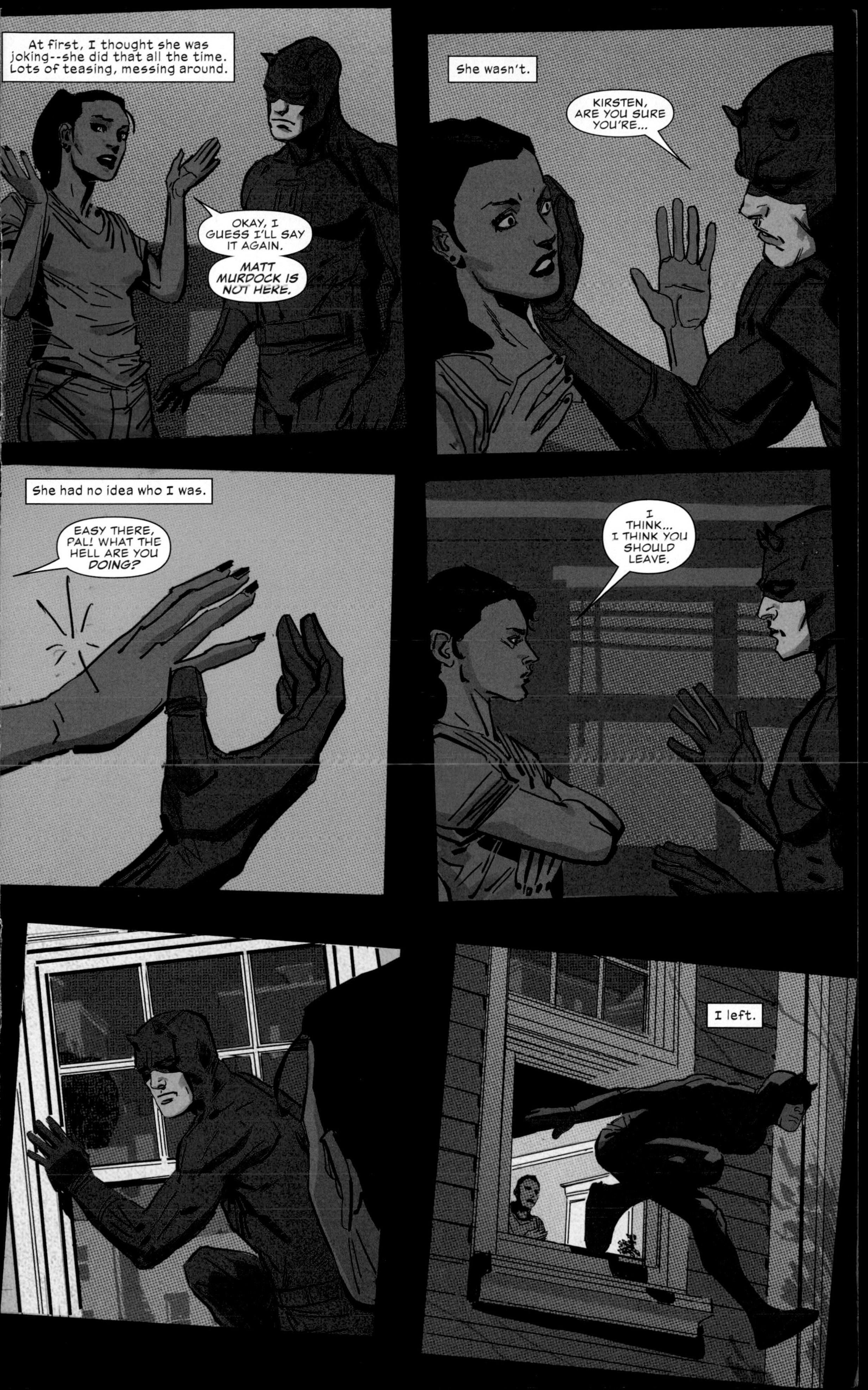
At first, I thought she was joking--she did that all the time. Lots of teasing, messing around.
OKAY, I GUESS I'LL SAY IT AGAIN.
MATT MURDOCK IS NOT HERE.
She wasn't.
KIRSTEN, ARE YOU SURE YOU'RE...
She had no idea who I was.
EASY THERE, PAL! WHAT THE HELL ARE YOU DOING?
I THINK... I THINK YOU SHOULD LEAVE.
I left.

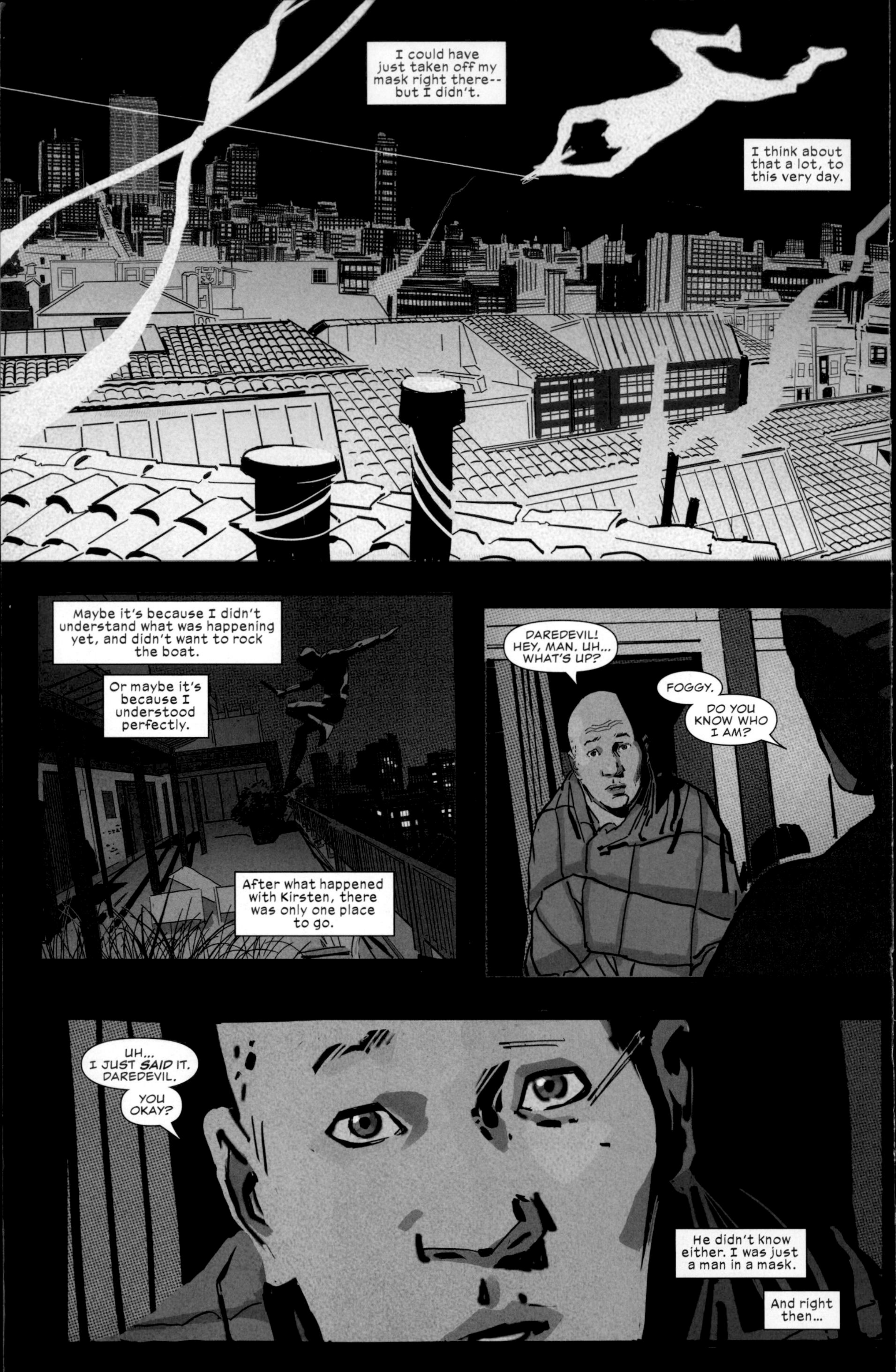
I could have just taken off my mask right there-- but I didn't.
I think about that a lot, to this very day.
Maybe it's because I didn't understand what was happening yet, and didn't want to rock the boat.
Or maybe it's because I understood perfectly.
After what happened with Kirsten, there was only one place to go.
DAREDEVIL! HEY, MAN. UH... WHAT'S UP?
FOGGY.
DO YOU KNOW WHO I AM?
UH... I JUST SAID IT. DAREDEVIL.
YOU OKAY?
He didn't know either. I was just a man in a mask.
And right then...

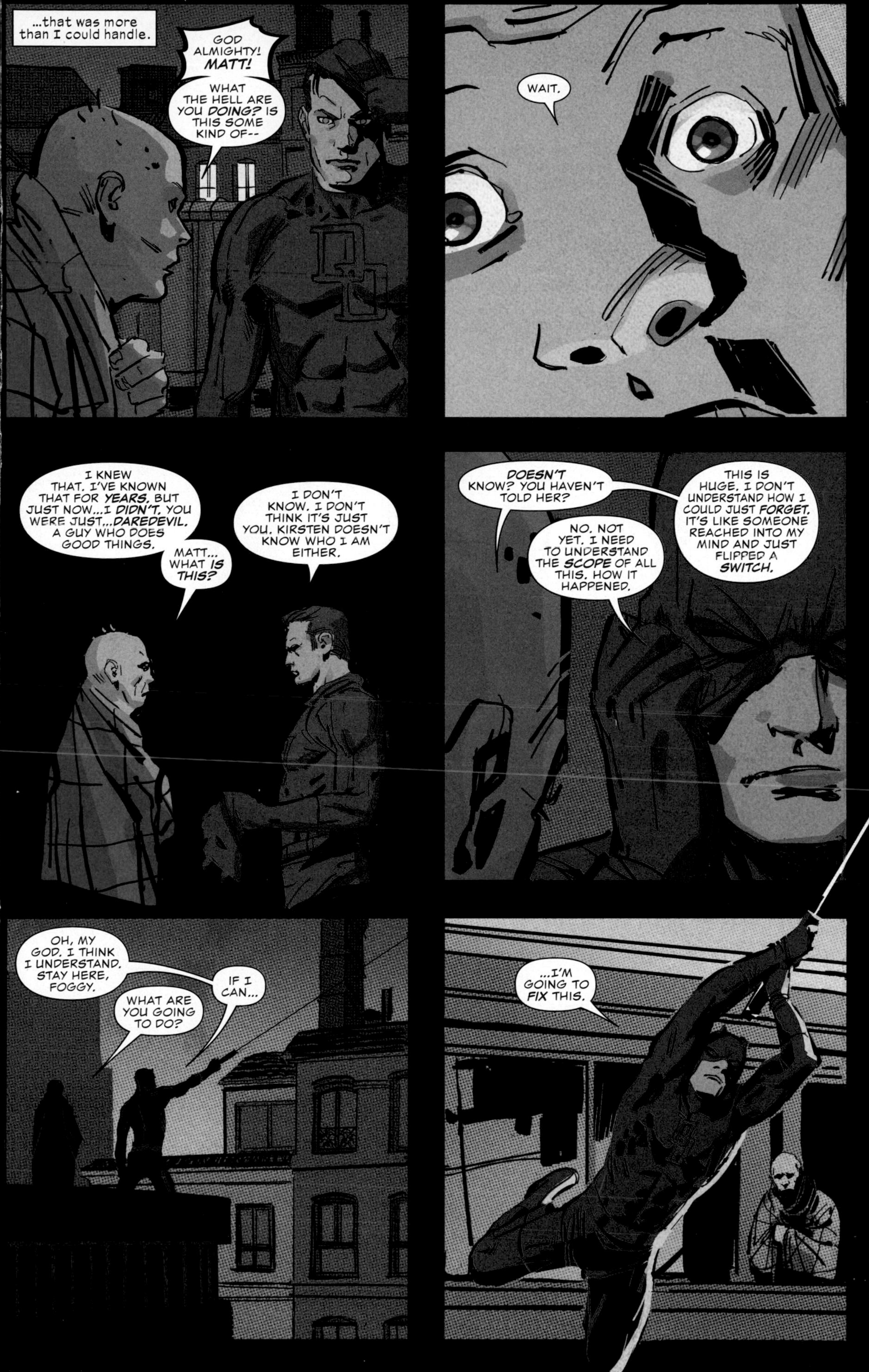
...that was more than I could handle.
GOD ALMIGHTY! MATT!
WHAT THE HELL ARE YOU DOING? IS THIS SOME KIND OF--
WAIT.
I KNEW THAT. I'VE KNOWN THAT FOR YEARS. BUT JUST NOW...I DIDN'T. YOU WERE JUST...DAREDEVIL. A GUY WHO DOES GOOD THINGS.
MATT... WHAT IS THIS?
I DON'T KNOW. I DON'T THINK IT'S JUST YOU. KIRSTEN DOESN'T KNOW WHO I AM EITHER.
DOESN'T KNOW? YOU HAVEN'T TOLD HER?
NO. NOT YET. I NEED TO UNDERSTAND THE SCOPE OF ALL THIS. HOW IT HAPPENED.
THIS IS HUGE. I DON'T UNDERSTAND HOW I COULD JUST FORGET. IT'S LIKE SOMEONE REACHED INTO MY MIND AND JUST FLIPPED A SWITCH.
OH, MY GOD. I THINK I UNDERSTAND. STAY HERE, FOGGY.
WHAT ARE YOU GOING TO DO?
IF I CAN...
...I'M GOING TO FIX THIS.

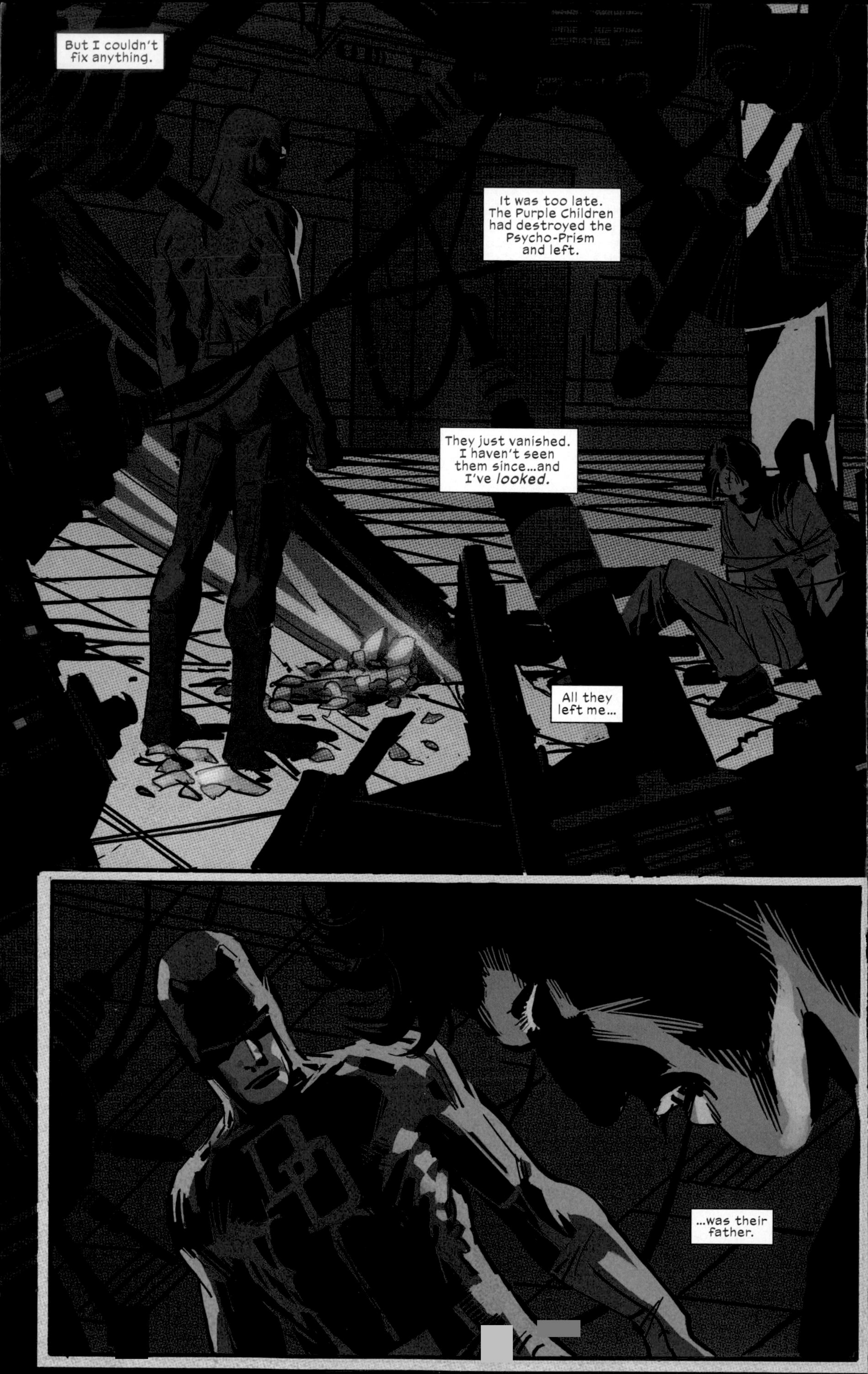
But I couldn't fix anything.
It was too late. The Purple Children had destroyed the Psycho-Prism and left.
They just vanished. I haven't seen them since...and I've *looked.*
All they left me...
...was their father.

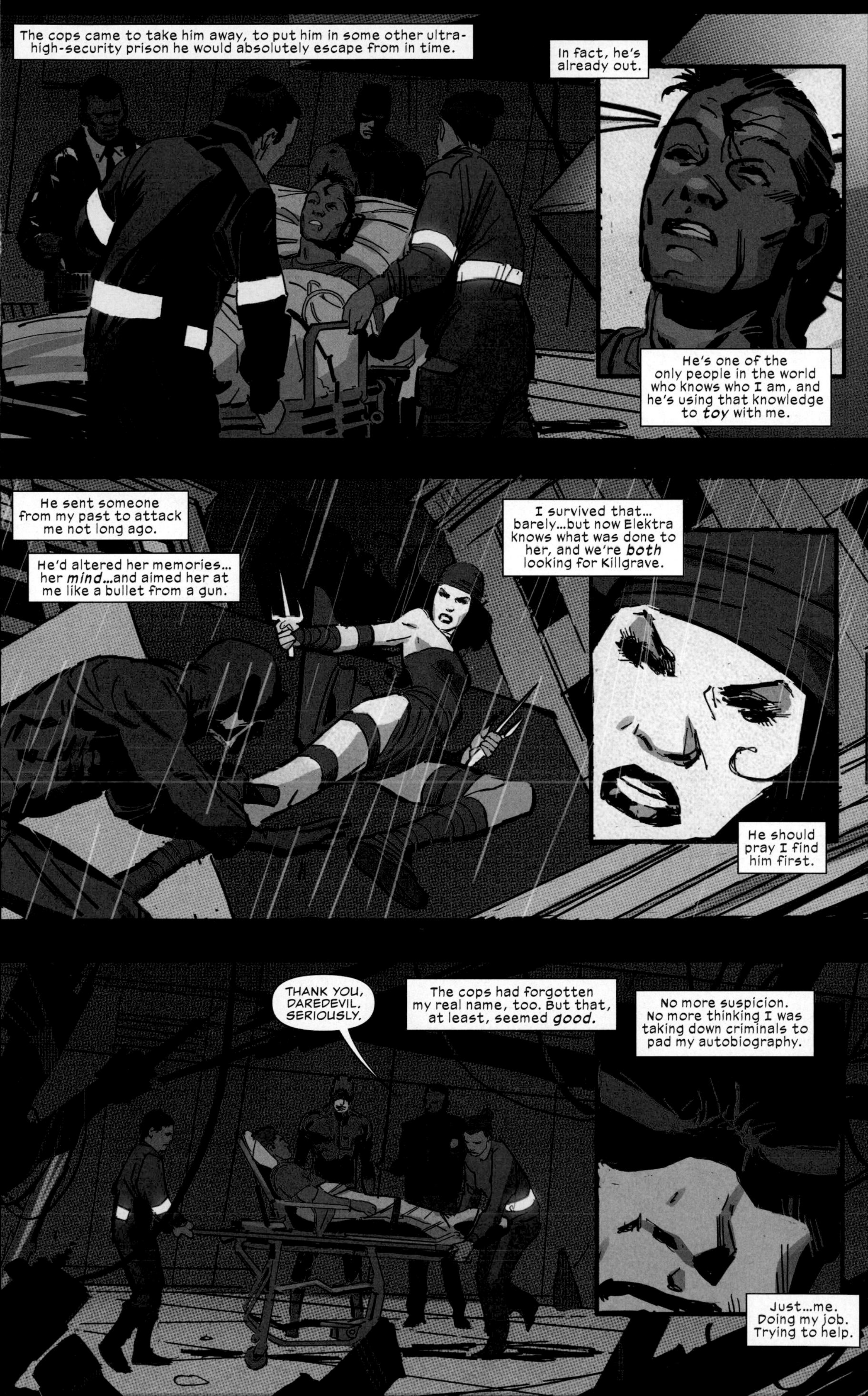
The cops came to take him away, to put him in some other ultra-high-security prison he would absolutely escape from in time.
In fact, he's already out.
He's one of the only people in the world who knows who I am, and he's using that knowledge to *toy* with me.
He sent someone from my past to attack me not long ago.
He'd altered her memories... her *mind*...and aimed her at me like a bullet from a gun.
I survived that... barely...but now Elektra knows what was done to her, and we're *both* looking for Killgrave.
He should pray I find him first.
THANK YOU, DAREDEVIL. SERIOUSLY.
The cops had forgotten my real name, too. But that, at least, seemed *good.*
No more suspicion. No more thinking I was taking down criminals to pad my autobiography.
Just...me. Doing my job. Trying to help.

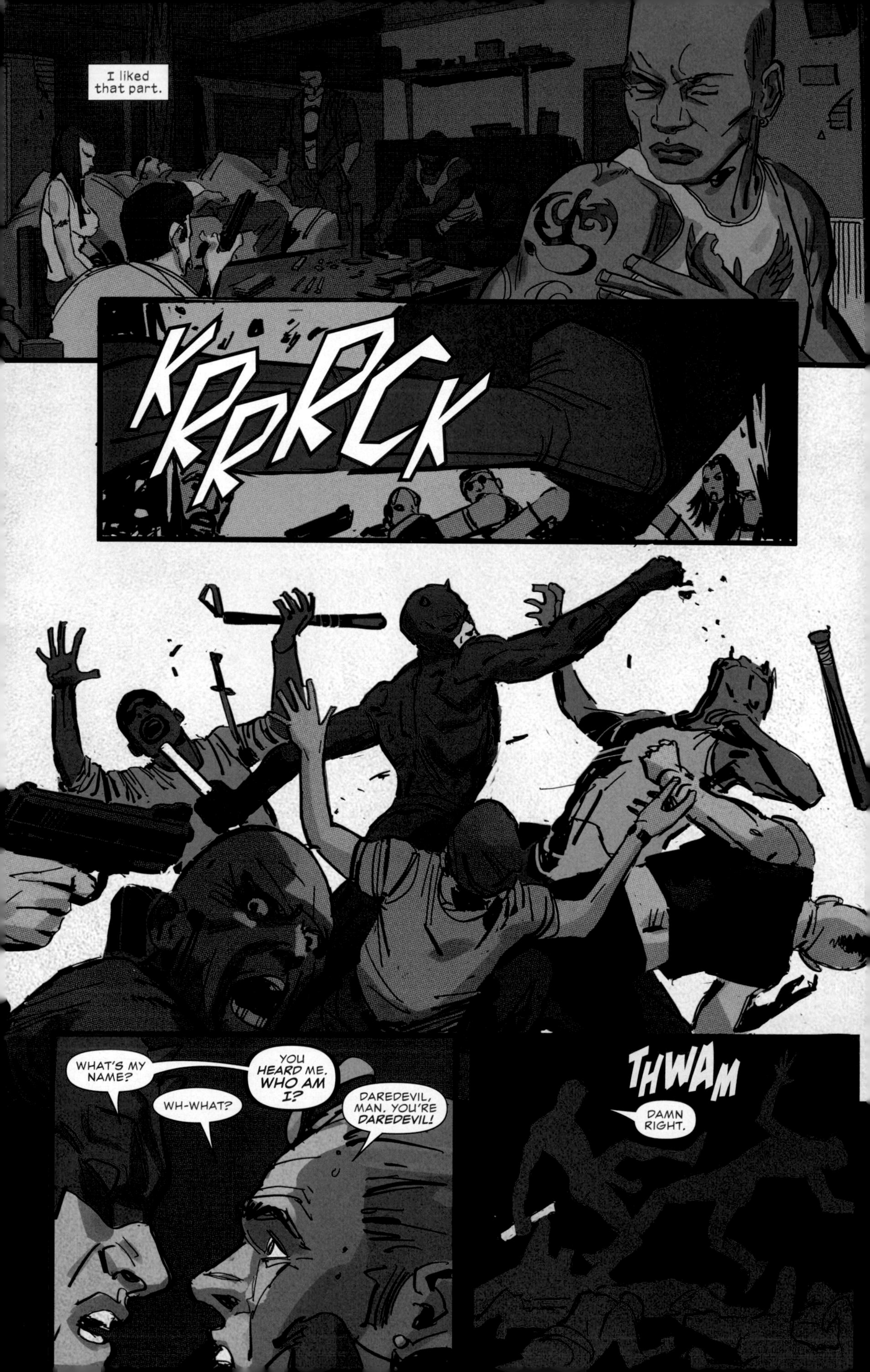
I liked that part.
KRRRRCK
WHAT'S MY NAME?
WH-WHAT?
YOU HEARD ME. WHO AM I?
DAREDEVIL, MAN. YOU'RE DAREDEVIL!
THWAM
DAMN RIGHT.

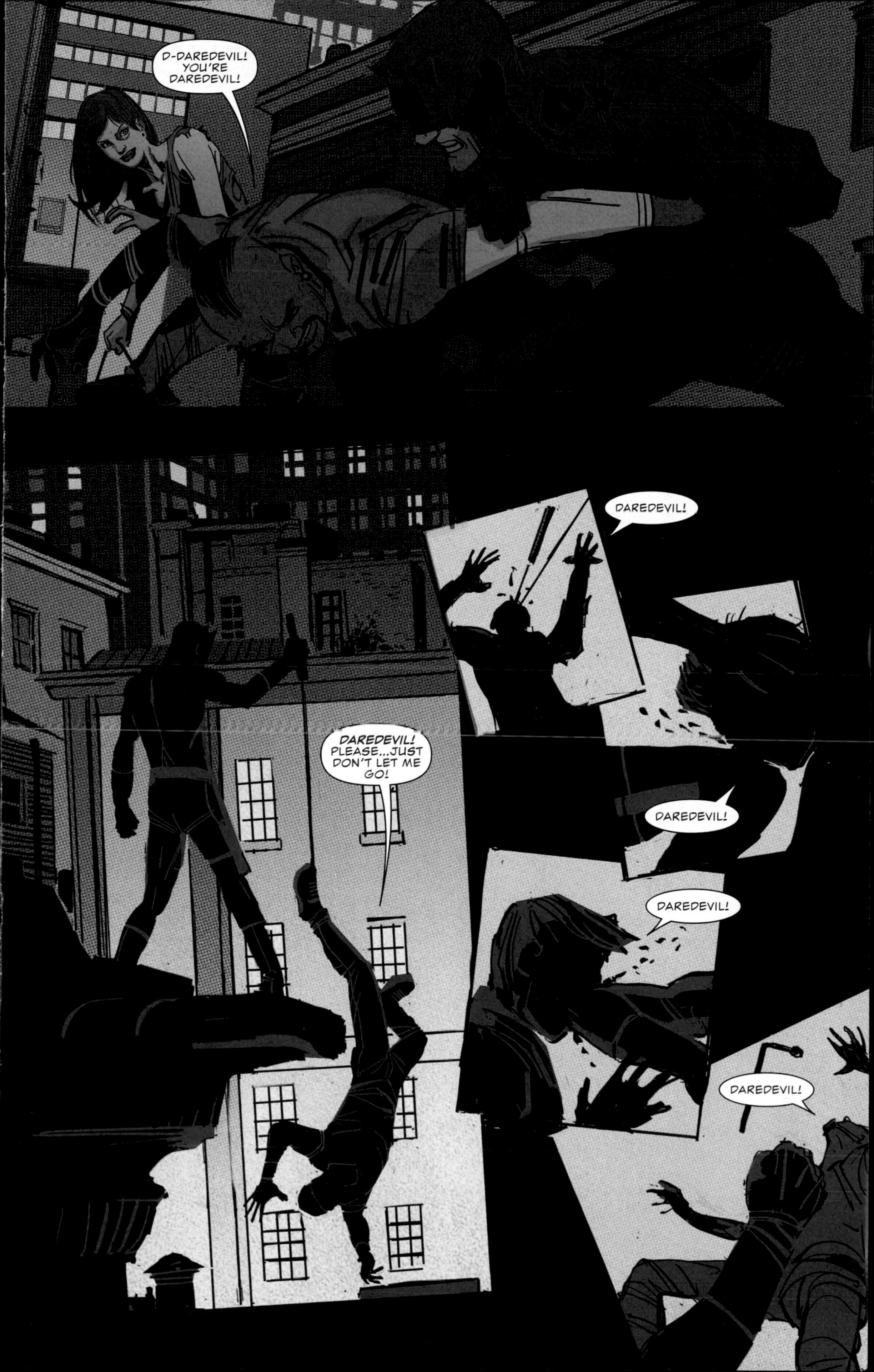

D-DAREDEVIL! YOU'RE DAREDEVIL!
DAREDEVIL! PLEASE...JUST DON'T LET ME GO!
DAREDEVIL!
DAREDEVIL!
DAREDEVIL!
DAREDEVIL!

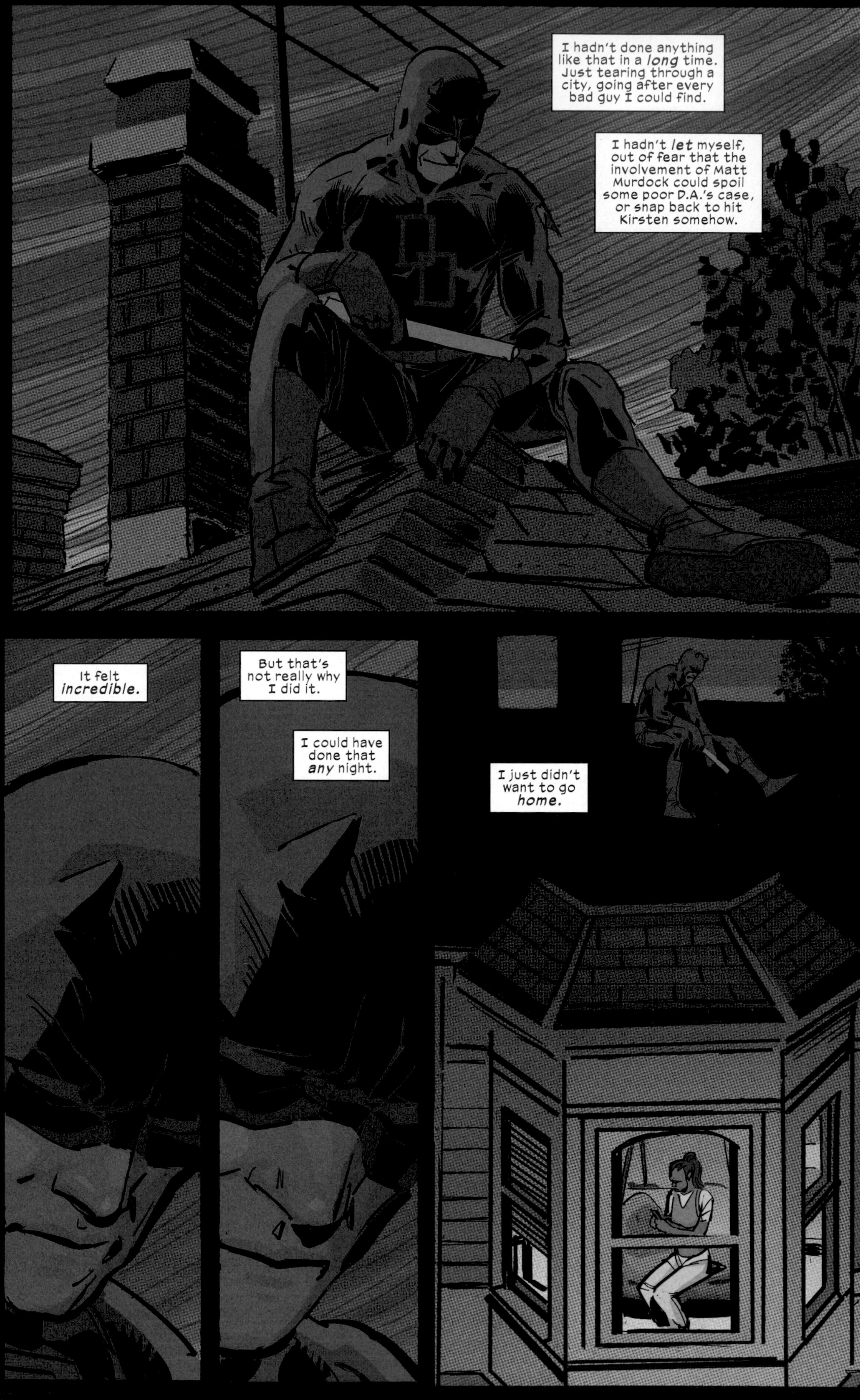

I hadn't done anything like that in a *long* time. Just tearing through a city, going after every bad guy I could find.
I hadn't *let* myself, out of fear that the involvement of Matt Murdock could spoil some poor D.A.'s case, or snap back to hit Kirsten somehow.
It felt *incredible.*
But that's not really why I did it.
I could have done that *any* night.
I just didn't want to go *home.*

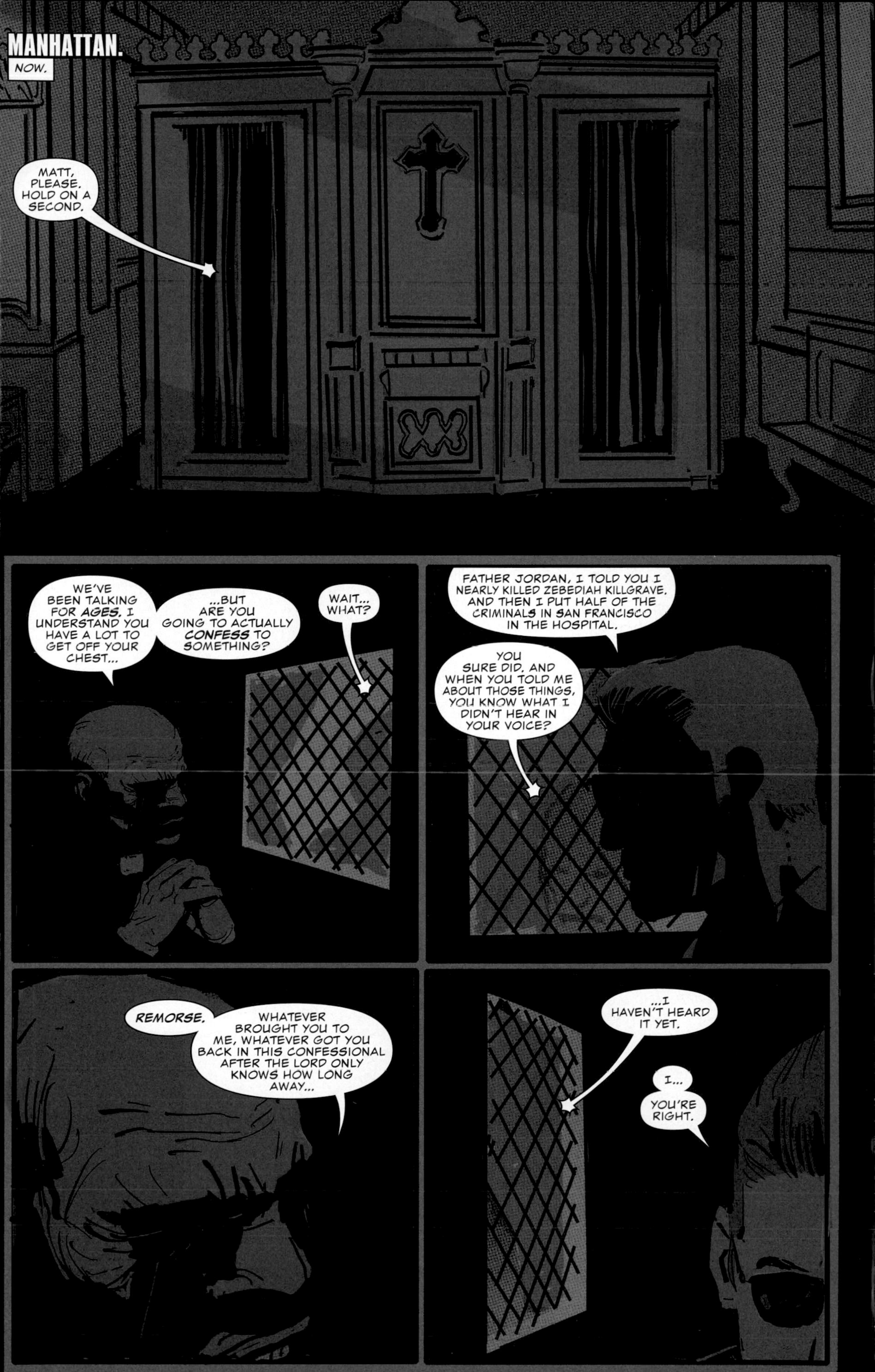
MANHATTAN.
NOW.
MATT, PLEASE. HOLD ON A SECOND.
WE'VE BEEN TALKING FOR AGES. I UNDERSTAND YOU HAVE A LOT TO GET OFF YOUR CHEST...
...BUT ARE YOU GOING TO ACTUALLY CONFESS TO SOMETHING?
WAIT... WHAT?
FATHER JORDAN, I TOLD YOU I NEARLY KILLED ZEBEDIAH KILLGRAVE, AND THEN I PUT HALF OF THE CRIMINALS IN SAN FRANCISCO IN THE HOSPITAL.
YOU SURE DID, AND WHEN YOU TOLD ME ABOUT THOSE THINGS, YOU KNOW WHAT I DIDN'T HEAR IN YOUR VOICE?
REMORSE.
WHATEVER BROUGHT YOU TO ME, WHATEVER GOT YOU BACK IN THIS CONFESSIONAL AFTER THE LORD ONLY KNOWS HOW LONG AWAY...
...I HAVEN'T HEARD IT YET.
I...
YOU'RE RIGHT.

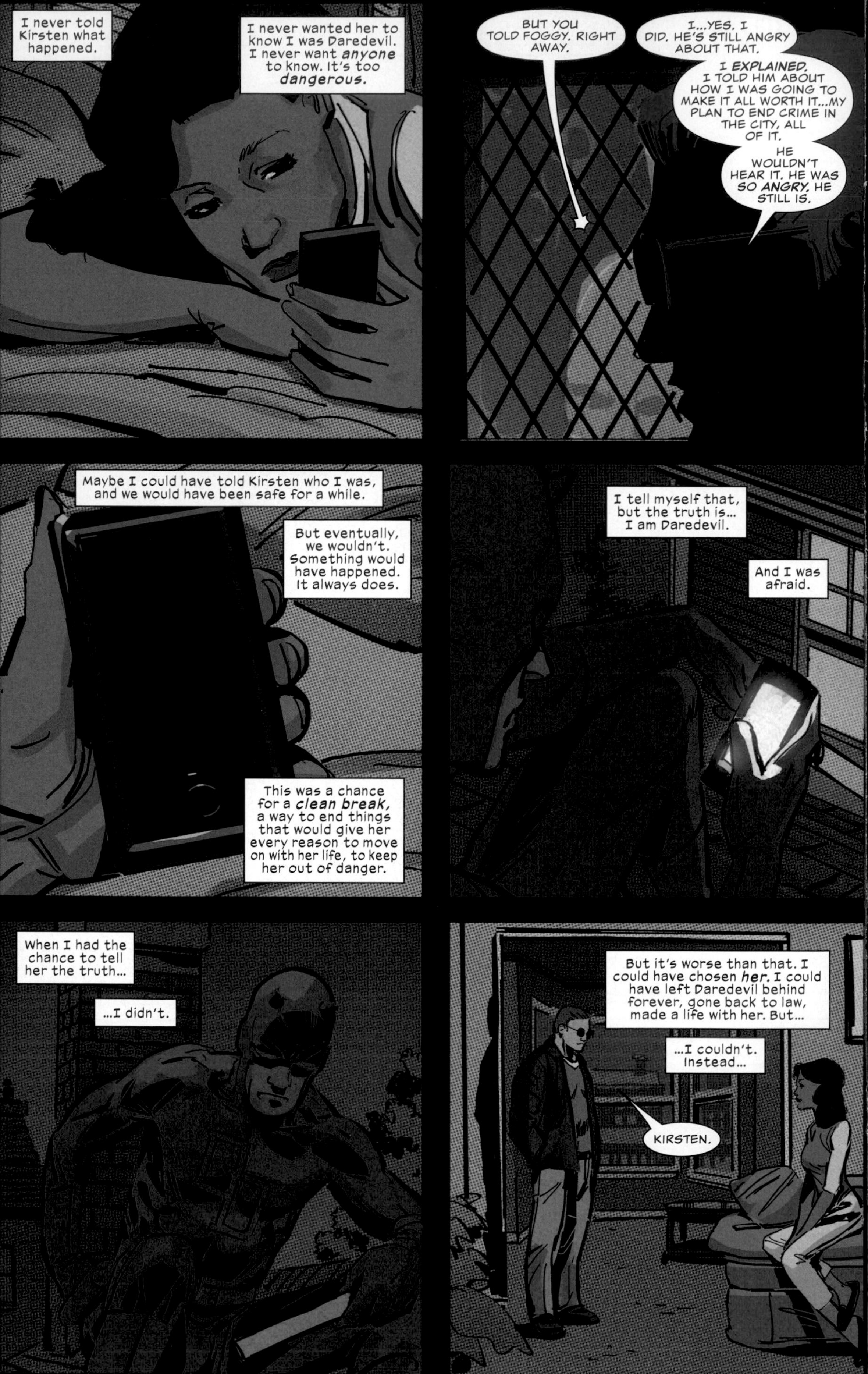
I never told Kirsten what happened.
I never wanted her to know I was Daredevil. I never want *anyone* to know. It's too *dangerous.*
BUT YOU TOLD FOGGY. RIGHT AWAY.
I...YES. I DID. HE'S STILL ANGRY ABOUT THAT.
I *EXPLAINED.* I TOLD HIM ABOUT HOW I WAS GOING TO MAKE IT ALL WORTH IT...MY PLAN TO END CRIME IN THE CITY, ALL OF IT.
HE WOULDN'T HEAR IT. HE WAS SO *ANGRY.* HE STILL IS.
Maybe I could have told Kirsten who I was, and we would have been safe for a while.
But eventually, we wouldn't. Something would have happened. It always does.
This was a chance for a *clean break,* a way to end things that would give her every reason to move on with her life, to keep her out of danger.
I tell myself that, but the truth is... I am Daredevil.
And I was afraid.
When I had the chance to tell her the truth...
...I didn't.
But it's worse than that. I could have chosen *her.* I could have left Daredevil behind forever, gone back to law, made a life with her. But...
...I couldn't. Instead...
KIRSTEN.

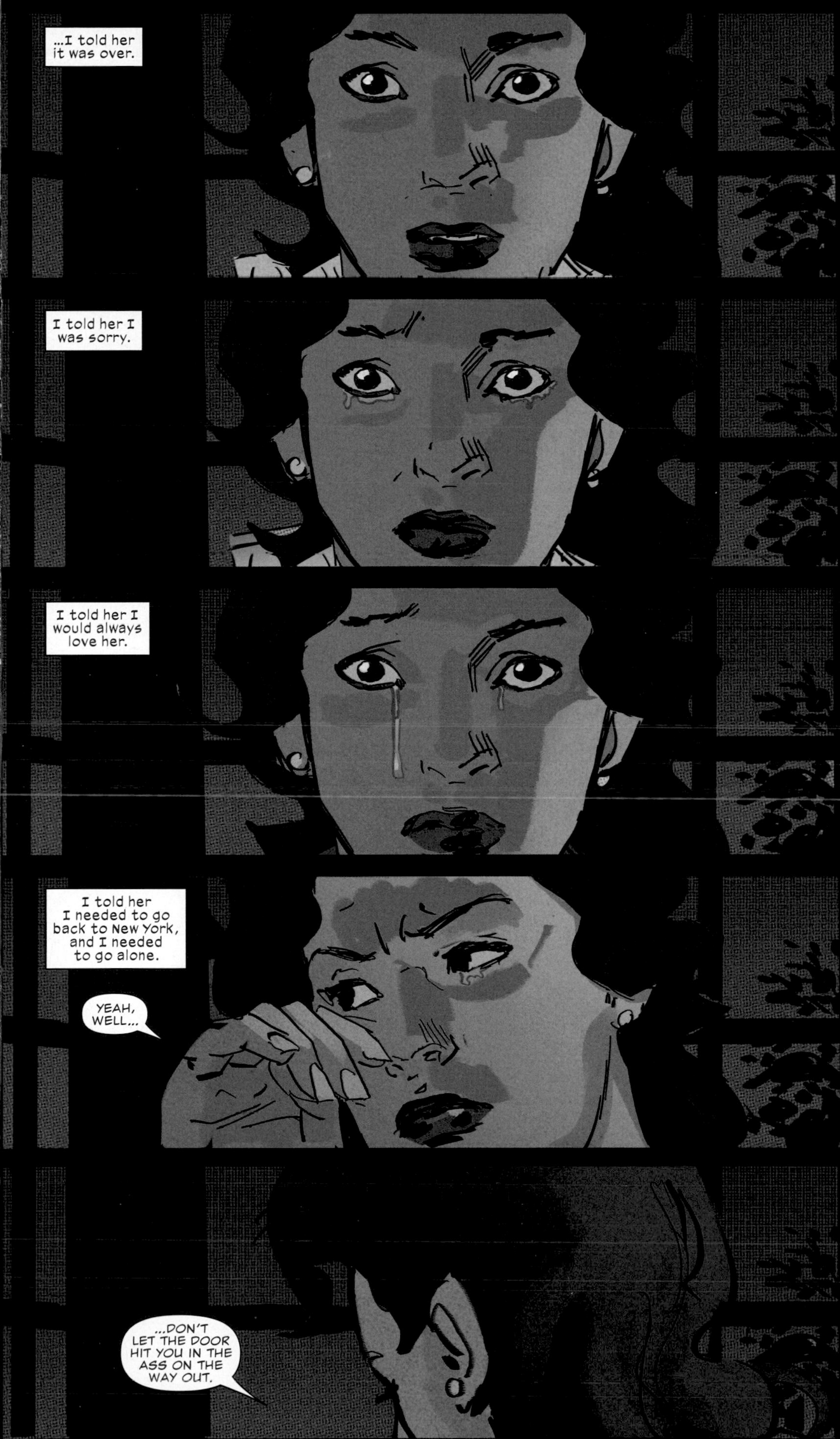
...I told her it was over.
I told her I was sorry.
I told her I would always love her.
I told her I needed to go back to New York, and I needed to go alone.
YEAH, WELL...
...DON'T LET THE DOOR HIT YOU IN THE ASS ON THE WAY OUT.

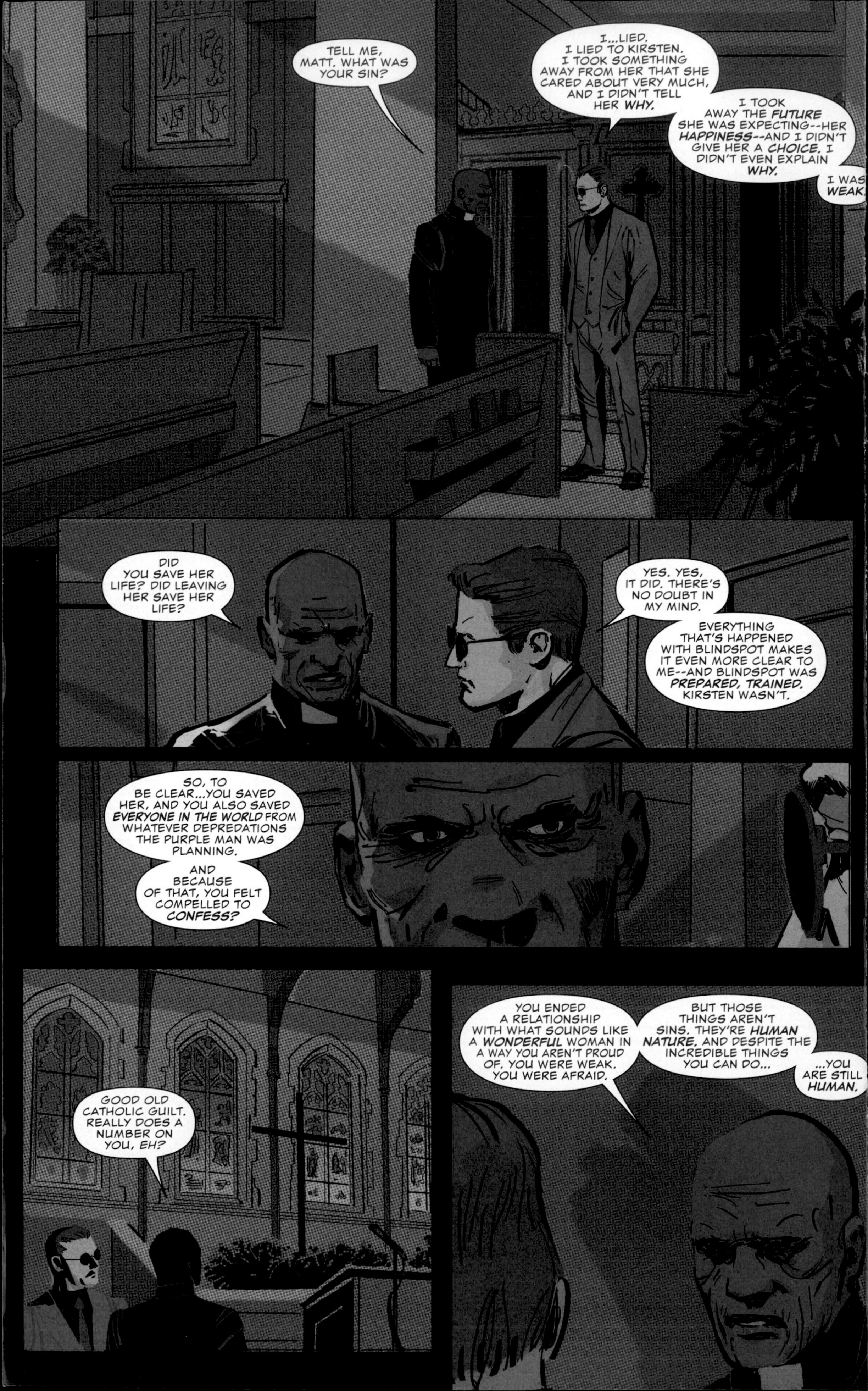
TELL ME, MATT. WHAT WAS YOUR SIN?
I...LIED. I LIED TO KIRSTEN. I TOOK SOMETHING AWAY FROM HER THAT SHE CARED ABOUT VERY MUCH, AND I DIDN'T TELL HER WHY.
I TOOK AWAY THE FUTURE SHE WAS EXPECTING--HER HAPPINESS--AND I DIDN'T GIVE HER A CHOICE. I DIDN'T EVEN EXPLAIN WHY.
I WAS WEAK.
DID YOU SAVE HER LIFE? DID LEAVING HER SAVE HER LIFE?
YES. YES, IT DID. THERE'S NO DOUBT IN MY MIND.
EVERYTHING THAT'S HAPPENED WITH BLINDSPOT MAKES IT EVEN MORE CLEAR TO ME--AND BLINDSPOT WAS PREPARED, TRAINED. KIRSTEN WASN'T.
SO, TO BE CLEAR...YOU SAVED HER, AND YOU ALSO SAVED EVERYONE IN THE WORLD FROM WHATEVER DEPREDATIONS THE PURPLE MAN WAS PLANNING.
AND BECAUSE OF THAT, YOU FELT COMPELLED TO CONFESS?
GOOD OLD CATHOLIC GUILT. REALLY DOES A NUMBER ON YOU, EH?
YOU ENDED A RELATIONSHIP WITH WHAT SOUNDS LIKE A WONDERFUL WOMAN IN A WAY YOU AREN'T PROUD OF. YOU WERE WEAK. YOU WERE AFRAID.
BUT THOSE THINGS AREN'T SINS. THEY'RE HUMAN NATURE, AND DESPITE THE INCREDIBLE THINGS YOU CAN DO...
...YOU ARE STILL HUMAN.

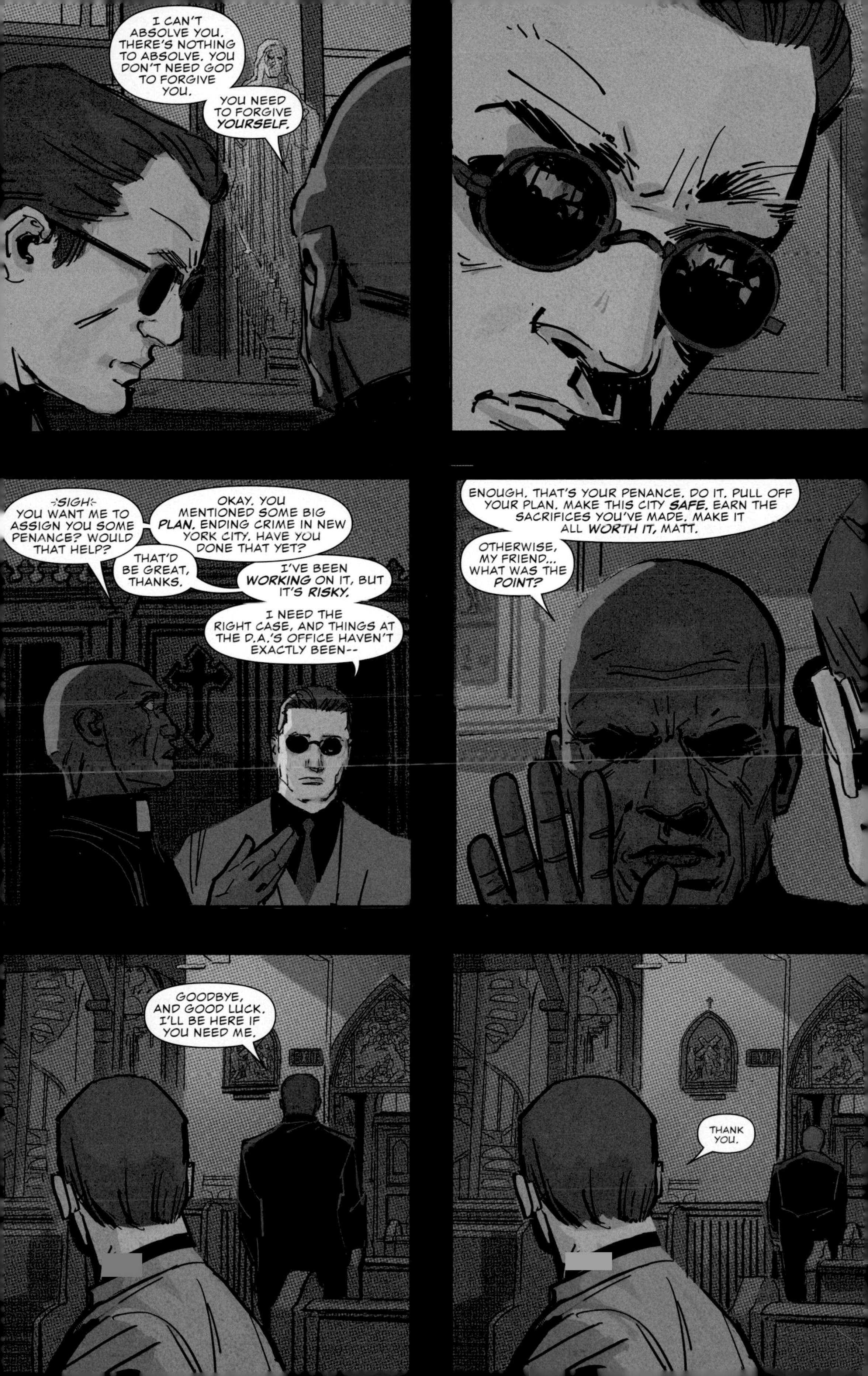
I CAN'T ABSOLVE YOU. THERE'S NOTHING TO ABSOLVE. YOU DON'T NEED GOD TO FORGIVE YOU.
YOU NEED TO FORGIVE YOURSELF.
-SIGH- YOU WANT ME TO ASSIGN YOU SOME PENANCE? WOULD THAT HELP?
OKAY. YOU MENTIONED SOME BIG PLAN. ENDING CRIME IN NEW YORK CITY. HAVE YOU DONE THAT YET?
THAT'D BE GREAT, THANKS.
I'VE BEEN WORKING ON IT, BUT IT'S RISKY.
I NEED THE RIGHT CASE, AND THINGS AT THE D.A.'S OFFICE HAVEN'T EXACTLY BEEN--
ENOUGH. THAT'S YOUR PENANCE. DO IT. PULL OFF YOUR PLAN. MAKE THIS CITY SAFE. EARN THE SACRIFICES YOU'VE MADE. MAKE IT ALL WORTH IT, MATT.
OTHERWISE, MY FRIEND... WHAT WAS THE POINT?
GOODBYE, AND GOOD LUCK. I'LL BE HERE IF YOU NEED ME.
THANK YOU.

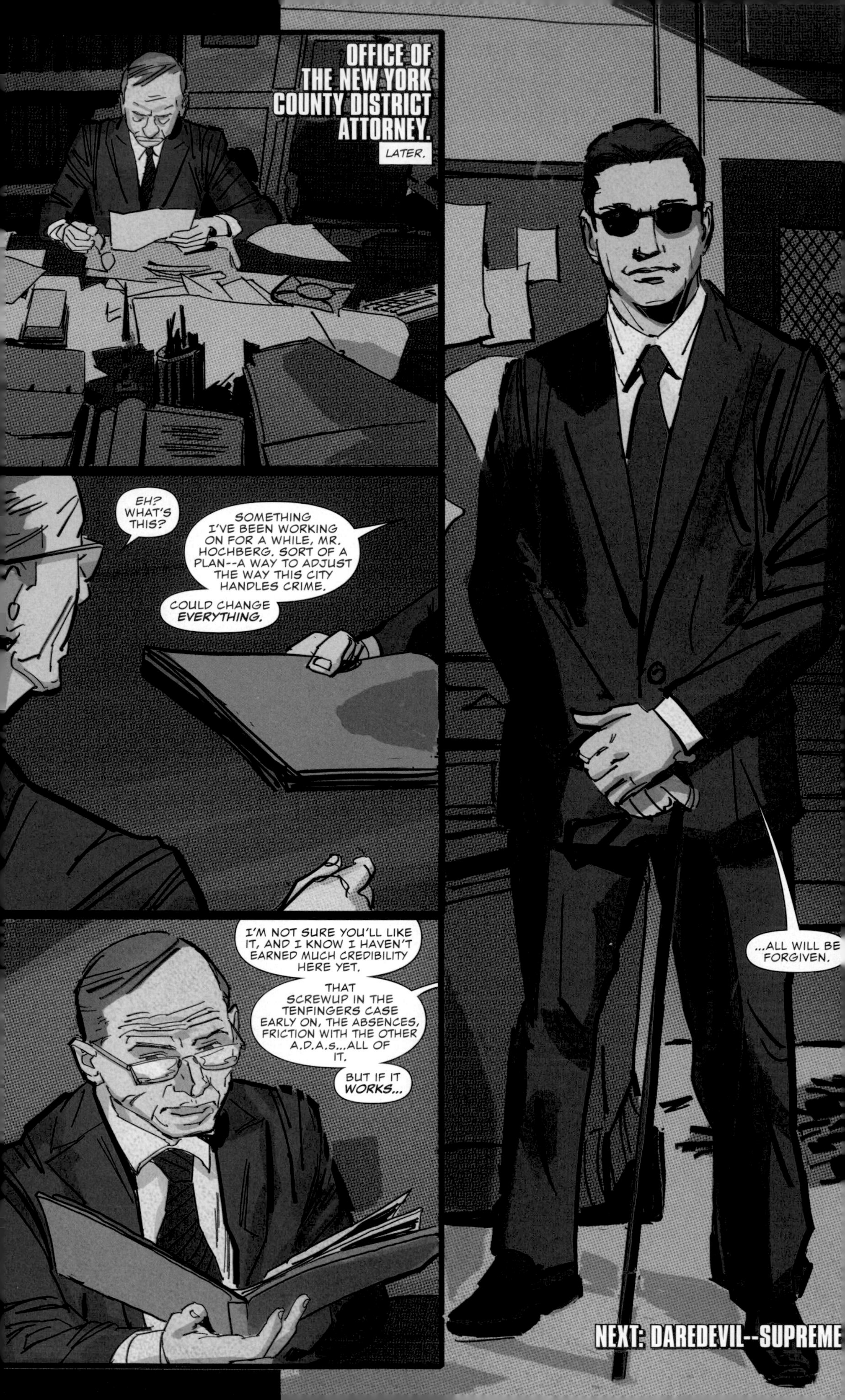
OFFICE OF THE NEW YORK COUNTY DISTRICT ATTORNEY.
LATER.
EH? WHAT'S THIS?
SOMETHING I'VE BEEN WORKING ON FOR A WHILE, MR. HOCHBERG. SORT OF A PLAN--A WAY TO ADJUST THE WAY THIS CITY HANDLES CRIME.
COULD CHANGE EVERYTHING.
I'M NOT SURE YOU'LL LIKE IT, AND I KNOW I HAVEN'T EARNED MUCH CREDIBILITY HERE YET.
THAT SCREWUP IN THE TENFINGERS CASE EARLY ON, THE ABSENCES, FRICTION WITH THE OTHER A.D.A.s...ALL OF IT.
BUT IF IT WORKS...
...ALL WILL BE FORGIVEN.
NEXT: DAREDEVIL--SUPREME

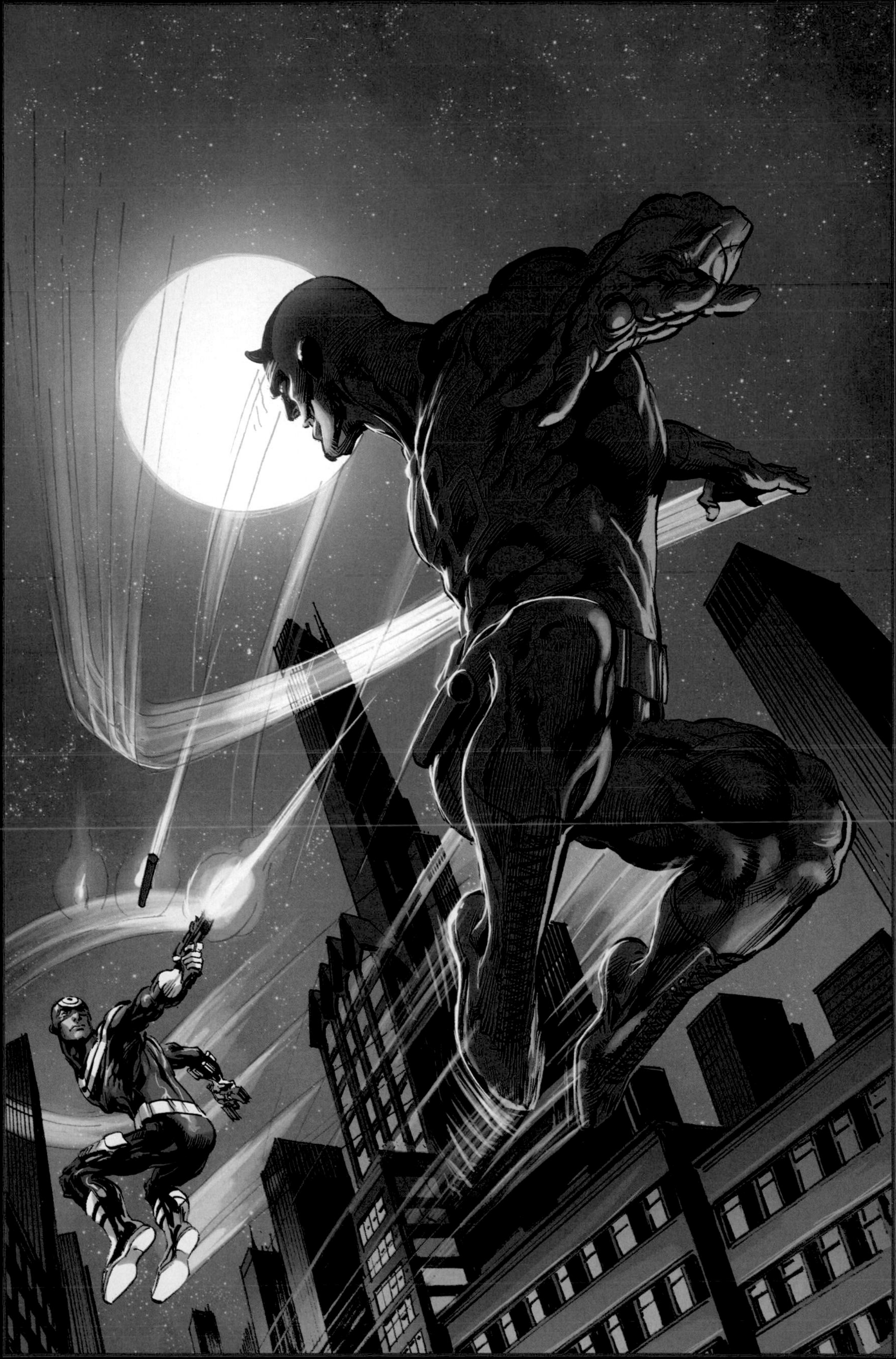

NEAL ADAMS & FRANK MARTIN

No. 15 VARIANT

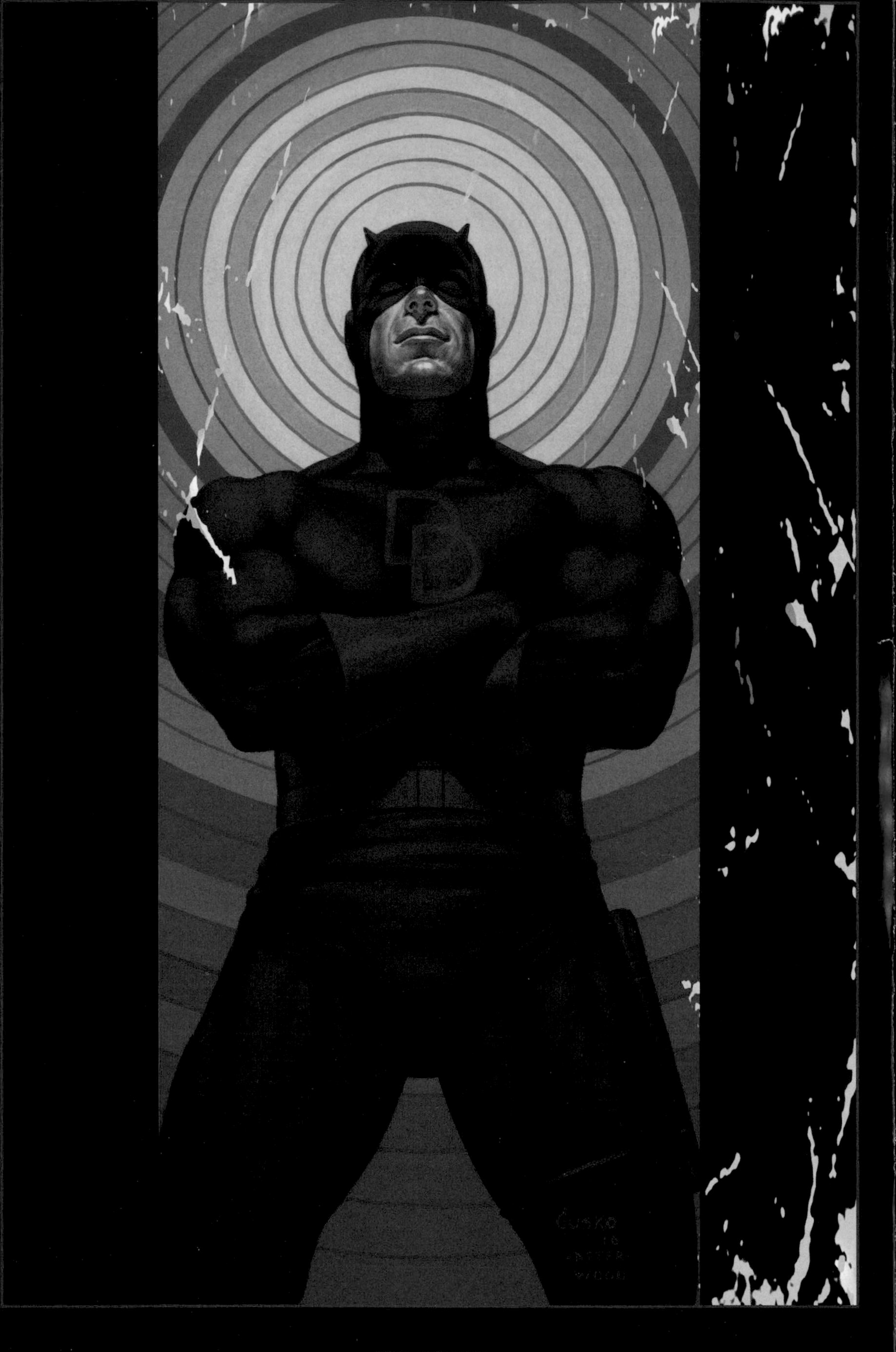

JOE JUSKO

No. 17 CORNER BOX VARIANT